KENT

A Chronicle of The Century

Volume Two: 1925-1949

by Bob Ogley

This is the second volume of Bob Ogley's Chronicle of the Century as it has affected his home county of Kent. It begins in those lively years of the "roaring twenties" when class distinctions were giving way to comradeship. It traces the story of Kent through the Great Strike, the depression of the thirties, the alarming rise of the Third Reich and the tyranny which followed. Here are the scandals, disasters, triumphs and dramas — the grim years of growing disquiet, the golden age of steam and screen. Remember the Crystal Palace, the abdication, the winter of '47 and the 'New Look'. Join us in this journey through Kent, back in time, with the help of more than 200 illustrations.

 **Froglets Publications**

Froglets Publications Ltd

Brasted Chart,
Westerham,
Kent TN16 1LY

Tel: 01959 562972
Fax: 01959 565365

ISBN Hardback 1 872337 84 8
ISBN Paperback 1 872337 89 9

© Bob Ogley

Front cover illustrations

Spitfires of 610 Squadron,
Austin 7,
Winston S. Churchill,
Sydney Wooderson and the
"invasion" of the hop-pickers.

This book was originated by Froglets Publications Ltd, scanned by Ashford Scanning, printed and perfect bound by Staples Printers (Rochester) Ltd, Neptune Close, Medway City Estate, Rochester, Kent ME2 4LT.
Casebound by Green Street Bindery, Oxford.

Jacket design and additional artwork by Alison Clark

FOREWORD

THE first volume of this Chronicle of Kent covered the years between 1900 and 1924 and, to my delight — and to the satisfaction of all those involved in the publication — it attracted enormous interest. Critics were also kind. The Kentish Times described it as a "five-star book of compulsive fare" and others said their "Christmas present list had been solved for the next three years".

The research, writing and design have been great fun; no county has a more dramatic story to tell. As the chief gateway to England, Kent has a matchless place in history — and especially the history of this century.

Like the first, this volume would not have been possible without the help and encouragement of many people. Fern Flynn was involved in all stages, Avril Oswald and Mark Laver read and corrected the text and made many useful suggestions. Local history departments, heritage centres, museum curators, local newspaper editors — and particularly their readers — responded to my appeal for information. Members of the public rang and even stopped me in the street to add another gem to the stories I was finding. There are too many people to name individually but they know I am grateful.

However, I would like to thank the following for their special help. Messrs Jonathan Balcon, D.E. Benjeyfield, David Cousins, Peter Finch, Arthur Galloway, Ken Jarvis, Jon Lindbergh, Nigel Nicolson, Anne Oakley, Ernest Rensch, John Rice, Chris Taylor, A.A. Tutton, John Williams, J.B. Snell, Barrie Wootton and Sydney Wooderson.

Richard Church in his most intimate history of Kent says that he, like Chaucer, was not a Man of Kent or Kentish Man but writes: *"Why should not another Cockney voice his adoration at a moment when Kent has suffered somewhat and had her beauty marred by front-line exposure to the ravages of the barbarian, who threatened to rape her, but did not succeed."*

This volume covers the second all-European conflict which began just 21 years after the first one ended. Next year I will concentrate on the more peaceful years — 1950-1975 — and I will be delighted to hear from all of you who have a relevant photograph or story.

I hope you will enjoy this volume well enough to place an order for the third (or first, if you have not seen it) and join our list of subscribers whose names are printed on page 195.

Bob Ogley

PHOTOGRAPH CREDITS

We are grateful to the following for the use of their copyright photographs. In some cases we have been unable to trace the copyright holder but have made every effort to do so. **Kent County Council Arts and Librarie**s: *Dover* (pages) 70, 169, 183, 188, 191. *Ramsgate* 74 (bottom), 85, 124 (top),192. *Folkestone* 11. *Canterbury* 12. *Deal* 16. *Gillingham* 46, 193. *Ashford* 73, 90, 139. *Gravesend* 63, 125. *Sittingbourne* 44. **Topham Picture Source** 3, 6, 15, 23, 28, 47, 50, 51, 52, 55, 57 (top), 61, 66, 75, 76, 84, 87, 89, 92, 95, 96/7, 101, 103, 104, 107, 109, 131, 143, 159, 166, 170, 172, 175, 179, 181, 182, 184, 185, 186/7, 190. **Kent Messenger** 7, 42, 98, 105, 106, 114, 115, 118 (bottom), 129, 142 (top), 153, 154, 162, 178. **Chris Taylor** (Kent Cricket Club archivist) 10, 19 (top), 31 (right), 53, 56, 69, 91, 137. **Imperial War Museum** 102, 113, 120, 122,123, 126, 127, 128,129, 130, 133, 148, 149, 150, 164, 165(all), 167, 180. **Bromley Library** 9, 32 (top), 62, 64, 81, 82, 83, 93 (top). **Dover Museum** 39, 111, 145, 146. **Mayfair Postcards** 13, 35, 138 (bottom). **Raleigh Industries** 41. **John Williams** 22, 67, 110, 173. **Barrie Wootton** 20, 29, 60, 99. **Pamlin Prints** 8, 45. **Rochester-upon-Medway Heritage Centre** 21, 67, 86 (Short Bros). **National Trust photographic archive** 78/9. **Deutches Museum** 157, 158 (bottom). **National Railway Museum** 48. **Maidstone Museum** 18, 58. **Romney, Hythe and Dymchurch Railway** 19 (bottom), 24. **Dean and Chapter, Canterbury Cathedral** 65, 74 (top). **Jonathan Balcon** 189, 191 (bottom).**Philip Lane** 37, 116. **Bexley Library** 121, 142 (bottom). **Rugby Aviation Group** 140, **David Cousins** 32 (bottom). **Mark Davison** 176/7. **Terry Rensch** 135. **D.E. Benjeyfield** 27. **Kent County Council** 59. **John Jago** 17. **Peter Finch** 183 (bottom). **Sydney Wooderson** 88. **Jon Lindbergh** 94, **A.A. Tutton** 174. **Robert Opie** 43 (Wills), 68 (Dunlop), 77 (Brylcreem). **J.E.Sims** 118. **Nigel Nicolson** 43. **Mr L. Lawrence** 25 (top).

1925: Hop-picking is once more the dominant industry in Kent, although the seasonal labour force has not, and perhaps never will attain the strength of pre-war days. Here are the skilled men on their special "Kentish shoes" stringing the poles that cannot be reached by the women. This will be followed by the twirling of young vines as they begin to run and then, in September, will come the invaders in their thousands. The Londoners will bring with them their grubby-faced children, grandads and grandmums, popular songs, high spirits and bad language. There will be fights and thefts; theirs is a necessary but unwelcome intrusion. For the locals, however, Kent's hop gardens remain somewhat akin to a sacred cult, and continue to enter deeply into the life of the people of the hop-growing villages. When the Londoners have left, the strange, haunting, bitter-sweet smell of the drying hops in their oast kilns will pervade the Kentish air.

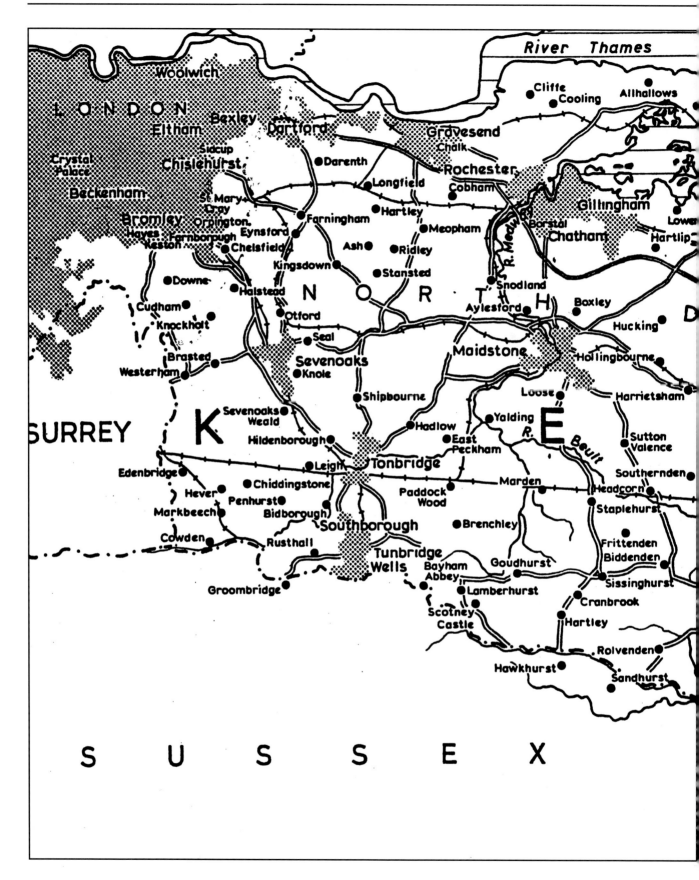

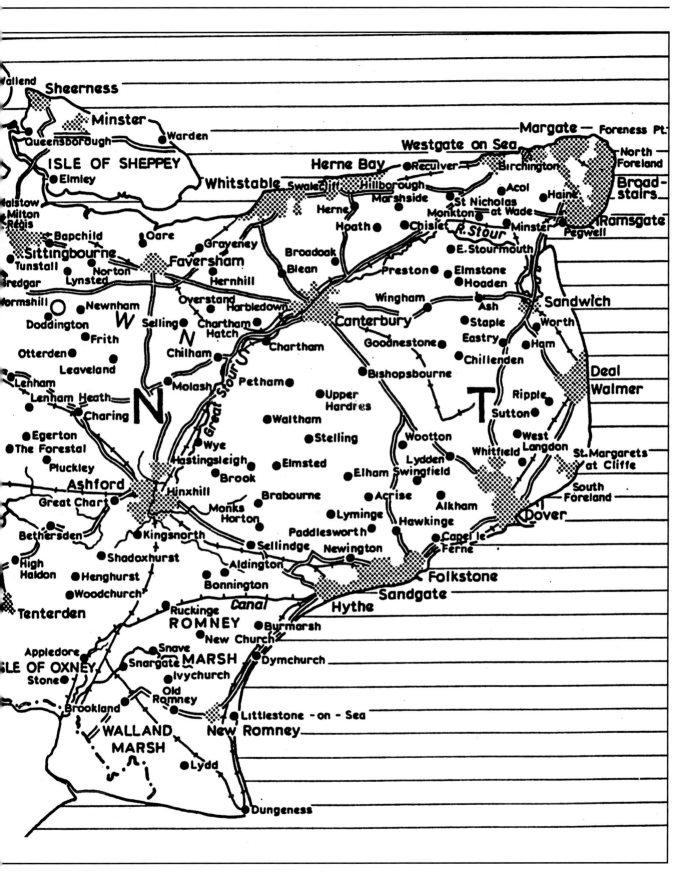

Pacifism and belonging — key words in these difficult, but happy, post-war years

1925: Kent has emerged from the Great War physically unscathed but mentally scarred. Thousands of local men died on the battlefield and the pain and bereavement can never be cured by either medicine or social amelioration. The burdens of peace are great but the monuments are in place, the treaties all signed and pacifism is flourishing.

These immediate post-war years have brought a stimulus to social consciousness. Class distinctions are fading away, women have the franchise and new families are moving into the county. More important the comradeship of war has given everyone a new sense of belonging — a desire to achieve a better social life and greater equality.

The mid-twenties may one day be called the age of the voluntary bodies.The British Legion, formed to represent the interests of ex-servicemen and women and their dependants, has branches in every town and village. The Rotary movement has moved from America and clubs are opening all over Kent (Margate, the first), Women's Institutes are flourishing and so are hundreds of other clubs, societies and Christian organisations. There are branches of the Toc H and Salvation Army in most towns and the scout and guide movement is at its peak. In the countryside almost everyone belongs to at least one club — from the hunt down to the rat and sparrow club or the cabbage-growers' society.

Within the home change is coming slowly. Domestic servants can still be found within most of the well-to-do households and many middle-class daughters still live at home after school age. No need to obtain regular employment — finding a husband is still the major priority.

Alongside this increased importance of group activity is a vast growth in the responsibility of local government. For some years now migrants have been moving into Kent in vast numbers from the depressed areas of the north. In partnership with Kent County Council, the 56 borough, urban and rural councils continue to concentrate on the provision of housing; however they are unable to keep pace with demand.

If municipal housing has a great influence on the landscape of Kent, then two other institutions are having an equal impact — the southern railway and the central electricity generating board.

Electrification of the railways is imminent. It will bring almost all parts of Kent to within commuting distance of London. Big housing projects are underway in Paddock Wood, Shorne, Newington, Edenbridge, Swanley and Staplehurst. Will this be enough to satisfy demand?

An example of insensitive placement of an electricity pylon — in a garden in Sidcup.

The clamour for electric power has meant the building of power stations and, even worse, a network of pylons and lines to take the electricity to every home. The great railway viaducts, such as that at Ford, near Folkestone, which were once considered such an intrusion on the landscape, are today viewed with much more tolerance. Will it ever be the same for the electric grid system?

Apart from the holiday industry, which is back to its pre-war levels, there are many old-fashioned firms providing employment which other counties envy. There is also the hop-growing and brewing industry for which Kent is famous and among the oldest brewing firms are Whitbreads, with 400 acres at Paddock Wood, Fremlins, Style and Winch, Westerham Ales and Shepherd Neame. "No sir," said Dr Johnson, "there is nothing which has yet been contrived by man by which so much happiness is produced as by a good tavern or inn."

There are something like 5,000 inns in Kent. It is a very happy county.

'I really understand how and why Vita likes the Bloomsbury people. They seems to appreciate her as she deserves' — Lady Sackville on her daughter's friendship with Virginia Woolf and friends.

January 1st: Despite a gallant rearguard innings of 50 at Sydney, which failed to save England who lost by 193 runs, Tich Freeman has been dropped for the second Test Match against Australia at Melbourne which begins today. The other two Kent cricketers in the touring party, Percy Chapman and Frank Woolley, are playing.

January 4th: The River Darent has burst its banks following torrential rain and Dartford town centre — now known as "Little Venice" has been badly flooded.

January 16th: Leon Trotsky, who played a leading part in the October revolution of 1917, has been deposed as leader of the Soviet Communist party.

February 14th: Low lying areas of Kent are under water following an intense rainstorm which raged without cessation throughout yesterday (Saturday). Mason's Brewery, Maidstone is flooded and the municipal sports ground at Tonbridge resembles a massive lake. Graziers in the Stour Valley, between Chartham and Canterbury, are trying to move their stock to safe quarters. The Isle of Oxney is an island again — approachable only by boat.

February 27th: Adolf Hitler, released from prison today, will speak at a mass meeting of his resurrected Nazi party. He has promised the Bavarian authorities that he will seek political power only through legal means and not force. Herr Hitler's "book of dreams" which he wrote in prison will be published in the summer under the title *Mein Kampf.*

May 1st: Britain today welcomes another British colony — Cyprus. The Mediterranean island was annexed during the war when Turkey sided with Germany but an agreement made in 1878, when the Ottoman Empire was "persuaded" to place Cyprus under British administration, takes effect from today.

A new dance is taking Kent's fashionable night spots by storm. It's called The Charleston and it is loved by "flappers" who turn in their toes, kick their legs and wave their arms in unison. Many are scandalised by such behaviour!

A number of Special Constables interested in aircraft identification and reporting have formed themselves into a special group or Corps at Cranbrook. They are hoping to expand across the county.

Summer: Sevenoaks urban council has acquired from Kent and Sussex Farmers Ltd the rights to the market in the High Street.

Chief Scout, Lord Baden Powell is seen here with Scout Commissioner Lord Brabourne. They are currently helping to plan a Scout Marathon to be held at The Friars, Aylesford next year and attended by scouts from all over the country.

Salvage work has begun on the hull of *HMS Glatton* which has been lying on the sea bed in Dover harbour since the ship was torpedoed in September 1918, with the loss of 100 lives.

August 8th: More than 40,000 members of a new secret society, which aims to protect white supremacy in America, today marched through Washington. The society calls itself the Ku Klux Klan.

September 9th: The Trades Union Council has voted against the amalgamation of all British trade unions.

September 29th: White traffic lines are to be painted on roads all over the country in an attempt to reduce accidents. In recent weeks there has been a spate of accidents in Kent.

A Grammar School for girls has been opened at Chislehurst.

October 6th: The Archbishop of Canterbury Dr Randall Davidson, commenting on low church attendances throughout the country, has blamed poor preaching.

October 13th: Seamen at Chatham and Dover have returned to work. They have been on strike for six weeks.

November 12th: The submarine, *Mi,* is lost in the Channel; it is feared the 68 crew have perished.

November 13th: The bandages that swathed a mummified body in Luxor have been removed. Investigations indicate that the body is that of King Tutankhamun who was about 15 when he died.

November 20th: Queen Alexandra, widow of King Edward VII, died at Sandringham today.

December 18th: For the first time more than a million passengers have passed through the port of Dover in one year.

A regular visitor this year to Long Barn, Sevenoaks Weald, the home of Vita and Harold Nicolson, has been the novelist Virginia Woolf whose new book *Mrs Dalloway* is hailed as brilliant and original.

Shoreham Mill, which once produced some of the finest hand-made ledger paper in the country, has closed. For more than 200 years the River Darent had supplied both the water and power necessary to produce the paper.

GREAT HITS OF 1925

*Show Me The Way
To Go Home*

Always

Montreal House memorial to a famous soldier

March: Following the recent death of the Fourth Earl, the Amherst family have decided to sell their stately home at Riverhead, Sevenoaks and move from the area. The new owner of the grand house, its park, gardens and vast estate is Mr J.J. Runge of Kippington Court.

The house was built by Jeffrey Amherst in 1776 and named Montreal in honour of his historic victory in Canada six years earlier. Following General Wolfe's capture of Quebec, General Amherst (an equally famous soldier) moved an army of nearly 8,000 men across wild country to the southern shores of Lake Ontario and then took them down the St Lawrence River to Montreal in a manoeuvre that has few equals in British military history. Days later the French Commander-in-Chief surrendered himself, his army and the whole of Canada to General Amherst.

The hero of England returned home to Kent four years after Canada's surrender and celebrated by building a new mansion. He became Commander-in-Chief of the British Army and was created Baron Amherst of Holmesdale. He then erected an obelisk as a memorial to a happy reunion with his brothers and entertained, among others, King George III and Queen Charlotte.

Sevenoaks has not entirely lost its connection with the Amhersts. A large public house in Riverhead is named after the hero of Canada.

Farewell to Sir David: a great inventor

April 19th: Sir David Lionel Salomons, Bart, scientist and inventor, the man who brought the first motor car to Kent and pioneered electric power for lighting and cooking in the home, has died in London. He will be buried in the family cemetery at Lower Green, Tunbridge Wells, near his home at Broomhill.

Sir David leaves behind an extensive collection of engravings and documents relating to mechanical locomotion comprising of some 5,352 pieces and it is his desire they should be presented to the Bibliothèque Nationale in Paris.

Engineering has been the overwhelming interest in Sir David's extraordinary life. His workshop at Broomhill contains 60,000 tools, by far the largest collection in the country. Adjoining the workshop is a theatre with seating for 150, the largest electrical organ in England — a Welte philharmonic installed at a cost of £4,000 — and a magnet which is the most powerful ever constructed.

Sir David is best known for his pioneering work with motor transport. He constructed the first motor car to be electrically propelled and brought to England the first Peugeot "horseless carriage" scorning the innate conservatism of the English and the scepticism that accompanied it. He formed the Self-Propelled Traffic Association, later to become the Royal Automobile Association and lobbied Parliament to remove speed restrictions on the highway.

His inventions covered a wide field and industrialists throughout the world owe much to the entrepreneurial ability of this outstanding man.

Today motoring is no longer a pursuit of the wealthy. Henry Ford, with his assembly-line mass production, was the first to introduce a cheap car, the Model T Ford — priced at £195 before the war. Now there is competition from William Morris with his Morris Cowley and Herbert Austin, whose Austin Seven (1922) was once a joke.

Great War artist Paul Nash, whose images of the scarred landscape of such places as the Ypres Salient and The Somme shocked the country because of their terrible truth, is to move from Dymchurch where he has been painting a series of pictures of the beach. Nash, who is 36 and suffers from asthma, hopes to find a home nearby in Rye.

As a soldier and later official war artist he came to public prominence following an exhibition of war drawings in 1918 and from April of that year was engaged on paintings commissioned by the Government, the most famous of which is The Menin Road. His Dymchurch paintings, which include Winter Sea and Dymchurch Steps, has inspired another artist, Ben Nicholson, to paint the view from the sea wall.

June 30th: *Queen Mary visited Chislehurst today and opened the new additions to Farringtons School for Girls which consist of assembly hall, new classrooms and the West House. Her Majesty was told that the total cost of the extensions was £60,000 of which £30,000 has been donated by the Rt Hon T.R. Ferens, the vice-chairman of the Governors. Farringtons was founded 12 years ago and is closely connected with the Wesleyan Church.*

No more novels says disillusioned Forster

March: Edward Morgan Forster, the popular author whose formative years were spent in Kent, has said he will not write any more novels. His latest book, *A Passage to India,* was published only last year but Forster has said that he feels out of touch with the world that came into existence after the Great War and the censor's refusal to allow him to write about homosexual relations is, apparently, the last straw.

This is a tragedy for those who admire his work. The former Tonbridge schoolboy, now aged 45, has frequently championed freedom and tolerance and exposed the weaknesses of the English middle classes. He is also well travelled and his earlier books *Where Angels Fear to Tread* and *A Room with A View* brilliantly compare the stubborn conventions of English surburban life with that of easy-going Italy.

Born in London, E.M. Forster lived for many years in Tunbridge Wells before studying at Cambridge where he was an outstanding scholar. His favourite novel, *The Longest Journey* presents the ideal of comradeship at school and university. *Howard's End* takes on a wider significance of social unity while *A Passage to India* reveals the great misunderstandings between east and west.

The censor's refusal to allow Forster to express individualism now means that his planned novel of homosexual love and the future of England as a classless society through the love of a stockbroker, Maurice, and a gamekeeper, Alec, may never be published in his lifetime.

Electric trains here at last — historic day for Orpington

July 10th: For many months past the engineers of the Southern Railway have been busily engaged in the first stage of the £8 million scheme to electrify the railway lines. The great change-over will take place on Sunday (July 12th) when the line from Victoria to Orpington, via Holborn Viaduct and Herne Hill, will be converted to electric traction.

High tension cables have been placed along railway embankments and cuttings to conduct a 600-volt current to the third rail made. Platforms have been lengthened and sub-stations established for the distribution of power from the main supply.

Meanwhile the men in the great railway workshops at Ashford have been working full time on the construction of new rolling-stock. A new receiving shed has been built at Orpington, and engineers claim it is the largest and best-equipped of any in the world, able to house 64 electric coaches or eight fully-equipped trains. Additionally 12 homes have been erected at Station Approach, Orpington for members of Southern Region's electrical staff.

The remaining sections comprising of lines from Charing Cross and Cannon Street to Beckenham, Hayes, Bromley and Orpington, from Deptford to Charlton, Lewisham, Woolwich, Blackheath, Bexleyheath and Dartford; and from Hither Green to Sidcup and Dartford are due to open in December. It constitutes the largest electric surburban system in the world, representing in all 647 miles of electrically operated track.

Haig ordered Cornwallis to play for Kent

June 6th: Captain W.S. Cornwallis, a former officer in the Cavalry Brigade, has started his second season as captain of Kent Cricket Club in great form. This week at Mote Park, Maidstone he took ten wickets against Gloucestershire and Kent won by an innings.

Cornwallis, who enjoyed a distinguished military career, played cricket for Eton and the Army and received an invitation to play for his county just after the Great War.

Treating the invitation as a joke he showed it to Lord Haig who ordered him to "accept it at once, Cornie".

Cornwallis, the second son of Lord Cornwallis of Linton Park, will eventually inherit his father's title as his elder brother was killed in 1921.

Meanwhile his greatest ambition is to to win the county championship. With such players as Chapman, Woolley, Freeman and Ashdown in the side he stands a great chance.

Earl of Ypres dies in Deal Castle

May 22nd: Field Marshal Sir John Denton Pinkstone French, Commander-in-Chief of the British Expeditionary Force, has died at his home in Deal Castle where he has lived since his appointment as Captain of Deal two years ago.

Sir John was a true Man of Kent, born at Ripple, Walmer in 1852 and will long be remembered as one of the country's most distinguished soldiers. When hostilities began in 1914 Sir John led one unit of four infantry divisions — some 70,000 men — into the bloodbath of Belgium and found the fighting skill and sheer numbers of the enemy too much. Britain, suffering heavy losses, pulled back. Sir John French resigned his command in 1915 and was succeeded by Sir Douglas Haig.

He became C-in-C of Home Command and later had another diffcult commission as Lord Lieutenant of Ireland during the Home Rule struggles. He was created Earl of Ypres in 1922.

The impressive twin towers of Saltwood Castle gatehouse.

British Legion takes over Preston Hall TB colony

April 1st: The institution at Aylesford, near Maidstone, known as the Preston Hall Colony for ex-servicemen suffering from tuberculosis, has been handed over to the British Legion. This great organisation which was established four years ago to represent the interests of men and women who served in the Great War will continue with the treatment and training but the mansion and the specially designed huts which surround it will now be known as the British Legion Village.

At a dinner given at Claridges Hotel to celebrate the transfer, Mr G. Reeves-Smith, the moving spirit in the formation of the Colony, said that 45 cottages have been built on the site and a further 25 are under construction. Among the trades and vocations taught to the sufferers are pig breeding, chicken-rearing, horticulture, agriculture and the making of furniture. The estate comprises about 150 acres.

In 1919 there were 35,000 ex-servicemen suffering from tuberculosis due to their war service and there was no machinery or accommodation for dealing with them. The Preston Hall estate of the late Mr H. Bassey, was purchased by the Industrial Settlements Corporation and in four years about 1,442 men have been treated.

Mr Neville Chamberlain, Minister of Health, has visited the site and is so impressed with what he has seen that he has secured a promise from the Prime Minister for a donation of £10,000 to the colony.

Saltwood Castle on the market

May 21st: Mr William Deedes is to sell Saltwood Castle, near Hythe — his home for many years. Since it was acquired by his great grandfather in 1791 the 14th century gatehouse has been restored, several additions made and a well-equipped country residence formed. The sale is being handled by Knight, Frank and Rutley.

The history of the Castle goes back to Roman and Saxon times and it was just before the Norman conquest that it was made over to Christ Church, Canterbury. In December 1170 it was the place of assembly of the four knights who rode to Canterbury to kill Thomas a Becket. It was rebuilt in the 14th century.

Archbishop Cranmer exchanged the castle with Henry VIII for other land, Queen Elizabeth stayed there and Henrietta Maria, wife of Charles 1st, drew an annual dowry from the estate. For some time Saltwood was the official residence of the Lord Warden of the Cinque Ports.

June 12th: The last moment of the old town hall at Herne Bay. Thanks to the prompt and energetic action of the staff assisted by volunteers, many important documents were saved.

Paper mill and town hall lost in two disastrous fires

October 19th: About 120 men have been thrown out of work as a result of a disastrous fire at the Bridge Paper Mills, Tovil early today. The fire started in the engine room, surging through the heater house and machine departments above. Fed by the chemicals used in the paper-making industry the flames leapt up greedily and lit up the surrounding countryside. The blaze could be seen for miles around.

The timber-built galleries used for hoisting pulp from the barges glowed with an eerie brilliance and cast a lurid reflection on the clear waters of the Medway. As the fire became a roaring furnace a series of explosions caused considerable alarm to a growing number of spectators. These are being attributed to the thick ferro-concrete flooring yielding to the intense heat and collapsing in several places.

Remarkably, the portions of flooring supporting numerous vats, rollers and machinery remained intact and thus prevented a greater debacle.

The Maidstone Fire Brigade worked heroically during the small hours and a number of men narrowly escaped death. With 1,700 feet of hose in use they played four one-inch jets onto the flames and, having subdued the flames, a small party of firemen made a precautionary inspection of the building. As they did so large quantities of concrete flooring crashed down from above. None was hurt.

This is the second massive blaze in Kent this year. On June 12th Herne Bay Town Hall caught fire and, despite all the efforts of the local brigade, the building was so badly damaged that it had to be demolished together with the fire station which formed part of the town hall complex.

A crowd of several thousand who watched the amazing scenes were almost lost in the dense volumes of smoke which poured into the High Street and William Street. They saw the flames sweep through the entrance hall with startling rapidity and then the sound of explosions caused by escaping gas, the crash of beams and the collapse of the gallery.

While firemen played their hoses onto the building frantic efforts were made by officials to save many important documents in the various municipal departments.

By the morning the town hall was just a blackened shell and the council chamber in ruins. They presented a sorry spectacle — scorched, smoke-stained and sodden with water.

'Not a penny off the pay. Not a minute off the day' — Arthur James Cook. Miners' Federation secretary, during the Great Strike.

January 5th: Post Offices across Kent paid out the first widows' pensions today.

January 15th: Prime Minister Stanley Baldwin has outlined plans for a new board which will co-ordinate electricity supplies and link them in a "national grid".

January 27th: Inventor John Logie Baird, who has a studio at Hastings, demonstrated to the Royal Institution today how moving pictures can be transmitted by wireless.

February 17th: The government is to give £2 million for the development of the Kent coalfields, it was announced today.

March 20th: England has been beaten by Scotland in the Calcutta Cup for the first time in the history of the competition between the two countries.

March 13th: Pilot Alan Cobham has completed an historic 16,000-mile flight from London to Cape Town and back. He hopes it may lead to the establishment of a commercial air route across Africa.

Shepway Cross, a beautifully sculpted stone cross, crowned with the figure of the Blessed Virgin and the Holy Child has been dedicated by the Archbishop of Canterbury. It stands at the top of Lympne Hill as a memorial to the men and women of the Cinque Ports who lost their lives in the Great War.

March 24th: A Royal Commission has recommended that miners' wages be cut and the 1924 minimum wage agreement be abolished. This has angered the Miners' Federation, whose new slogan is "not a penny off the pay, not a minute on the day".

April 21st: The Duchess of York has given birth to a baby daughter, Elizabeth.

April 30th: A national coal strike begins today with most of Britain's miners under notice of lockout. The employers' final offer is a return to the 1921 minimum wage structure.

May 1st: The TUC has called a General Strike of essential services

September: The Southern Railway Company, in a bid to create a faster and more efficient service, has introduced a Golden Arrow service between London and Paris. The Golden Arrow consists entirely of Pulman cars, named after George Mortimer Pulman who made high-class carriages for the Chicago-Alton railroad in 1859. Southern Railway's Golden Arrow, with its restaurant car, is a great attraction as it steams through the countryside.

in sympathy with miners. The BBC has refused to allow the Archbishop of Canterbury, Dr Randall Davidson, to broadcast about the strike because of his socialist tendencies.

May 8th: For the duration of the strike Winston Churchill, Chancellor of the Exchequer, is to be the editor of *The British Gazette*, which will provide daily and officially approved news in the ab-

sence of ordinary newspapers.

May 12th: The TUC has called off the General Strike.

June 18th: Whitefriars Press, the largest printing works in Tonbridge which employs more than 400 people, has been destroyed by fire in what the local newspaper describes as "the greatest calamity that has occurred in the town within living

memory". As great cascades of molten metal poured down three storeys, firemen worked through the night but the firm, well-known for printing the humorous magazine, *Punch*, could not be saved. The printers, having barely recovered from the effects of the General Strike, have been laid off until rented premises can be found.

July 26th: A huge viaduct requiring more than two million bricks has been built over the Margate Road, Ramsgate to serve a new railway station.

October 1st: The long-distance pilot, Alan Cobham has added another record to his long list of aviation successes. Today he landed his seaplane on the Thames after completing a 28,000-mile round trip to Australia.

The Herne Bay roller-skating team has won the world title for the second time. They took the honours and the Victoria Cup at the championships in the Grand Pier pavilion rink at Herne Bay.

October 14th: Christopher Robin, the most celebrated child in juvenile literature, reappeared today with his teddy bear in his father's second book, *Winnie-the-Pooh*. The first book, *When We Were Verry Young* ran to 14 editions in two years.

Bowaters has opened a new paper mill at Northfleet. It has been built on 27 acres of land.

October 20th: The Duke and Duchess of York visited Ashford today to lay the foundation stone of the town's new hospital.

November 12th: The six-month-old coal dispute ended today when the miners agreed to the employers' demand that working hours be increased from seven to eight.

The mansion at Eastwell Park, near Ashford has been rebuilt in Jacobean style.

New church: St John the Evangelist, Welling

GREAT HIT OF 1926

Bye Bye Blackbird

Kent stays calm in the General Strike

May 8th: As the first week of the General Strike draws to a close, Kent is facing the position with quiet fortitude. Industry in England has been paralysed but from all parts of our county come reports of orderly behaviour on the part of strikers and great resourcefulness by the general public. There has been a rush to volunteer for help in the maintenance of the county's services and the position is steadily improving.

The first general strike in British history began at midnight on Tuesday (May 1st) when the general council of the Trades Union Congress backed the miners following a breakdown in their negotiations with the mine owners. A state of emergency was declared and the country was immediately divided into areas with emergency arrangements run by civil commissioners.

On Saturday (May 8th) the first issue of *The British Gazette* appeared under the editorship of Winston Churchill, Chancellor of the Exchequer, who lives in West Kent. He demands unconditional surrender by the strikers and describes them as "the enemy".

In Maidstone, with normal supplies of lighting and power from both gas and electrical undertakings, many local industries are carrying on almost as before. A committee of Maidstone coal merchants has been formed with the mayor as chairman. They will control the stock of coal and ensure no-one receives more than one hundredweight without obtaining a permit.

On Wednesday morning a procession of strikers marched up the High Street and demanded that the Town Council find accommodation for their meetings. They were immediately given the use of the Concert Hall at a reduced rate. Encouraged by John Reith, managing director of the BBC, who has said that "peace on earth comes to all men of goodwill" everyone is doing their best to ensure there is no conflict or violence.

This is the situation in Kent:

Sittingbourne: More than 2,000 men employed by Edward Lloyd's paper mills are on strike. The firm has arranged for sports and games competitions to be played and Mr A.J.Evans, Kent and England cricketer, is in charge of the organisation.

Sheerness: Ships of the Atlantic fleet, including the battleship *Royal Sovereign*, went to sea as soon as possible before the strike was called.

Dover: An armed guard of 30 soldiers is on duty at the electricity works. Cross Channel passengers for London have chartered local taxis to take them to their destination. All the boats of the Southern Railway Company have come into dock and the Orange buses have been taken over by the Government for use in another district.

Folkestone: About 500 men are on strike, most of them railwaymen. There has been a rush of volunteers to man vital services and many have signed as special constables

Tonbridge: Printers, bricklayers and railwaymen are out but the strike has had little effect. The train service is rapidly improving and both Autocar and Redcar bus services are running to the ordinary timetable. Colonel Spender Clay MP, addressing an informal meeting at the Empire Picture Palace, said that the strike would only hinder Britain's trade and increase the cost of living. He urged the men to return to work.

Sevenoaks: The only difficulty facing tradesmen is getting goods delivered. Strikers are extremely well behaved and one would hardly know there is a crisis.

Gravesend and Northfleet: The demeanour of everyone is splendid. There is a mere skeleton of railway staff but city businessmen are taking the bus to London. There are no shortages, the postal staff has maintained a regular service and Bowaters Paper Mills has been commandeered by the Government for the manufacture of paper for essential purposes.

Rochester and Chatham: Tramwaymen assert their intention of seeing the dispute through to a close . The dockyard unions have felt unable to give any support to the strike and work proceeds as usual. There are actually reports that the yard is being used for strike breaking. Large amounts of dockyard coal, bought for powering ships, are being conveyed to various power stations.

Lorry overturned by angry mob of strikers

May 12th: The general strike is over to the dismay of the miners who are extremely bitter at the way they have been "deserted". In calling for a show of solidarity, the TUC quickly realised they had neither the will nor the means to maintain a lasting challenge to the Government's authority. The three-week old coal dispute, however, continues.

There was one dramatic moment yesterday when a lorry was intercepted on its way to Biggin Hill airfield and overturned by a band of strikers. The police telephoned the station commander and warned that a mob was marching to the station.

They are angry because the *The British Gazette* is being distributed from Biggin Hill. Each evening an army lorry delivers the newspapers which are then transferred to three Vimys. With the rear cockpits crammed and the occupant perched on top, the Vimys take off on a night paper round dropping the bundles over towns and villages of the south.

During this period all leave has been cancelled and a cordon of armed sentries thrown around the station.

The mob, marching to the station, dispersed well before they reached Biggin Hill. The only excitement was the arrest of a civilian taking a short cut home across the airfield in the dark.

May 16th: *It may have been quiet in Kent but mobs in London have driven many vehicles off the road in scenes of great violence. This motorbus, en route for Dulwich and Penge, was set on fire — presumably because it was being driven by a volunteer. The chassis and engine of this bus was made in the Victoria works of Messrs Tilling-Stevens at Maidstone which has been a major employer in the county town since W.A. Stevens, who specialised in converting motor cars to electric power, collaborated with the Tilling bus company of Peckham.*

Tilmanstone wants 2,000 m

November 17th: The six-month coal strike is over. More than 700 men reported to work at Tilmanstone Colliery for the early shift today following the news that the Government and miners' leaders have reached an agreement. Working hours will be increased from seven to eight but the employers have promised that wages will not be cut below pre-April levels.

The men at Tilmanstone are aware that the wages in Kent coalfields are good by national standards. But they say working conditions are appalling and the accident rate is unusually high. They were given 48 hours to sign on, otherwise they could not be guaranteed their old job.

The colliery, however, is still desperately short of men and intends to advertise in Northern and Midland newspapers for 2,000 more workers.

So ends a bitter dispute. The Kent miners came out in May and survived only through private charities to which many local people subscribed. Many of the men found work in the fruit orchards and hop fields.

Miners' leaders this week told how the men of Tilmanstone and Chislet ceased work immediately the strike was called. They were followed by those at Betteshanger and Snowdown where only sinking was in progress.

During the duration of the General Strike there was considerable hostility towards the miners and the men responded by picketing in the area in some force. The most violent scenes were at Dover Marine Station where a cross-

Tilmanstone miners back after the collapse of the coal strike. The smiling faces do not reveal the true story for there is still discontent and recently the deputies again went on strike. Six have been dismissed.

Channel service was run by 150 Dover volunteers and a large number of Cambridge undergraduates. Several violent scuffles took place and the police arrested several men.

The Kent mining community is now bracing itself for an influx of men from other parts of England — particularly those who have been black-listed in other collieries and intend to travel south with assumed names.

They are encouraged by the fact that in future all agreements are to be negotiated locally and not nationally.

More electric lines: steam enthusiasts devastated

May: More and more steam trains are disappearing from Kent's railways. Following the electrification of the line from Victoria to Orpington, which was completed last year, comes news that hundreds of miles of track will be converted to the new system. Already an electric service runs from Charing Cross and Cannon Street to Bromley North and there is now a third rail to Dartford. This will soon be extended to Gravesend. The £3 million improvement scheme promises a better service but steam enthusiasts throughout the county are dismayed.

As the old South Eastern Railway and the London

Chatham and Dover lines are finally rationalised to serve the changing needs of rail users, improvements are also being made to the Isle of Thanet railway system. The Ramsgate Town to Margate Sands line has closed and a new station for Ramsgate is due to open on July 26th.

Already a huge viaduct has been built over the Margate Road by the Derby Arms and more than two million bricks have been used in its construction. In addition, 500,000 tons of chalk has been excavated to accommodate the Dumpton Park section of the line which now covers all the major towns on the island from Birchington to Minster.

Lady Olive buys "the loveliest castle in the world"

The Hon Lady Olive Cecilia, eldest daughter of the Baron of Queenborough, part of the fabulously rich American Whitney family has fallen in love with what Lord Conway of Allington describes as "the loveliest castle in the world" and she has bought it. Leeds Castle, a few miles east of Maidstone and one of the most romantic stately homes in England, has been on the market since death duties forced the family of the late Mr Cornwallis Wykeham-Martin to sell.

Her Ladyship, who is just 26, intends to lavish much money on improving the property. She is fully aware of the American connection, for Leeds has been owned in turn by the St Legers, the Culpeppers and the Fairfaxes who all played a major role in settling the colonies in the New World. Thomas Culpepper was the first governor of Virginia in 1680 and his son was a friend of George Washington.

Leeds Castle was first built by a Norman baron and became the home of six medieval kings. Lady Baillie will renovate and refurbish the house and then turn her attention to the garden which has been much neglected since it was originally laid out by Capability Brown.

Associated Portland Cement Manufacurers, better known as "The Combine", are completely rebuilding their works at Northfleet. They are also introducing a new deep-water jetty and four new rotary kilns which will be the largest in Europe. Before the turn of the century there were scores of individually-owned cement works near the river at Northfleet but most of them, together with barges, cooperages and staveyards, were taken over by APCM. Workmen are currently clearing the site to erect a new grinding mill near the mouth of the Ebbsfleet before it flows into the Thames close to the Huggins Arms pub. Here the clinker will be ground down, given its additives and made into Portland cement.

HMS Kent the eighth is launched at Chatham

March 16th: *HMS Kent*, a class cruiser and the eighth ship to bear the name of the county, was launched today by Countess Stanhope, wife of the Lord of the Admiralty.

For Chatham Dockyard, once the largest industrial centre in Kent and the main naval station in the kingdom, this is truly a red-letter day. For alongside *HMS Kent* work continues on the submarine *Oberon*, also due to be completed this year and built with Pacific operations in mind.

Three special gangs have been employed — two for the cruiser and one for the submarine and the activity at Chatham since the contract was secured in 1924 has been reminiscent of the good old days. *HMS Kent* is a magnificent flagship and will carry a full complement of 770 officers and men. The cost of building is close to £2 million and there is still much fitting to complete. She will be capable of a speed of 31.5 knots and carries eight Yarrow small tube boilers with superheaters for burning oil fuel and accommodation for 3,300 tons of oil. Her overall length is 630 feet.

The crowds who gathered on the bridge for the official opening ceremony

38,672 vehicles a week means a new bridge for Maidstone

July 1st: The bridge over the River Medway at Maidstone has been widened and improved in order to meet the astonishing increase in modern-day traffic. Improvement costs of £53,000 have been shared between the Ministry of Transport, the Rochester Bridge Wardens and the Maidstone town council.

The decision to strengthen the bridge follows a census taken a few months ago which revealed that 38,672 motor vehicles are crossing the river at this point each week. Made up of 20,347 cars, 8,042 motor cycles and 10,283 lorries this represents an increase of more than seven and a half times the volume of motor traffic recorded in 1913.

It is incredible to think that just 25 years ago horse-drawn vehicles and the occasional motor were using the bridge and most people were sceptical about the future of the automobile. Today horses are still very much in evidence but they are a traffic hazard and have caused many accidents.

The railway bridge over the Medway by Maidstone East is to be renewed as part of Southern Railway's scheme to enable the Swanley to Ashford line to be used as an alternative boat train route when the trains are worked by engines of the "King Arthur Class".

In order to enable the present bridge to carry the heavy engines it is being supported by temporary staging which will also be available for the construction of the new bridge.

Memorial in Gillingham for Will Adams

A memorial clock has been erected in Gillingham in memory of William (Will) Adams, the Elizabethan navigator and adventurer who sailed to Japan in 1600, gained the confidence of the ruthless Shogun, Tokugawa Ieyasu and became the only European to be ennobled as a Samurai.

Will Adams, who was born in Gillingham in 1564, was a remarkable man. He virtually founded the Japanese navy and, in gratitude, the Japanese maintain two shrines in his memory. He never returned to England, although the East India Company did offer a passage after Ieyasu's death in 1616.

By this time Adams had married a Japanese girl and had two children by her but still continued to write to his wife, Mary, in England.

Six Cockburn, two coronas and the Ashes — what a summer!

August 18th: The brilliant amateur cricketer, Mr A.P.F. (Percy) Chapman is the toast of all England, despite having only played one full season of county cricket. Selected to captain his country against Australia, Chapman and his young lions have regained the Ashes after 14 years with an emphatic victory by 289 runs at the Oval. The first four Tests were all drawn.

Chapman is lucky to be playing cricket at all. In 1924 he was thrown from his motorbike in a freak accident when his raincoat became caught in the back wheels of the machine. He was thrown off and escaped with shock and severe bruises.

England's hero was born in Reading, educated at Uppingham and Cambridge University and qualified to play for Kent by residence when he came to live in Hythe and work as an

underbrewer at H. Simmonds, Mackeson's brewery.

The same year he made his first appearance for England in this country against South Africa, although he had already toured with an MCC side in 1922-3.

In 1924 he played for Hythe on three occasions scoring 129, 112 and 174. He also made at least one appearance with the brewery cricket team.

Chapman played five games for Kent last season and nine this season. In May a colleague at the brewery offered him two bottles of port for each 50 he could score and bet him 50 cigars he wouldn't score a century. In the first championship match at Southampton, Chapman hit a brilliant 159 and immediately sent a telegram to his colleagues: *"Six Cockburn 1886 and two large coronas. Percy."*

The men of the construction gang look well pleased with their work. A bridge outside Hythe is completed, the line of the track determined and all is set fair for the laying of the rails, the completion of the terminus and the opening of the smallest public railway in the world. The line will have a gauge of only 15 inches and will eventually run between Hythe and New Romney and then, perhaps, on to Dungeness. See page 24.

Woman swims Channel faster than any man

August 31st: It has been a triumphant month for the fair sex. Two women have successfully swum the Channel from Cap Gris Nez to the Kent coast while a third only abandoned her attempt because of dense fog and freezing conditions.

The achievement of being the first, however, belongs to Gertrude Ederle, a 19-year-old New York athlete who overcame the cold, strength-sapping tides and strong current on August 6th to make the crossing in 14 hours 31 minutes. It was more than two hours quicker than the previous record time set by Sebastian Tirabocchi three years ago. Miss Ederle was a bronze medallist in the Paris Olympic Games.

Two weeks later, Miss Corson, a 27-year-old mother from New York, also beat all male records with her swim of 15 hours 28 minutes. She landed on Dover's western beach where an enthusiastic party gave her an ecstatic welcome.

Uncle Mac and his minstrels are enjoying another great season on the sands at Broadstairs. One local boy who has won an Uncle Mac singing competition is Frank Muir.

Airliner crashes in flames at Hildenborough

October 2nd: A four-engined Bleriot French airliner caught fire while flying over Tonbridge on Saturday and crashed in flames in a field at Westwood, near Hildenborough. The five British passengers — three women and two men — and the French pilot and mechanic all perished.

The plane was flying from Paris to Croydon but it was over the Sports ground at Tonbridge that people first saw the flames spurting out from the tail. These died down then appeared again and the machine came down to earth with startling velocity in a field at the rear of Southwood house on Westwood Farm just inside the parish of Leigh.

A *Sevenoaks Chronicle* reporter, attending the sale of livestock in Weald village, was one of the first on the scene. He mounted his motor cycle, found the field within minutes and began to extract bodies from the wreckage with the help of several local people.

The aeroplane was a Bleriot 155, fitted with four Renault water-cooled engines. It appears that one of the petrol tanks burst and that the escaping petrol caught fire. As smoking was strictly prohibited inside the plane the cause of the fire remains a mystery.

The aeroplane disaster at Hildenborough follows three other crashes in Kent this year. On June 24th a French Fokker (F-NACL) came down in the sea off Seabrook and was dragged ashore by onlookers. On the same day a French Farman Goliath nose-dived onto Littlestone Golf Course, the passengers and crew escaping with injuries.

On August 18th a French Bleriot — identical to the one that crashed at Hildenborough — came down at College Farm, near Aldington with the loss of four lives. The pilot was M. Jean Emile de Lisle who, by a sad coincidence, died at almost the same time as the French government was awarding him the Croix de Chevalier de Legion d'Honneur.

'The drowned and desolate world lies dumb and white in a trance of snow '
— Elizabeth Chase, 1896

1927

January 9th: Four men have been killed and 11 seriously injured during blasting operations at Betteshanger Colliery.

February 4th: Malcolm Campbell who lives at Chislehurst, has raised the world land-speed record to an incredible 174.224 mph. He achieved the feat today in his car Bluebird along the Pendine Sands in West Wales.

February 12th: Ten vessels collided today in a fogbound English Channel. Three of them sank.

The London brewers, Samuel Whitbread — who have hop farms in Kent — have taken over the famous Phoenix Brewery which has been making Wateringbury ales for more than 150 years. Trading since 1895 under the name Frederick Leney and Sons, all shares have been sold and control passes to Whitbread.

March 1st: 53 miners are feared dead in an explosion in a pit at Ebbw Vale, Wales. Another 150 are trapped below ground. Rescue work continues.

March 15th: Petrol prices have dropped to 1s 4° d a gallon.

April 13th: The Goverment today promised to give the vote to all women over the age of 21.

April 19th: American actress Miss Mae West has been found guilty of indecent behaviour in her production of *Sex on Broadway*. She has been sentenced to 10 days in jail and fined $500.

May 21st: Captain Charles Lindbergh today completed the first non-stop solo flight between New York and Paris. Flying a Ryan NYP monoplane, *The Spirit of St Louis*, he touched down in front of a crowd of 10,000 people at Le Bourget airport. His 3,600 mile flight took 33 hours. The Leas Cliff Hall at Folkestone

SOUVENIR PHOTOGRAPH of SIR ALAN & LADY COBHAMS 20,000 MILES FLIGHT ROUND AFRICA IN THE "SHORT'S ROLLS ROYCE (COPYRIGHT) SINGAPORE" FLYING BOAT. NOV 1927. WILLIS 67 HIGH ST CHATHAM.

November 24th: News was received today that the famous aviator, Alan Cobham, who left Rochester last week in a Short's Singapore Rolls Royce flying boat has completed his pioneering flight round Africa. Cobham, accompanied by his wife, was caught in a heavy storm and forced to crash-land in the sea off Malta but engineers from Rochester travelled overland and repaired the aircraft.

has been opened to great acclaim.

June 19th: More than 20,000 young people are taking part in the Festival of Youth at Crystal Palace.

A pioneer parachutist, Corporal East has been killed at Biggin Hill attempting a world record for a delayed drop from a Vicker's Vimy. A large crowd watched with horror as his parachute failed to open.

August 1st: Torrential rain in Kent has made the Bank Holiday one of the wettest ever known.

August: New covered-top buses have been introduced in London.

August 24th: Coal has been lifted for the first time from Betteshanger Colliery in East Kent.

August 25th: The famous Time Ball on top of the Semaphore Station adjacent to the Admiralty Dockyard in Deal has been withdrawn from service. It was first erected in 1855 to give the correct time to ships passing through the Channel.

Barge races, so popular on both the Thames and the Medway in the early years of the century have been revived. The *Harold Margetts*, owned by APCM and skippered by Jack Waterhouse, won the River Class in the

Thames Match and deadheated with the *Plinlimmon* in the Medway Match.

October 6th: Warner Brothers' production of *The Jazz Singer,* starring Al Jolson, includes the first spoken dialogue in films ever heard.

October 29th: There are now 1,729,000 motor vehicles registered in Britain compared with 127,248 horse-drawn carriages. These figures released today show there is now one vehicle to every 26 people.

Louis Brennan, the great inventor who lived in Gillingham between 1883 and 1912, has achieved another sensational engineering triumph — an aircraft with rotating blades which can lift itself off the ground vertically. Brennan, who heads a small design team at the Royal Aircraft Establishment, Farnborough, is applying for a patent.

November 15th: Leon Trotsky and Grigori Zinoviev have been expelled from the Soviet Communist Party by Joseph Stalin.

December 15th: The House of Commons today voted to reject the new Book of Common Prayer. The most controversial change in the proposed book is a clause in the marriage service in which a wife no longer has to promise to obey her husband. Supporters fear the vote may lead to the disestablishment of the Church of England.

The largest paper mill in the world, Lloyds at Sittingbourne, has been sold to Allied Newspapers. *The Daily Chronicle* is printed at Lloyds.

GREAT HITS OF 1927
Ain't She Sweet

Among My Souvenirs

Sometimes, I'm Happy

Everest hero tells of tragedy near the summit

March: Captain John Noel, one of the heroes of the courageous but ill-fated attempts to conquer Mount Everest in 1922 and 1924, has written a book about the two expeditions. Because of the overwhelming interest in every attempt to climb the world's highest peak, the book is tipped to be a national best-seller.

On both occasions Noel was the expedition cinematographer and his book has helped to immortalise the mystery of the loss of George Leigh Mallory and Andrew Irvine high on Everest's north-east ridge in June 1924. He explains how the two climbers were less than 1,000 feet from the 29,028 foot summit and going strong when bad weather came down and the support team lost sight of them in a swirling snowstorm.

Captain Noel, who lives in Brenzett, on Romney Marsh writes: "Up and up into the blue sky they had gone higher and higher — higher than any man had reached before. We had a glimpse of them 600 feet from the summit and still going up. Then they disappared from sight. Hour after hour we watched the mountain with our telescopes. Had they slipped and been hurled down the precipice? Had they reached the summit and then been frozen to death? Will we ever know?"

Noel and his team remained at 23,000 feet for 10 days without oxygen and all the time he was filming, using a cine-camera which is now in the Science Museum. He said: "I now realise how hard and cruelly this mountain fights. She had allowed the men to come on and, at the last moment had killed them. Maybe she had killed in revenge after they had attained their victory. Who knows? She alone holds the secret."

Captain Noel's book called "Through Tibet to Everest" is published by Hodder and Stoughton.

June 24th: A portrait of the mayor of Margate, Mrs M.H.S. Hatfeild with some of the town's bathing beauties after today's opening of the Margate Lido Pool.

Seven new towns for East Kent?

April: Following the publication of a Government-sponsored report by Professor Abercrombie, East Kent is bracing itself for a population explosion which has no precedent in Britain. "By 1955," says the professor, "300,000 more people will be living in the villages around Dover and Deal."

The reason for the violent change is the proposed creation of 18 new mining pits, all worked by electricity from a common generating plant and the erection of a vast steelworks near Dover.

Professor Abercrombie feels it is unwise to build small communities dependent on one industry so he has suggested that new towns be created; two the size of Folkestone, three as big as Canterbury and two similar to Deal. A port at Reculver, he says, should be considered.

Alarm bells in East Kent have been ringing furiously. There are fears of hundreds of colliery chimneys pouring out black smoke and iron foundries spreading across the Garden of England. There are predictions of slag heaps similar in size to those seen in Wales.

Pearson, Dorman and Young, who have the controlling interest in mineral rights, say there are 100 million tons of iron ore near Dover. To work the iron ore it will be necessary to build blast and steel furnaces, taking a large proportion of the East Kent coal output.

As Kent considers the impact of the report, miners from Wales, East Midlands, Durham and Nottinghamshire are flooding in by rail. Some are even walking to Kent in search of work. Advertisements in local papers are now telling the men not to proceed to Kent without direct engagements.

William Willett, a memorial to his memory.

Petts Wood honours its 'summer time' hero

May 21st: William Willett, the man who introduced daylight saving to England, has been honoured at last . Eleven years since the clocks were first advanced by one hour as a wartime measure, a memorial has been unveiled at Petts Wood where the dedicated campaigner lived until his death in 1915 aged 58.

The memorial is in the form of a sundial and bears the Latin inscription *'horos non numero nisi aestivas'* — 'I will only tell the summer hours'. On the north side of the stone is the legend: 'This wood was purchased by public subscription as a tribute to the memory of William Willett.'

Marquess Camden, Lord Lieutenant of Kent unveiled the sundial and William Willett's widow said: "Nothing would have given my husband greater pleasure than to have known that this wood belongs to the nation and will forever be

associated with his name."

Willett came to live in the area in 1890 when he bought the Camden Park estate at Chislehurst which had been the residence of Napoleon III of France and Empress Eugenie during their exile in England. Later Willett moved to The Cedars in Camden Park Road.

As a keen horseman, each morning before breakfast he would ride through Petts Wood. It was during one of these canters that the idea of daylight saving came to him. There was support for his idea from Sir Arthur Conan Doyle, Lord Avebury and Winston Churchill but it was not until May 21st, 1916, the year after his death, that daylight saving was introduced as a wartime measure. It became permanent in the "1925 Summer Time Act."

The appeal to buy 72 acres of Petts Wood and hand it over to the National Trust was launched at a dinner last year.

Family dies as fire sweeps through Tudor home

October 17th: Captain Richard Booth Leslie Bazley-White, his wife Katherine, son John and a nurse, Rose Weekes have perished in a fire which swept through their rambling Tudor house, The Hall, Wateringbury today.

The blaze broke out at about midnight in the study, a gas-lit room where the Captain was reading before retiring to bed. Because the only telephone was in the study and there were no others nearby it was more than an hour later before Maidstone Fire Brigade was alerted and by that time the house was well on fire.

It was first noticed by Mrs Bazley-White. She woke other members of the household who included four servants and then rushed along the corridor to save her four-year-old son and his nurse. The servants escaped. Edith Whitfield, the cook, found it was impossible to go downstairs because of the flames and so jumped out of the window onto the gravel path below and set off for her father's house nearby to raise the alarm.

Meanwhile the entire family were trapped upstairs. They made no attempt to jump and died of smoke suffocation.

TERRIBLE FIRE DISASTER
Captain and Mrs Bazley-White, their Child and Nurse Burned to Death

The headline in the *Kent Messenger*

Flashback to August 6th, 1926. The Duke of York, on the footplate with Captain Jack Howey, was driving the inaugural train on the smallest public railway in the world.

Open at last — 'the railway line that Jack built'

July 16th: Miniature railway enthusiast Captain John (Jack) Howey has finally realised his great dream — to build, own and run his own railway. The Romney, Hythe and Dymchurch Railway opened to the general public yesterday in the presence of the Lord Warden of the Cinque Ports, Earl Beauchamp KG who came along in full regalia. It was an historic moment and one that has put Romney Marsh well and truly on the map.

For the official party it was an unforgettable experience. They took their seats in the special train of 20 four-wheeled coaches pulled by a powerful little engine — all true scaled-down replicas of main-line express trains, one third of the size — and covered the nine miles at about 25 miles-an-hour.

It was some years ago that Howey and his friend Count Louis Zborowski made a pact to give up motor racing and start a 15-inch gauge miniature railway together. Tragically Zborowski was killed at the Italian Grand Prix and did not live to see the fruition of the plans, but Howey and his engineering friend Henry Greenly, who designed and constructed the rolling stock, pressed on, overcame vociferous local opposition, won the support of Southern Railway and were delighted when the 15-inch gauge line received its Light Railway Order from Parliament in 1926.

The Light Railway is certain to be a great attraction among holidaymakers in this delightful area of southern Kent.

August 25th: The people of Sevenoaks and district have witnessed two horrific accidents within a few days of each other. On Sunday a Dutch airliner came down at St Julians, a large country house near the village of Underriver. Yesterday (Tuesday), 12 people were killed at Riverhead when an express train hit the Shoreham Lane bridge. See P26.

The crash scene at Riverhead. One witness said it was reminiscent of the flow of wounded along the duck boards at Flanders. Most of the dead and injured came from Folkestone, Deal and Dover.

Express train derailed at high speed: 13 killed

August 25th: Sevenoaks and district is reeling under the shock of the awful disaster which occurred on the Southern Railway yesterday evening (Wednesday) at Shoreham Lane Bridge, Riverhead, when an express train was derailed at high speed. Thirteen people were killed and 30 badly injured.

The train was the 5 pm express from Cannon Street to Ashford, Folkestone, Dover and Deal. It was seen to be rocking violently as it took the straight elevated stretch after Dunton Green and left the rails after passing the catch-points near the bridge which carries traffic from Montreal Park to the Maidstone Road. The cause of the accident has not been ascertained but a railway worker said he noticed the shingle on the down track was loose, possibly caused by the recent heavy rain.

Immediately after the accident, the scene on the railway was like a battlefield. The "River Cray" engine was lying on the bank on the downward side with steam rising in clouds. Piled up behind was all that remained of a coach which carried one passenger who miraculously escaped. He was flung through the windows and bounced along the grass verge, suffering only bruises.

Other coaches were hanging at crazy angles and one entirely filled the archway of the bridge. Cushions, newspapers, magazines and huge pieces of woodwork were strewn across the line. The evening papers were later used to cover the dead as they were placed in a long row, a grim sight indeed.

Police, passengers, railwaymen and doctors were among more than 100 rescuers at this tragic scene. Also among them were nurses and other women taking their part in the work of mercy amid scenes of utter carnage.

Digging for victory. A shovel gang at Biggin Hill finds the main road under seven feet of snow.

Boxing Day blizzard rivals the greatest known

December 27th: A great blizzard which swept across the western part of the county yesterday has completely paralysed scores of towns and villages. Roads are hopelessly blocked, trains snowbound, vehicles buried and search-parties are doing their utmost to locate those in distress. The snow has stopped but, in many places, it lies 15 feet deep and people will be imprisoned in their homes for many days to come. Without doubt it rivals the greatest blizzards of the last century and will be talked about for many years to come.

There was no indication on Christmas Day of the dramatic events to follow. It rained hard for most of the day but, overnight, a cutting north-east wind turned the rain into driving, blinding snow. On the North Downs at Biggin Hill, Cudham and Knockholt homes were buried up to their roofs. People desperately tried to dig their way out but the wind whipped up the snow. One man, attempting to reach a bungalow which had virtually disappeared, fell into a drift up to his neck and only saved himself by clinging onto a tree branch.

Yesterday afternoon a rescue party tried to get to Biggin Hill. They found the road over Keston Common completely lost, reported that the blown snow was in excess of 18 feet deep and abandoned their mission. Later today a light aircraft will attempt to take off from Biggin Hill with supplies of food. The BBC has asked people to lay out black clothes in the snow "not less than 15 feet in diameter to help pilots pin-point people in need".

It's the same story at Toys Hill, Ide Hill and villages along the Greensand Ridge. One couple attempting to walk from Sevenoaks Station to Goathurst Common with their eight-year-old son found the going so hard that they thought they would perish. Fortunately, although it was past midnight, the landlord of The Woodman Inn heard their shouts and helped to dig a path to his pub.

Between Kemsing and Otford a train was buried when masses of snow above the railway cutting collapsed onto the line. At Polhill, Sevenoaks, scores of cars have been buried and a Maidstone and District bus has been lost "somewhere on Seal Chart".

In East Kent there was little snow but three inches of rain fell in just over 24 hours.

August 4th: Mr Winston Churchill, accompanied by his debutante daughter, Diana and his parliamentary private secretary, Mr Bob Boothby on his way to the House of Commons with his despatch box which contains his budget secrets. Mr Churchill has been Chancellor of the Exchequer since the end of 1924 but it is at Chartwell that he relaxes, swims, paints and prepares speeches. The April budget (his fourth) is widely predicted as one that will break new ground and is already hailed as Winston's "industrial lifebuoy".

'A.P. Freeman, the only man to take 300 wickets in a season, is almost small enough to go into your waistcoat pocket, yet this philosopher of the slapstick is endowed with dignity' — Denzil Batchelor.

January 5th: Queues have been developing at post offices in Kent as those over the age of 65 receive their first state pensions of ten shillings a week.

February 6th: A woman has arrived in New York on board the liner *Berengaria* today claiming that she is the youngest daughter of the murdered Russian Czar. Mrs Anastasia Chaikovsky says she survived the bloody massacre of the Russian Royal family at the hands of the Bolshelviks in 1918.

February 19th: Mr Malcolm Campbell of Bonchester, Chislehurst has set a land-speed record of 206.35 mph in his car *Bluebird* at Daytona beach, Florida.

February 28th: During dense fog last night the German ship, *S S Olive* collided with the South Goodwin lightship, smashing the stern of the lightship.

March 19th: Skullcaps of gold and silver tissue were unveiled at today's Women's Wear Exhibition. It is predicted that the fashionable women of Kent, whose hair has been getting shorter and shorter over the past few years, will enjoy wearing the skullcaps and the new skirts which are only just below the knee.

Berry Wiggins has bought the 323 acre site once occupied by the airship factory at Kingsnorth for its crude oil refinery. Building will begin soon.

March 29th: The campaign by the Suffragettes is over. The House of Commons today passed the Equal Franchise Bill giving the vote to all women aged 21 or over.

April 6-7th: The newly-formed Cinque Ports Flying Club held its first meeting at Lympne airport this weekend. The event attracted 30 visiting aircraft and 6,000 people turned up, many enjoying joy rides for 5/-.

April 14th: Anxiety is growing in Sevenoaks over the "ill-considered" shop building development adjacent to Bligh's Hotel in the High Street. Mr C.R. Ashbee has written to *The Times*

July 14th: Captain H.H.Balfour, MP for Thanet and Councillor Bing, chairman of the council, today opened the new road into Broadstairs which has cost £15,412. The opening ceremony was followed by a grand cavalcade of cars.

complaining that Sevenoaks has suffered greatly in the spoiling of old buildings and the destruction of parks and he asks for the newspaper's support in the "saving of the High Street."

May 1st: A sight for astonished eyes in Kent is the trolleybus, seen for the first time this week in Maidstone on the well-used route to Barming. Northern cities have been using the trolleybus for several years but a regular service in London has still to be introduced. If the Maidstone experiment is a success a trolleybus will also run to Loose.

May 12th: Part of the cliff and esplanade overlooking The Garden On The Sands at Broadstairs has collapsed leaving three homes in a perilous position.

July 22nd: Dame Ellen Terry, illustrious lady of the theatre and a resident at Smallhythe Place near Tenterden for 29 years, died at home yesterday aged 81. Also known for her association with Sir Henry Irving, she enjoyed playing a huge variety of roles — many to universal acclaim. Her last appearance on the stage was at the Lyric Theatre, Hammersmith in Walter de la Mare's *Crossings* (1926). Her daughter, Edith, plans to turn the 16th-century house at Smallhythe into a memorial for her mother.

Ashford Hospital in King's Road has been completed.

August 12th: The Olympic Games has ended. Amsterdam welcomed more than 3,000

competitors from 46 countries. Lord Burleigh, heir to the Marquess of Exeter, became the first non-American to win the 400m hurdles.

August 27th: Delegates from 15 countries met in Paris today to sign a pact of the Renunciation of War. First to sign was Herr Gustav Stresemann, the German Foreign Minister.

September 19th: Work is nearing conclusion on a new paper works and village at Kemsley, near Sittingbourne.

September 30th: Professor Alexander Fleming of Queen Mary's Hospital has discovered a mould which attacks many different kinds of harmful bacteria. He has identified it as Penicillium Notatum which often grows on stale bread. It will be some time before it is available for medical use.

October 9th: The BBC has rejected the idea of a trial television service following several tests.

Admiral Sir John Jellicoe, who was in command of the most powerful fleet ever assembled and won a decisive naval battle at Jutland in May 1916, has been given the Freedom of the City of Canterbury during a service at the Cathedral. In the Battle of Jutland, Britain lost a battleship, cruiser and five destroyers. The Germans lost a battleship, cruiser, destroyer and 2,500 men.

November 28th: The first one pound and ten shilling notes have come into circulation.

December 20th: Kent cricketer Mr Percy Chapman has led England to massive victories in the first two Test Matches. Australia lost by 675 runs at Brisbane and then by eight wickets at Sydney.

December 28th: The East Goodwin lightship which is protecting shipping in the notorious Downs drifted four miles north of its station today after the cable snapped.

GREAT HITS OF 1928

Ol' Man River

A Room with a View

Overcome by fatigue or famine, a victim is carried through the Canterbury floods to a waiting ambulance.

Catastrophe in Canterbury as river bursts its banks

January 1st: The depression from the Atlantic which brought the greatest blizzard ever known to West Kent on Boxing Day also affected the eastern part of the county. But the results are different and, in many places, far more catastrophic — for hundreds of thousands of acres are now under water.

Right along the Thames embankment from Woolwich to Gravesend and beyond, fast-flowing floodwater has invaded towns and villages. Lush valleys are lost beneath the swirling torrents, farms inundated, road and rail traffic dislocated and telephonic communications are chaotically disrupted. In London 14 people have been drowned, including four young sisters in their basement home, and hundreds more are homeless.

Other riverside towns in Kent have not escaped. The Medway has burst its banks at Tonbridge and, in Maidstone, where the water is almost as high as the lamp posts on the embankment, a relief fund has been established to help families in distress.

In Canterbury, the city is experiencing what the mayor describes as "its greatest natural disaster ever known". The torrential rain just after Christmas coincided with a full moon and spring tides and an abnormal amount of water began to drain into the valleys from the uplands. By New Year's Eve the villages along the Stour Valley and the ancient city itself were under several feet of water and hundreds of inhabitants were imprisoned in their quarters without food or heating.

The water has continued to rise. In St Peter's Place it is too deep for a horse and cart to approach the marooned people and, tragically, all the boats which ply the Stour have been sunk. The Salvation Army has sent to Whitstable for more boats — one for every street — and soup kitchens have been set up for those rescued.

The mayor of Canterbury has now opened a fund for those who have lost possessions and suffered flood damage and a souvenir newspaper called *Canterbury's Catastrophe* is soon to be published.

Welcome provisions are handed to a family in St Peter's Place, Canterbury. In many parts of the town people have lived for days on bread and butter alone and families living in upstairs rooms have waited patiently for the rescue parties to bring food and water by boat. At Sturry the owner of two mills, Mr Prosser attempted to open his sluices and run the mill races at full bore but they couldn't cope with the volume of water and the two branches of the river joined forces to create havoc. One car was swept into the mill pool, the passengers just escaping in time.

300 wickets in one season for the wizard called 'Tich'

September 16th: Kent and England's slow right arm googly bowler, Alfred Percy Freeman, has achieved a bowling feat that may never be equalled in the history of cricket.

Freeman, 40, who is just 5ft 2in tall and better known as "Tich", yesterday took his 300th wicket this season for Kent in the championship match against Lancashire. In reaching this extraordinary milestone Freeman has helped to secure Kent's place as runners-up in the Championship and has set a standard of sensational proportions.

Tich was born in Lewisham, joined the Kent staff before the war and played his first match for the county at 26. In fact, he took over where Colin Blythe left off and for a number of seasons has shouldered, with Woolley, the burden of the Kent attack.

He played his first Test Match for England in England in 1924 and is certain to be selected on many occasions in the future. Tich has been awarded a benefit for the 1929 season.

Whenever they drive or walk around Looking Glass Corner, the people of Beckenham and district cannot believe their eyes. There in the middle of the road, at the end of Hayes Lane, sits a new garage that looks more in keeping with the suburbs of Shanghai or Peking than London. The garage, built in eastern style by the Beckenham firm of Hand Taylor to serve the new Langley estate, has won a newspaper competition for the most original filling station. Local people have started to call it The Chinese Garage.

Hales Place to be demolished by gelignite

April 7th: Hales Place, Hackington, Canterbury, the impressive, seventeenth century mansion latterly occupied by the Jesuit community, is to be razed to the ground by explosives.

The demolition will commence on Tuesday (April 11th) when the walls will be brought down by gelignite in order to preserve intact as many bricks as possible.

The fabric has been bought for £4,900 by a demolition company and the site by Mr Radford Arthur Dagnall, a property speculator, who intends to lay out a new estate, complete with country club.

Attempts by the Jesuits to sell Hales Place as a school or institution have proved fruitless in the present economic climate, so despite considerable opposition, they have been forced to sell the site as a building plot.

The great mansion, built partly

with stone from St Augustine's Abbey, contains 135 rooms and is 535 feet long. It is named after the original owner of the house, Sir Edward Hales, a friend of James II who was King for less than four years and who fled to France after his failed attempts to turn England into a Roman Catholic country.

Although the mansion and its theatre will be pulled down there are no plans to demolish the Jesuit burial ground and chapel, where Mass will continue to be celebrated annually.

A horse- drawn wagon bearing the coffin of Lord Sackville proceeds at walking pace through Knole Park.

Lady Sackville 'boycotts' her husband's funeral

January: When Lionel and Victoria Sackville-West returned to Sevenoaks following the great "illegitimacy trial" of 1912 local people turned out in their thousands to watch the happy couple make their triumphant journey to Knole. How times have changed!

At Lord Sackville's funeral on Thursday — he died at Knole a week ago — Victoria was notable by her absence. The couple had been on the coldest of terms for many years and when Victoria discovered that her (former) friend Olive Rubens was his mistress, the relationship abruptly ended. Lionel requested a divorce but she refused him time and time again.

Lord Sackville has been buried in the family tomb in Withyham church. The coffin was borne from the doorway of Knole by a horse-drawn estate wagon which moved at walking pace through the great park to the main gates in Sevenoaks.

Among the chief mourners was the Sackville's daughter Vita who was accompanied by her husband Harold and her friend, the author Virginia Woolf. Also present was Vita's cousin Major General Charles John Sackville-West, nephew to Lionel, who inherits both Knole and the peerage.

In a letter this week to the new Lord Sackville, Miss Woolf writes: "Vita has answered 300 letters about her father but I'm afraid it's a dismal affair for her. Your aunt's (Lady Sackville) behaviour could only be tolerated in an Elizabethan play. That she may take a dagger to her own throat or drink broken glass is rather my hope, I admit."

Death-trap theatre destroyed by fire

Concerned inhabitants of Herne Bay who have campaigned hard for the removal of the Pier Theatre, Herne Bay, which has long been considered a fire hazard, have had their prayers answered in the most ironical way. Last week it burnt to the ground; arson is not suspected.

The campaign to demolish the building was led by the Herne Bay Guardian who this week expressed a feeling of great relief, because the fire occurred at night and the theatre was empty.

In an editorial the Guardian said: "Please sir, we had no knowledge of the fire.....With similar strangeness of coincidence, a councillor told a friend that the theatre would be 'down' in a month. Now a good deal of banter is coming our way and we were told in Canterbury the other day that we had 'timed our stunt' to the right minute."

The theatre, which stood at the entrance to the Grand Pavilion, will not be replaced. Not only was it a death trap but an eyesore.

Primate resigns over new prayer book

November 12th: Randall Davidson has resigned as Archbishop of Canterbury. For years he has been advocating the introduction of a revised Book of Common Prayer and its rejection — for the second time — by the House of Commons has left him bitterly disappointed.

Dr Davidson, 80, who has enjoyed 25 distinguished years as head of the Church of England, leaves today on his golden wedding anniversary. In his sermon at Canterbury on Sunday he said: "It may seem to be a paradox but it is true that these prayer book discussions — until some jarring notes caused trouble at the end — have evolved a deeper and more thoughtful spirit of unity in purpose and in prayer than any we have known before."

His departure will not end the controversy, for Dr Davidson is succeeded by Bishop Cosmo Lang, the chief advocate of the revised book and an outspoken member of the House of Lords. His enthronement will take place on December 4th. The Home Secretary, Sir William Joynson-Hicks who is a leading opponent of the revisions, has called for Lang to devote himself to "the evangelization of the people, the real call of the church".

The controversy over the revised book has split the Church of England.

The Rev Edmund Arbuthnott Knox, Bishop of Bromley who led the evangelical fight against the new prayer book has been supported by *The Times* newspaper. He believes the bill, had it been passed, would have destroyed some of the most valuable elements of life in the Church of England.

50 bishops but no Roman Catholics at enthronement

December 5th: The enthronement of Archbishop Cosmo Lang which took place at Canterbury yesterday was masterminded by the Dean, Dr George Bell and attended by thousands of people including some 50 bishops and the whole of the Diocesan clergy. Church representatives included Greek Orthodox, Russian Orthodox, German Lutheran and the Armenian Church but no invitation was extended to any representative of the Roman Catholic Church.

The BBC covered the occasion — "their biggest effort so far", The Southern Railway Company, at the request of Dean Bell, arranged a special train from London and Vaughan Williams composed a "Te Deum" for the ceremony.

The outgoing Archbishop, Dr Davison has now taken his seat in the House of Lords as Lord Davison of Lambeth and the Prime Minister, Mr Stanley Baldwin, has presented him with a cheque for £14,500 as "a national tribute of gratitude and respect".

15 lifeboatmen perish in heavy seas off Dungeness

November 15th: In the worst single lifeboat tragedy ever known, 15 men have perished in stormy waters about three miles south-west of Dungeness.

The victims are the entire crew of the Rye Harbour lifeboat, *The Mary Stanford,* which responded to a distress call in the early hours of this morning from the Latvian steamer, *The Alice,* which was taking in water and drifting in the heavy seas.

Although the wind was blowing at hurricane force *The Mary Stanford* was launched at 6.45 am and the crew began the daunting task of rowing through mountainous seas on their life-saving mission. At 6.50 am Rye coastguards heard that the crew of *The Alice* had been rescued by a passing steamer and gave the recall signal but the lifeboatmen were unable to see or hear it.

Fears grew all this morning as the lifeboat failed to return and it was not until 12 noon that she was seen, bottom upwards, floating towards the shore. Some of the men were entangled beneath the boat; others were washed ashore one by one. This morning's great tragedy unfolded slowly.

In the small but close-knit community of Rye Harbour eleven children are now fatherless and nearly every family is affected.

Police urged: Prosecute those who ignore 20 mph speed limit

November: Figures released this week show that traffic accidents in Kent continue to soar at an alarming rate, prompting demands for new laws to control the mania for private motoring. Councillors throughout the county are pressing parliament to introduce a driving test and others are urging police to prosecute those who ignore the speed limit of 20 mph. Nationally, 5,329 people died on the roads last year and the sight of mangled vehicles by the roadside is commonplace.

The notion that only rich people own motor cars is changing with the introduction of smaller, cheaper cars. The Austin Seven (first introduced in 1922) at a price of £225) is seen all over Kent and next year William Morris will introduce his 7 hp economy car to be called the Minor.

January 3rd: The BBC is to form a permanent symphony orchestra with Sir Thomas Beecham as conductor.

January 13th: Today the death occurred of the legendary Wyatt Earp, former Marshal of Dodge City, who assumed the role of law-enforcer. He was 80.

February 14th: Seven men have been murdered in a Chigago side street by gangsters believed to be led by Al Capone. The mob was defending their monopoly of boot-legged liquor, extortion and prostitution in the city.

March 11th: Major Henry Segrave has set a new land speed record of 231 mph in his *"Golden Arrow"* at Daytona Beach, Florida.

May 10th: The General Election campaign began today when the King dissolved Parliament.

June 3rd: Actor Douglas Fairbanks Jnr, 19, has married actress Joan Crawford, 23.

The Royal School of Church Music has opened at St Nicholas College, Chislehurst.

June 7th: Ramsay MacDonald announced today the composition of Britain's second Labour Government. Among MPs elected are 13 women including Lloyd-George's daughter, Megan.

All bridge tolls over the Swale between Sittingbourne and Sheerness have been lifted by the railway company, following compensation of £50,000 paid by Kent County Council.

July: The Isle of Grain has been given a new name — "The Isle of Grin and Bear It" — so called because of the big gun naval firing range established by the War Office at Yantlet by the far end of the Medway mud-flats. Residents claim the massive guns have brought down walls and ceilings in scores of homes and the village is strewn with broken tiles and pieces of glass from blown out windows. Life in Grain, they claim, is unbearable .

Christopher Robin, the son of author A.A.Milne was a member of the cast of a glittering pageant, staged at Kidbrooke Park, Lewisham in the summer. The producer was Gwen Lally and the programme included verses written by Vita Sackville-West and a sketch by Milne, whose book Winnie-the-Pooh, *is the delight of children all over the country.* The Pageant of Ashdown Forest, *as it was called was presented in eight episodes.*

July 19th: On the 136th rainless day of the year, water boards in Kent have suspended the use of water for gardens and motor cars. The prolonged drought is thought to be a serious menace to health.

August 21st: Mahatma Ghandi has been elected President of the Indian National Congress. He has refused to accept the position.

August 29th: The German airship, *Graf Zeppelin* returned to New Jersey today after a historic 21-day trip round the world.

September 7th: The Schneider Air Race has been won by Britain. Flying Officer Waghorn in a Supermarine Rolls-Royce S6 flew at a speed in excess of 300 mph proving that this country is the leading force in aircraft design.

September 12th: An aerial ropeway has been erected at Tilmanstone to connect the colliery with Dover Harbour.

September 13th: Traffic lights, now in use in 21 British cities, are to be standardised. A trial has shown that red should signal stop, green go and amber warn of a coming change. They are also proving unsuitable where horse-drawn traffic still abounds.

October 14th: People in the northern Kent boroughs saw the R101, the world's biggest airship, make her maiden voyage yesterday over London.

A twice daily cross Channel flying boat service between Dover and Calais has been introduced. The journey takes about 20 minutes either way.

October 24th: Thirteen million shares changed hands on the New York Stock Exchange today in an unprecedented wave of fear and panic. Police riot squads were called to try and disperse the hysterical crowds gathering in Wall Street. The crash is certain to have an affect on the economy all over the Western world.

Sir Philip Sassoon, MP for Hythe and Under Secretary of State for Air, has flown to India to survey a route for Imperial Airways passenger lines.

December 1st: Public telephone boxes were introduced today in London.

Pressure is mounting for a by-pass around Maidstone. The council, with the backing of KCC, has argued the case to the Minister of Transport and it is likely that the scheme will soon be approved. The greatest problem is in Week Street where the volume and speed of traffic causes great concern. One-way systems have been experimented with and a set of traffic lights installed at the bottom of the High Street.

New church:
St Andrew's Bromley.
New cinema:
The Plaza, Gravesend.

GREAT HITS OF 1929

Stardust
Tiptoe Through The Tulips

February 16th: Kent is experiencing one of the coldest Februaries ever known. Up to this morning there has been more than 120 hours of continuous frost and the mercury yesterday fell to 9F (-13C) — so cold that the sea at Whitstable froze solid.

In these arctic conditions there have been power cuts and burst pipes. Unemployed men have been engaged to help Corporation workers grit the roads, where conditions are lethal.

At Folkestone no-one remembers it being so cold. Schools have closed and people advised to stay indoors. Such warnings have been ignored by many children, especially small boys who have flocked to Caesar's Camp, Folkestone with their toboggans or to the Military Canal where skating conditions are perfect.

Singing MP wins his seat — but "Stanley-boy" is a loser

May 31st: Kent is no longer a solid Conservative county. The general election returns show that two seats (Dartford and Chatham) have been gained by Labour and, more surprising, the Liberals have captured Ashford, overturning a 10,000 Tory majority.

Other than these, there are few shocks. Sevenoaks is once more a safe Conservative seat and Mr Waldron Smithers of Knockholt has increased his majority at Chislehurst — thanks to his singing. During the campaign, Smithers composed new lyrics to the Al Johnson song Sonny Boy and serenaded his constituents with the words "We love you Stanley boy".

It may have worked at Chislehurst but nationally, the general election ended in stalemate. Stanley Baldwin secured the most votes but Ramsay MacDonald's Labour party won the most seats with the Liberals holding the balance of power.

Tonight it appears the three-way tally will be: Labour 288, Tories 260 and Liberals 59. This means that MacDonald will be forming Britain's second Labour Government.

The safest seat in Kent is Dover where Major J.J. Astor of Hever, who is chairman of *The Times* publishing company and President of Kent British Legion, gained a majority of almost 12,000.
Results are as follows:

Ashford: Kedward (L) 15,753, Steel (C) 14.579, Follick (Lab) 3,885 (Liberal majority 1,174).

Bromley: James (C) 25,449, Fordham (L) 18,372, Ashworth (Lab) 10,105 (Unionist majority 7,077).

Chatham: Markham (Lab) 13,007, Moore-Brabazon (C) 12,221, Bryans (L) 5,284 (Lab majority 786).

results continued

Passengers escape as steamer sinks

February 29th: There was great drama in Dover Harbour on Monday when a passenger steamer, the *Ville de Liege* struck the shore between the Marine Station and the South Pier and turned broadside. Rockets were fired but the harbour board tugs could not get near owing to the shallowness of the water.

Eventually a motor-boat was launched from the beach, the ship's lifeboats were lowered and together they brought the 40 passengers to the steps of the Hotel de Paris.

The stricken ship was towed to a position just outside the Mole Rocks where it slowly sank.

Imperial Airways has become one of the most famous trail-blazing companies in civil aviation. Since the company was established in 1924 it has flown from Croydon to every major airport in the Commonwealth and Europe. There have, however, been many crashes and forced-landings including this one that occurred in a field at Chelsfield.

Smarden taxi takes gold bullion to London

August 1st: There is growing concern at the number of crashes among civilian airliners en route to and from the Continent. Yesterday a French Farman Goliath carrying about £100,000 of gold bullion, made an emergency landing at Smarden. There was no loss of life but the aircraft was badly damaged. It is believed the gold was driven to London in a Smarden taxi.

Just over a month ago a Handley Page airliner *"City of Ottawa"* suffered engine failure and crashed in the sea off Dungeness. Four people were drowned. Other airliners have come down at the emergency landing grounds at Marden, Penshurst and Littlestone without mishap, apart from considerable shock to the passengers. Since civilian aviation began after the Great War there have been more than a dozen such scares.

As civil aviation bodies look at ways of improving safety, pilots and navigators have said how useful it is to have the names of towns painted on the roofs of Tonbridge, Redhill and Ashford railway stations. All airliners are now obliged to land and refuel at Lympne, the main customs clearance station. Here there is wireless communication with St Inglevert aerodrome in France.

Canterbury: Wayland (C) 19,181, Carnegie (L) 9,937, Eastman (Lab) 4,703 (Unionist majority 9,244).

Chislehurst: Smithers (C) 16,909, Bateman (L) 9,025, Thompson (Lab) 5,445 (Unionist majority 7,884).

Dartford: Mills (Lab) 26,871, Edwards (C) 16,568, Williamson (L) 9,689 (Lab majority 10,303).

Dover: Astor (C) 20,572, McKeag (Lab) 8,864 Baxter (L) 8,188 (Unionist majority 11,708).

Faversham: Maitland (C) 16,219, Aman (Lab) 15,275, Gerothwohl (L) 7,782 (Unionist majority 944).

Gillingham: Gower (C) 13,612, Blizard (Lab) 11,207, Tyrer (L) 3,856 (Unionist majority 2,405).

Gravesend: Albery (C) 14,644, Humphreys (Lab) 12,871, Kershaw (L) 4,220 (Unionist majority 1,773).

Hythe: Sassoon (C) 12,982, Holland (L) 6,912, Colman (Lab) 2,597 (Unionist majority 6,070).

Maidstone: Bellairs (C) 14,254, Morgan (Lab) 10,419, Day (L) 10,222 (Unionist majority 3,835).

Sevenoaks: Young (C) 16,767, Liddiard (L) 7,844 Fyfe (Lab) 6,634 (Unionist majority 8,923).

Tonbridge: Spender-Clay (C) 19,018, Alchin (L) 10,025, Toynbee (Lab) 9,149 (Unionist majority 8,993).

Thanet: Balfour (C) 22,595, Svenson-Taylor (L) 15,648, Paisted (Lab) 4,490 (Unionist majority 6,947).

'Firemen's wedding' ends in tragedy

July 11th: A disaster which has shaken, not only Kent, but the entire nation, occurred at Gillingham Park yesterday when 15 people — firemen, sea-scouts and naval cadets — were burned to death, many beyond recognition, in front of their horrified relatives and hundreds of spectators.

The precise cause of the disaster remains a mystery and may never be solved, for the person who made the fatal mistake also died in the flames. The irony of this terrible tragedy was obvious for all to see.

It happened during the annual fete in aid of the St Bartholomew's Hospital Fund which is staged over two days. The climax and the highspot of the programme should have been the exciting rescue by the Gillingham Fire Brigade of a wedding party who were taking part in a mock marriage in a large make-believe house.

Firemen, dressed up as the bride and bridegroom with sea scouts and naval cadets pretending to be the wedding guests made their way to the "house" where the "reception" was due to be held. At a pre-arranged signal the appearance of a fire was to be simulated by displaying red flares behind the windows.

Thousands of people packed the streets for the funeral procession which began at the council chambers in Green Street and went to the cemetery by way of Copenhagen Road, Gillingham Road and Livingstone Road. Ten draped coffins were carried on fire appliances which were covered in wreaths and five more draped coffins were borne on carriages.

Never before had an accident occurred during this well-rehearsed display. But as darkness was falling over Gillingham Park, something went horribly wrong. Flames appeared from the ground floor, mushroomed upwards almost immediately and blocked all the exits. Within seconds the "reception house" was a roaring inferno. Many of the spectators did not realise that the "make-believe" fire had become a real tragedy and they continued to be "entertained" by the antics of the figures on the roof.

When these people, enveloped in flames, leapt into the blazing wreckage below, the full horror became immediately apparent. Chief Officer Frederick White of Gillingham ordered two motor-pumps standing nearby into action. As water was pumped from a special dam holding 1,200 gallons, and rescue attempts were made with ladders and escapes, women in the crowd fainted and men were in tears.

Although the fire was put out within minutes none of the 15 in the building escaped. Firemen, police and members of the St John Ambulance Brigade who were present also tried to enter the blazing house but were beaten back by the intensity of the flames. Many were severely burnt.

The disaster has stunned the people of Gillingham. This morning the mayor received a telegram from Buckingham Palace which read: "The King and Queen are shocked and distressed by this terrible disaster, resulting in the loss of so many lives, the majority of them being boys of promise."

It is only with the utmost difficulty that the bodies have been identified. In the case of Fireman Nicholls his body was burnt beyond recognition but identification has been made by the mayor from Nicholls' dentures. Councillor Treacher is a dentist.

He said last night: "We can only guess at the possible cause. One suggestion is that someone in a fit of aberration fired half-a-dozen tar barrels which were in the lower storey. It was a terrible sight to see them hanging out of windows imploring help in earnest, but everyone thought it was make-believe". The mayor went on to say that the local authority has seven families to support. "In the case of the three firemen, their families will get 10/- a week."

Sassoon presents trophy for air-speed record

September 7th: Sir Philip Sassoon, MP for Folkestone and Hythe and President of the Royal Aero Club, saw Britain win the Schneider Trophy today with speeds never before attained in the air.

Writing in the *Folkestone Herald*, the former Under Secretary of State for Air said that Britain leads the way in aircraft design and the whole nation thanks the team for the magnificent manner in which they have maintained British prestige.

The winning pilot was Flying Officer H.R.D. Waghorn who took his Supermarine Rolls-Royce S6 round the circuit over the Solent at a speed in excess of 300 mph.

Sir Philip writes: "The roar of his engine followed after him and almost before its reverberations had died away the seaplane was hurtling back towards us on the long straight leg past Stokes Bay, leaping down upon us like a destroying angel with the speed of light and the sound of whirlwinds."

Sir Philip said that as he banked the plane there was a 1,080 lb force on his body. "The machine turned over till its wings were vertical and rising slightly swung round through an angle of 135 degrees in a beautifully even curve."

With Sir Philip was Sir Henry Royce, whose advanced engine powered the seaplane, the Prime Minister Mr Ramsay MacDonald and the Prince of Wales. More than two million people watched the great race.

Townsend's new ferry service undercuts SR by 50 per cent

December: Captain Stuart Townsend, whose new ferry service between Dover and Calais has been such a success, now plans to introduce a bigger and better ship which can carry over 300 passengers — and 28 cars.

He hopes to obtain a passenger certificate, launch the new service in the spring of next year and, in order to finance the whole operation, float a new private company. Townsend is confident that traffic across the Channel will continue to increase "in leaps and bounds."

It was only in July of last year that Captain Townsend chartered the small 386-ton Newcastle-owned coastal collier *Artificer* for one month and launched his service. He wanted the backing of the AA or the RAC but both motoring organisations refused to support him. They felt the Southern Railway Company's Channel crossing service was adequate.

Townsend, however, believed that SR was incompetent. Cars were frequently damaged in transit and vehicle owners were constantly harassed by the loading gangs who demanded tips. In addition the railway company could not carry cars with petrol and hundreds of gallons had to be poured into the sea.

He commissioned a feasibility study and found it was possible to undercut the Southern Railway car rates by 50 per cent and still make a profit.

Using a berth in the Camber at Dover's Eastern Docks and another at the Quai Paul Devot, Calais, the *Artificer*

A car is lowered onto Townsend's new ferry, The Ford.

carried 15 crane-loaded cars and 12 passengers.

Townsend said: "The charter was for one month with the option of a further month. I argued that it would take SR a month to appreciate what I was doing and another month to act by reducing their rates. As this was my original objective I intended then to cease trading if it were achieved."

The Artificer was always full. The rates were £2 single and £3.15s return as against the £5. 15s single by Southern Railway. Townsend won the support of the Dover Harbour Board.

His new ship is *The Ford,* currently being converted. Services will leave daily at 11.30 and again two hours later. It will take an hour and a half to arrive in Calais.

You ain't heard nothin' yet, says Al Jolson

April: Some people are calling it the eighth wonder of the world and others say it is a passing novelty but a few hundred people from Maidstone were in raptures yesterday as the rather indistinct voice of Al Jolson, echoing around the auditorium of the Central Cinema in King Street, uttered his already-famous line: "You ain't heard nothin' yet". Talkies have arrived in Kent.

Although the film *The Jazz Singer* has been seen in London this was the county town's introduction to live dialogue — and it brought the audience to its feet with rapturous applause. Jolson, hailed as King of Broadway and the star of the film, sings *Sonny Boy* among other numbers. The film is produced by Warner Brothers.

The Central, with its 1,250-seat auditorium distempered in cream and beige, was packed to capacity and, judging by the comments from the audience as they left the cinema, talkies are definitely here to stay.

Cinema managers throughout Kent are already discussing ways of going over to the talkies permanently. Many have already introduced sound on disc phonograph films — music shorts with elaborately synchronised sound. The Savoy Theatre at Folkestone is urging its patrons "to come and hear the wonderful singing and talking spectacle *The Broadway Melody*". That is due to open in July.

The Hippodrome, Margate, where so many silent film epics have been shown, will soon be showing *Bulldog Drummond* and the Dreamland Cinema in the same town is being wired-up for sound. The Chatham Empire starts the new era on July 15th with the famous talkie *The Singing Fool.* On the same day talkies will be introduced at Chatham's New Regent.

The Pavilion Theatre, Tonbridge (700 seats) will join the talkie craze in August, also with *The Singing Fool* and The Capitol will follow a few weeks later.

Within a few years Kent's Super Cinemas will all be showing talkies with the accompanying glamour, tinsel and wonderful musical numbers. Stars like Joan Crawford and

Douglas Fairbanks Jnr, who are to marry soon, Sweden's Greta Garbo and France's Maurice Chevalier will be entertaining the people of this county every night. The silver screen is entering a golden age.

New Dover cinema is named after a town in Spain

December 18th: The inhabitants of Dover are wondering why their new cinema, which opens soon, is to be named after a town in Spain. There is a simple explanation. Sidney Bernstein, on a recent walking holiday in southern Spain came across the town of Granada and was so taken with the architecture that he decided to design his new cinema in Moorish style and call it Granada.

The opening of the cinema in Castle Street is accompanied by a huge advertising campaign. Signs are appearing on the side of trams in Dover with the words: "Start saying Granada" and newspaper notices describe

the new cinema as "gay without gaudiness" and "magnificent without ponderosity".

It certainly looks like a Moorish palace with a large entrance hall overlooked by a balcony. Inside there is a huge cut-glass chandelier and Spanish shawls hang from the carved stone balustrades.

The Granada will open on January 8th, 1930 with the Norma Shearer talkie, *The Last of Mrs Cheyney.* Pathe Pictorial, British Movietone News and Mickey Mouse will be in support. If it is a success, Mr Bernstein plans to open more Granadas in Kent.

'They smash gramophone records over each other's heads and roll on the floor. Do people of apparent breeding really do these things'? — Daily Telegraph on Coward's new play *Private Lives*.

February 22nd: The Canadian-born newspaper owner, Lord Beaverbrook, today launched the United Empire Party in collaboration with his fellow Press baron, Lord Rothermere. He plans to field election candidates against official Tory ones.

February 23rd: Government plans to build a bridge across the Thames at Charing Cross have led to the resignation of Sir Edward Lutyens from the Royal Institute of British Architects. The project has been widely criticised and Lutyens, designer of the bridge, feels his reputation has suffered.

April 9th: 200 people gathered outside the gates of Maidstone Prison today to read the notice concerning the hanging of Sydney Fox, aged 29, for the murder of his mother — the first man to be sentenced to death for matricide in over 50 years. The execution was followed by an inquest. The Coroner said he hoped it would be the last time "such a distasteful business would be necessary within these walls".

April 24th: Amy Johnson, aged 27, has become the first woman to fly solo from Britain to Australia. She left Croydon 19 days ago in a second hand Gipsy Moth, made several forced landings on the way, flew blind through sandstorms and finally arrived in Darwin to a tremendous reception.

The Boards of Guardians, which for centuries have looked after the welfare of inmates of Kent's workhouses, have been disbanded.

The people of Eynsford are devasted by the news that Philip Arnold Heseltine, better known as Peter Warlock the musical composer, has taken his own life. Warlock was well-known in the village, where he lived in a converted bakehouse; the Five Bells across the road was a favourite haunt. His friend Arthur Mee said that Peter was the type of wild genius which the world of music traditionally breeds. He would shut himself in his cottage for days and would be heard at all times at the piano; for money, he cared not a jot. Mee said: "Eynsford afforded him some

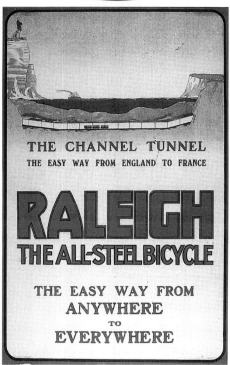

June 5th: This delightful advertisement for Raleigh All-Steel bicycles accompanies the latest attempt to get a Channel Tunnel Bill through Parliament. The Bill failed today.

lighter moments in an existence perpetually overshadowed by the ultimate climax of it."

May 24th: A new planet, discovered in February, has been named Pluto.

June 1st: The proposal for a by-pass through Shortlands Valley in order to relieve congestion in Bromley High Street, particularly in the narrow section by the Market Square, has forced the well-known children's author Enid Blyton to leave her cottage in Shortlands Road.

The 13th-century Priory which stands on the edge of the historic village of Aylesford has been destroyed by fire. The Priory, once occupied by Carmelite monks, until Henry VIII's dissolution of the monasteries, was occupied for the last 200 years by the Earls of Aylesford. It was the Carmelites who built the beautiful stone bridge over the Medway at Aylesford.

September 15th: Adolf Hitler's National Socialists have become the second largest party in Germany behind the Socialists. The mounting economic crisis is blamed for swinging voters towards the extreme. Many people are suggesting that Hitler should now be made Chancellor.
Bligh's Meadow, a disused hop field in the centre of Sevenoaks, is to become the site of the town's new bus station.

October 5th: The R101, the world's biggest airship, exploded in a ball of flames yesterday after hitting a French hillside near Beauvais. 44 people were killed.

The military hospital at Sidcup, formerly known as Frognal which specialises in plastic surgery, has been sold to London County Council. It is to be renamed Queen Mary's Hospital.

October 28th: Dr Edward Whitehead-Reid, senior surgeon at the Kent and Canterbury Hospital died today from injuries received in a flying accident. His monoplane crashed into trees at East Sutton Park, Detling two days ago. Dr Whitehead-Reid was a pioneer brain surgeon, a Flight Lieutenant in the medical branch of 601 Squadron and President of the Kent Gliding Club. He was known as "The Flying Doctor."

The nationally-known Norman Cycle Company has acquired a 34-acre site for new works at Beaver Road, Ashford.

Well-known Kent poet, Frank Kendon, has published *The Small Years* — a book set in the 1890's in and around Winchet Hill near Goudhurst. It depicts Kent rural life before the onslaught of the 20th century. The introduction is written by Walter de la Mare.

The 1930 Road Traffic Act is accompanied by a warning from the Minister of Transport concerning the high number of new motor coach and bus services which he feels are superfluous to the needs of the travelling public. Among them is a non-stop Greenline coach from London to Westerham, via Bromley and to Edenbridge, via Croydon.

New cinemas in Kent: Regal, Beckenham; Plaza, Deal; Theatre Royal, Deal; Gem Picture Theatre, Gravesend.

GREAT HITS OF 1930

On The Sunny Side Of The Street

The King's Horses

Eastwell Manor and the legend of Richard Plantagenet

May: Eastwell Manor, the historic mansion which lies in a 3,000-acre parkland three miles north of Ashford, is on the market just three years after being pulled down and entirely re-built. The vendor is Sir John de Fontblaque Pennefether who acquired the property some years ago.

The sale is already attracting enormous interest from would-be buyers all over the county anxious to own a property that has been so closely associated with the British royal family.

It was in 1878 that Eastwell, then owned by the Earl of Winchelsea, was leased to the Duke of Edinburgh, second son of Queen Victoria. The Duke built the Edinburgh portico towers which stand by the entrance to the park. His two daughters, the princesses Marie and Beatrice were born in the great house and spent much of their childhood playing in the grounds. Queen Victoria was a visitor and her son, Edward VII, a regular guest.

Eastwell is believed to be the final resting place of the last member of the royal House of York. He was the illegitimate son of King Richard III who summoned him to Bosworth field the day before he (Richard) was slain by Henry Tudor. The young man fled and earned his living as a workman, helping to rebuild the mansion in 1545 and living anonymously in the grounds. The legend unfolded after he died.

Ashford's association with royalty continues today. Princess Beatrice is the Infanta of Spain while Princess Marie is Queen of Roumania having married King Ferdinand. She made her last visit to the great house in 1924 when she said "the very name Eastwell is still a joy". And she wrote in her memoirs: "Eastwell is a big grey house in a huge beautiful English park with woods, great stretches of grass, wide undulating horizons; not grand or austere but lovely, quiet and noble."

July: The new Dover lifeboat, named after the founder of the RNLI, Sir William Hilary, was launched today by the Prince of Wales. Designed and built at a cost of £18,446 she is believed to be the largest lifeboat in service anywhere in the world. She is 64 feet by 14 feet and has a speed in excess of 17 knots. The Prince was astounded to learn that she could carry about 100 people.

Maidstone Corporation buys Mote Park for £50,000

April: The beautiful and historic Mote Park, which was bought by Maidstone Corporation from Lord Bearsted for £50,000 last year, will be available for public recreation for the entire summer — and for many more years to come.

For the inhabitants of Maidstone, who have always thirsted for more outdoor facilities, the availability of this large area of open fields with its great lake makes a welcome improvement to their quality of life. They can now play tennis and golf, fish or enjoy boating and, as an extra bonus, a running-track is being laid out.

The Kent Cricket Club ground which is situated in Mote Park was not included in the offer. It was Lord Bearsted's intention to safeguard the ground in the interests of cricket and it is his desire that county matches should continue to played there annually.

In an extra offer of generosity Lord Bearsted has given the Corporation £10,000 towards the expense of converting Mote House into a convalescent home.

Vita and Harold sitting on the steps of the tower at their new home, Sissinghurst Castle.

Sportsmen and women are appearing this year on advertisements for Wills's Gold Flake cigarettes. One of them is Miss Diane Fishwick, who lives at St Peter's, Thanet and is a member of the North Forelands Golf Club. Diane won the British Ladies Open Championship at Formby and, during a celebration dinner at the Savoy Hotel, the actor Mr Douglas Fairbanks presented Diane, just 19, with a silver tray

Nicolsons move into derelict castle

May 21st: Sir Harold Nicolson and his famous wife, the novelist Vita Sackville-West, have decided to lease their beautiful 14th-century house, Long Barn, Sevenoaks Weald and buy a ruined tower and some broken down farm buildings in a derelict field about a mile from the village of Sissinghurst. It is priced at £12,000 and it will cost them at least double that amount to restore it.

Friends are saying that the decision to purchase this dilapidated site is an act of gambler's madness. Apparently Sir Harold has resigned from the Foreign Office and Vita has renounced the income of £1,600 a year due to her from a trust fund because of her mother, Lady Sackville's continuing belligerence. The couple have little capital but they consider the whole venture an irresistible creative challenge.

The buildings — all isolated from each other — are not inhabited apart from the entrance-range which is shared by cart-horses and a few farm labourers. Alongside is an Elizabethan tower which was once part of a larger castle, pulled down in the early nineteenth century.

There is a strong connection with Knole. The castle was once given by Queen Elizabeth to her cousin, Sir Thomas Sackville, the 1st Duke of Dorset. Vita believes that the blood of the Sackville dynasty runs through the veins of Sissinghurst and she has said she is captivated by its beauty and history.

The garden is completely overgrown with weeds and scarred with little broken-down sheds and fallen fencing but Vita has written to friends: "When I first saw the place it caught instantly at my heart and my imagination. I fell in love at first sight. I saw what might be made of it. It was Sleeping Beauty's Garden: but a garden crying out for rescue."

This is just what Sir Harold and Vita intend to do — rescue this waste ground of brambles and weeds and rotting old sheds and design a formal, yet romantic garden.

With so much combustible industry in Sittingbourne it has become imperative that the town has a modern appliance and all the necessary fire-fighting equipment. Photograph shows a huge crowd gathering for the official opening of the new station in Crescent Street.

Kent prospers as industrial crisis bites

August 7th: Unemployment figures released today show that more than two million are now out of work which is the biggest number since 1921. The period of hectic boom which followed the Great Strike of 1926 appears to be over and pundits are suggesting that the country is on course for the worst economic crisis ever known. Certainly the Wall Street crash last year and the collapse in US confidence has badly hit world trade generally.

Kent seems to be escaping the worst of the depression. Unemployment figures are well below the national average and, in fact, correspondents to the Kent Messenger are predicting that the county's chances of increased prosperity are extremely rosy.

The best news lies in the manufacture of Portland cement. Ten years ago road engineers and surveyors could not be persuaded to use it but today the cement factories can hardly keep up with the demand and there is no-one in the country who can equal the quality produced on the shores of the Rivers Thames and Medway.

Kent also continues to hold the premier position in the manufacture of bricks thanks to the deposits discovered by the Romans 2,000 years ago. Kent's famous red bricks can be seen all over the country but particularly in Greater London. They are as sound in quality and as perfect in colour as they were when they were made. Mr George Andrews, chairman of the Stock Brick Association, says the deposits available in the Sittingbourne district are unbelievable. "The area," he said, "hums with an industrial activity immeasurably greater than any known in the past."

Sittingbourne also boasts the country's largest paper-making firm. Edward Lloyd of Kemsley is now employing more than 2,000 people and they have just installed the biggest power-plant in England, if not the world.

The industrial crisis has seriously affected coal — but not in Kent. Nearly 4,000 workers are employed at the four mines at Snowdown, Tilmanstone, Chislet and Betteshanger and the demand for labour is steadily increasing as more shafts are sunk. There is little unemployment of reliable men, although a certain number, with unfamiliar accents, have drifted into the district in search of work, proved unsuitable and are now on the books of local labour exchanges.

Kent's foremost industry is, and always will be, agriculture and here there is little cheerful news, for farmers have taken some bad knocks. However sheep have made money in Romney Marsh, there is a good fruit crop on the belt between Sittingbourne and Faversham, broccoli is proving profitable in Thanet and the big hop and barley growers have done well. In other areas, though, farmers have felt the pinch.

As the country goes into a downward spiral the people of Kent can comfort themselves that they live in a county which has, it appears, preserved its prosperity and self-confidence.

Above: The centre at Ashford in the summer of 1930. Like many Kent towns, particularly Maidstone, Ashford is suffering badly from town centre congestion caused by the great expansion of vehicle ownership and the growing availability of more motor-bus services to take people from their homes to shops, factories and offices, The answer, say planners, is to build a by-pass.

Maidstone, in fact, has already drawn up proposals for a relief road which they will be presenting to the Minister of Transport but there are no such plans at Ashford. In Orpington the route of the by-pass has already been designated and the work entrusted to local builders, Fordyce Bros. Picture on the right shows the Orpington Tar Gang at work a few years ago.

"HERE LIE THE BODIES OF CHATHAM AND DIST." R.I.P.

October 1st: Medway's great tram age ended yesterday when the Chatham Traction Company's double-decker buses were officially introduced and the old trams removed to a reserve section of the track at Watling Street to await disposal. Trams have been running from Chatham, Rochester, Strood, Old Brompton and Gillingham for 28 years but in recent years they have not been able to compete with the cheaply-run individually-owned motor bus firms which now ply most of the routes. In 1902 the Medway Tramway Company (run by the Chatham and district light railway) began with 25 double-decker tramcars and were so popular that the fleet soon grew to more than 40. A sad fate now awaits the old trams which served the area so well. As the caption says: "rest in peace".

Coward joins the writers on the Marsh

March: The witty and often outrageous playwright Noel Coward, whose own performances in the West End have been widely acclaimed, has acquired a weekend country home on the boundaries of Romney Marsh — an area which he simply adores.

Goldenhurst sits in the hills overlooking the Military Canal, only a stone's throw from where the Romney, Hythe, and Dymchurch light railway is currently being constructed. Coward was drawn to the area through his friendship with Edith Nesbit (who died in 1924) and her husband Thomas Tucker. He has already entertained several distinguished guests at his new home including Rebecca West, Binkie Beaumont, the theatrical impresario, and Charlie Chaplin.

Coward, born in 1899, found fame when he starred in his own play *The Vortex* in 1924. By the following year he had no less than three plays on in the West End — *The Vortex*, *Fallen Angel* and *Hay Fever*.

Romney Marsh is rich in literature and many distinguished writers have chosen to live there. Among them are: the Rev. Richard Barham, who wrote the *Ingoldsby Legends* when he was Rector of Snargate, H.G.Wells, who came to live at Sandgate in 1900, the poet Ford Madox Ford lived at Appledore, Russell Thorndike, author of the *Dr Syn* novels, had a house at Dymchurch, Joseph Conrad, author of *Lord Jim* and *Heart of Darkness* frequently visited the area and Henry James lived just over the border in Lamb House, Rye until his death in 1916.

'I rejoice to think that Canterbury gave Mahatma Ghandi a little hospitality at this rather bitter period of his life.... I have seldom met a more lovable man' — Dr Hewlett Johnson, Dean of Canterbury.

January 1st: The Road Traffic Act, which comes into force today will make third-party insurance compulsory and introduce traffic police.

February 5th: Captain Malcolm Campbell has set a new world land speed record on the sands at Daytona, Florida. Chislehurst's speed hero drove his specially-built Bluebird car at 245 mph.

February 28th: Sir Oswald Mosely, who resigned from the Government last year, has formed a New Party, dedicated to complete revision of Parliament.

April 14th: Spain has been declared a Republic and King Alfonso has abdicated.

June 22nd-27th: An historical pageant presented by the City of Rochester in the Castle Grounds has been an overwhelming success. Depicting the main events in history from 43 AD, there were hundreds taking part and the floodlighting of the Castle Keep was a dramatic and memorable sight.

June 28th: Residents of Park Langley, near Bromley have told a public meeting that they object to a parade of shops being built on their estate. They say developers had promised to keep the area purely residential.

July 1st: Trolley-buses have begun regular services in London, 20 years after being introduced in Yorkshire. The first suburbs to switch from trams to trolleys are Kingston and Twickenham

July 6th: UK census results just released show the population of the country to be 44.8 million — the lowest ten-year rate of increase since 1801.

July: Mr F.S. Smythe of Maidstone, whose father was a well-known local timber merchant, has led the successful British Himalayas Expedition to Mount Khamet — at 25,447 feet, the highest yet reached by man. Nine previous attempts to scale this summit have failed.

August 24th: A Coalition Government has been formed to deal with the worst financial crisis ever known. The Labour Goverment has fallen and Ramsay MacDonald has been ousted from the party.

September 20th: Britain has been forced to prevent further withdrawals of gold and to stop foreign speculation against the pound. The move will lead to a 30 per cent devaluation of sterling. The Stock Exchange has been closed for two days.

The Dartford Tunnel scheme has been postponed as an economy measure in the financial crisis. A Bill, passed through parliament last year for the construction of the Dartford-Purfleet tunnel, estimated the cost at £3.5 million.

September 30th: Austerity measures taken by the Government have led to many strikes. Yesterday in London there were clashes between police and demonstrators followed by a riot in Battersea as 5,000 people demanded the restoration of full unemployment pay.

October: There has been an unprecedented and extraordinary rush for wireless licences in Bromley. The reason, says the *Bromley Times,* is the appearance this month of the BBC licence detector van in some of the most fashionable roads.

December 18th: Traffic lights are to be introduced to Kent following the London experiment, which was a great success.

Nine electric lamps on poles have been introduced in Orpington High Street. Local people describe it as "Orpington's Great White Way".

Obituary: Sir Edward Sharp, founder of Sharp and Co Ltd, confectioners and makers of the famous 'Kreemy' toffee. He was interred in Maidstone Cemetery, Sutton Road, Maidstone.

Obituary: Harold Copping, painter and illustrator and member of the group of "Shoreham artists". His pictures of bible scenes have been used in churches and Sunday Schools and in mission stations in the colonies.

New cinemas in Kent this year: Trocadero, Tankerton; Majestic, Gravesend; Astoria Dance Salon, Northfleet; Plaza, Gillingham.

GREAT HITS OF 1931

*Just One More Chance
Goodbye*

A report this year shows that the children of Kent are much healthier, thanks to a daily supply of milk, costing only one penny, and an improvement in nutrition and environmental conditions. Infant mortality in Kent is down to 55 per 1,000 births.

January: No passengers on the Whitstable to Canterbury line but freight continues to roll by. Here is a goods train (modified for the C and W) crossing the Kent coast line as the Sir John Dodinas le Savage express from Victoria to Ramsgate thunders into view.

No more passengers on the Invicta line

January 1st: Passengers will no longer be able to travel on the historic railway line between Whitstable and Canterbury. This famous stretch of rail, which once carried Stevenson's *Invicta* and 20 wagons on the thrilling 10-mile run in the pioneering days of steam, has closed to all but a few goods trains.

There was little fuss to greet the end of an epoch-making era; in fact it was in complete contrast to the grand occasion in 1830 when the line was opened for a sum in excess of £83,000 following three acts of Parliament.

Then, the wagons pulled by the *Invicta* were brimfull of people for Canterbury, who remained in the ancient city until a cannon boomed the time of departure. The *Invicta* left to the sound of the Canterbury bells.

The Stevenson brothers, George and Robert, were present at the inaugural run, proud that theirs was the first passenger steam train in the world. Tyler Hill provided the first tunnel.

The *Invicta* lasted for about a year and was then withdrawn because the engine wasn't really powerful enough. South Eastern eventually brought the line in 1853.

Deal's farewell to a great mission station

The Downs Mission Station at Deal, used for Sunday services, boatmen's recreation and, more important, for the reception of shipwrecked mariners, has closed after 72 years of providing spiritual and material comfort to seamen of all nationalities.

The mission station, built at the top of Exchange Street with stones from the demolished Sandown Castle in 1859, was in use all the time that the Downs — that anchorage of deep water to the west of the Goodwin Sands — remained a vital sea route for shipping.

Its popularity only began to wane after the death of the chaplain, Rev Thomas Treanor, in 1910. Last years the Mission's only real duty was to deliver Christmas hampers to the Goodwin Lightship.

In its heyday, however, the Mission looked after coastguard stations and lightships as well as 800 Deal boatmen. During one year the Rev Treaner spent almost 300 days afloat visiting 890 ships. Whenever the Goodwin Sands, the great "shippe swallower", claimed another victim, Treaner and his colleagues would remain ashore waiting to greet the survivors.

July 26th: *Crowds of people were in attendance at Knole Park, Sevenoaks today to hear the Conservative leader, Mr Stanley Baldwin predict a huge Tory victory at the next general election.*

Labour routed but coalition government stays in power

October 28th: Once again every parliamentary division in Kent is represented by a Conservative member. Tuesday's general election has resulted in huge majorities for the Tories with Labour losing two seats and the Liberals one.

Nationally, it is the largest election landslide in history and the Coalition Government, formed to deal with the growing financial crisis, stays in power with Mr Ramsay MacDonald as titular Prime Minister.

Supporting him are 473 Conservative MPs and just 13 from Mr Ramsay's party; in fact every member of the former Labour Cabinet, bar one, has lost his seat and the Liberals, who won 288 seats two years ago, are down to 68.

In Kent the rout is so decisive that there is little excitement. There are Conservative gains at Ashford, Chatham and Dartford and in five other constituencies — Canterbury, Chislehurst, Tonbridge, Thanet and Maidstone — the Tories have romped home with a 20,000-plus majority. In Bromley Mr E.T. Campbell has turned a marginal seat into one with a Conservative majority of 37,812.

Ghandi meets the Dean at Canterbury Cathedral

September 20th: **The Indian nationalist leader, Mahatma Ghandi, who is in this country to demand that India be given independence, visited Canterbury Cathedral as guest of the Dean, Dr Hewlett Johnson.**

Earlier in the week Mr Ghandi put his proposals to the Round Table Conference at St James' Palace when he said that India was held not by force but a silken cord of love.

The Dean said afterwards: "I have seldom met a more lovable man, a more understanding man, a more simple man. He sat beside me in the chancel of the cathedral and I rejoice to think that Canterbury showed him a little hospitality at this rather bitter period of his life. I pray that his influence will save India from further calamity".

Mr Ghandi has been invited to take tea with the King and Queen at Buckingham Palace next month and he intends to dress, as he always does, in his simple loin cloth and torn woollen shawl.

George V, of course, is Emperor of India.

Hoppers at Paddock Wood — their day's duty over.

Conditions in Kent makes Orwell hopping-mad

November: A man who has spent four years as a vagrant in London and Paris has surprised many people by joining the hop-pickers in Kent and then writing an essay about the cruelty and the unfair conditions under which most of them work. The man's name is Eric Blair but he has written under the pseudonym of George Orwell.

Mr Orwell was living rough in London with a 26-year-old ex-Borstal boy called Ginger, a 20-year-old orphan called Young Ginger and an 18-year-old Liverpool Jew when they decided to go hopping at Blests' Farm, Wateringbury in September.

The unlikely group soon realised it was a bad year for Kent hops. With the depression at its deepest, the acreage had fallen to its lowest-ever level and they observed many drunken fights taking place between pickers and villagers in local pubs.

Orwell, in his essay, advocates a pickers' union to give them strength against employers but he then suggests there is little point in forming a union when half the pickers are "women and gipsies and too stupid to see the advantage of it".

The young writer says the rules of the farm where he worked are designed to reduce a picker more or less to a slave. He describes the tin huts, 10 feet across, where up to eight people are accommodated. He observes that laws about child labour are disregarded utterly and comments on the habit of heavy measuring. Theoretically, it is claimed a picker can earn 30/- a week but personally he doubts if any one picker earns more than 15/-.

Orwell, who is 28, has had an unusual life. He was educated at Eton and his first job was with the British police in Burma — entirely unsuitable for a man with his political sympathies. He reacted by spending the next four years in vagrancy and says he is at work on a book to be called *Down and Out in Paris and London.*

Although he is a committed socialist he dislikes repressive orthodoxy of any kind. Certainly he hates the hop farmers and most of the people in Paddock Wood. "Getting a bath in the village," he writes, "is about as easy as buying a tame whale."

Hop-picking is thirsty work so the few minutes allowed for lunch is thoroughly enjoyed. If conditions on the farm are appalling, for many of the Londoners they are no worse than their normal living conditions throughout the rest of the year. On occasions, however, they have to live in wet clothes and sleep for days on rotting straw; this has led to all kinds of diseases and epidemics. Today, the children of the hoppers have a hospital of their own — thanks to Father Richard Wilson of St Augustine's Church, Stepney who has acquired an old disused pub at Five Oak Green, near Paddock Wood and transformed the former skittles alley into The Little Hoppers' Hospital. It could not have come at a more opportune moment, for this year Father Wilson and his nurses have been busy coping with an outbreak of smallpox which has hit the locality.

Charlie Chaplin is a frequent visitor to Kent. Here he is pictured with (left to right) Amy Johnson, Lady Astor and George Bernard Shaw.

Charlie Chaplin — guest at Chartwell

September 14th: Charlie Chaplin, the great comic actor of the silent cinema made another one of his many visits to Kent yesterday — this time to meet Winston Churchill, MP who has been out of office since the Conservatives were beaten in 1929. Since then the former Chancellor who lives at Chartwell, near Westerham has been painting and writing and travelling extensively.

Chaplin and Churchill know each other well. They first met at a dinner party in 1929 given by the film actress Marion Davies and sat up talking until 3 am. Churchill later wrote: "You could not help liking him. He is a marvellous comedian, bolshy in politics and delightful in conversation. He is still out to prove that the silent drama or pantomime is superior to the new talkies."

The comedian was born in London and first made his name in the Keystone company's short slapstick films when he improvised the costume of baggy trousers, a walking-cane, bowler-hat and moustache which soon provided both his trademark and character.

Chaplin has visited Kent often. He is a friend of Sir Philip Sassoon, MP for Hythe and has stayed frequently at Port Lympne and, on occasions, entertained the guests there. He has also appeared at the Marlowe Theatre in Canterbury.

All saved as giant airliner crash-lands near Tonbridge

August: A four-engined Hannibal airliner of the Imperial fleet made a dramatic crash landing yesterday at Tatlingbury Farm, Tudeley, near Tonbridge.

The aeroplane, one of the biggest in the world, lost height among the rain clouds and came down by the George and Dragon pub tearing down a telegraph pole and leaving its tail behind.

Thanks to the skill of the pilot, Captain F.W. Dinsmore of Simpson's Road, Bromley, passengers and crew survived.

Lawn-tennis pioneer dies at Lullingstone

July: Sir William, Hart-Dyke, the veteran Victorian statesman who died yesterday, was one of the pioneers of lawn-tennis in this country. In fact he helped to work out the rules of the great game on his lawn at Lullingstone Castle, Eynsford.

It was in 1873 that Sir William, an English racquets champion, laid down what is believed to be the first tennis-court in England at Lullingstone and saw the game achieve such rapid popularity that the all-England Croquet Club at Wimbledon held a tennis championship in 1877.

He was a friend of King Edward VII and often played tennis with him when he was the Prince of Wales.

Sir William, aged 93, was the oldest ex-minister of the Crown still living. The height of his career was spent in the heyday of late Victorian politics with Disraeli and Gladstone the dominant personalities. He was the Conservative Chief Whip, a schools minister for many years and was the man responsible for carrying through the act which established free education.

During his political career he sat in nine Parliaments, under five Speakers, through 13 Governments and represented Dartford, Maidstone, West Kent and Mid-Kent at various times.

'Cricket has done more to consolidate the Empire than any other influence' — Lord Harris, founder of Kent Cricket Club, who died this year.

January 27th: The Royal Navy submarine, *M2* sank today with the loss of 52 lives.

January 31st: Advancing Japanese forces have captured the Chinese city of Shanghai as a preliminary to a possible full-scale invasion. British, French and Italian forces have been despatched to help defend the country.

Louis Brennan, who lived in Gillingham for 29 years and invented the monorail, the helicopter, a gyroscopically-controlled motor-car, ascending stairs for physically-handicapped people and the Brenagraph pocket typewriter among others, has died in Switzerland. He was knocked down by a car.

February 24th: Chislehurst speed king Malcolm Campbell has beaten his own land speed record at Daytona, reaching 253mph.

March 2nd: The baby son of aviation hero Charles Lindbergh has been kidnapped from his home in New Jersey. Lindbergh and his wife, Anne, were dining at the time and knew nothing of the incident until the nanny found the child's cot empty. A ransom of $50,000 has been demanded.

March 15th: The BBC today made its first broadcast from the new Broadcasting House, Portland Place, Regent Street.

March 18th: The Sydney Harbour Bridge, the world's longest single-arch span, has been opened today.

March 26th: A new attraction in Canterbury for visitors and tourists is the Friars' Ferry, inaugurated today. Passengers will now be able to see some of the ancient city's hidden beauty spots from the River Stour.

April 10th: Paul von Hindenburg has been elected President in the German elections. Adolf Hitler, the fanatical Nazi leader, increased his share of the vote to more than 13 million. His campaign has been helped by funds donated by Ruhr industrialists.

Lord Harris, the founding father of Kent Cricket Club, died at his home Belmont, Faversham in March.

April 27th: Imperial Airways has begun a regular service between Croydon and Cape Town.

May 10th: President Paul Doumer of France was assassinated today in Paris. The killer is believed to be Paul Gorguloff, a White Russian emigre.

The Royal Crown Hotel — once the pride of Sevenoaks — has been demolished to make way for a new cinema — the Majestic.

May 12th: The body of Charles Lindbergh's kidnapped baby son was found in a wood today, five miles from the aviation hero's home.

The Old Rectory at Beckenham has been enlarged and opened as the new Town Hall.

June 11th: Lord Darnley of Cobham opened Gravesend's ter-centenary celebrations today.

July: More than 20,000 people attended the opening of a new greyhound stadium at Catford. Names of the stakes included Bromley, Bickley, Beckenham, Keston, Hayes and Dulwich.

An unusual event, organised by the *Kent Messenger* newspaper was the race this month between a homeing pigeon and the new Golden Arrow train. They set off from Victoria at the same time and the pigeon took an impressive lead. The train, however, worked up enough steam to overtake the pigeon in East Kent and win by just a few minutes.

August 14th: Tommy Hampson won the 800 metres gold medal

for Britain in the Olympic Games at Los Angeles.

September: A Quincentenary Speech Day has been held at Sevenoaks School to celebrate the 500th anniversary of one of the oldest schools in the country. It was in 1432 that William Sennocke, former Lord Mayor of London and a contemporary of Dick Whittington left an endowment for the establishment of a free school in Sevenoaks.

Hundreds of people have enjoyed their first flights in an aeroplane this summer thanks to the well-known aviator Alan Cobham, who has taken his famous "flying circus" to Maidstone, Gravesend, Sevenoaks and Dover. The entertainment includes a spectacular "wing walking" exhibition by Mr M.N.Hearne.

October 30th: A 15,000-strong rally in Trafalgar Square against means tests and mass unemployment ended in violence today between police and supporters of the hunger marches.

A ship's bell has been presented by the citizens of Rochester to *HMS Rochester.*

November 8th: Franklin D. Roosevelt is the new Democratic President of the United States. He has defeated the sitting Republican, Herbert Hoover, by winning all but six of the 48 states.

November 22nd: Gordon Richards has made sure of retaining his title as champion jockey today by riding his 188th winner of the year. He has been top jockey five times in the last seven years.

December 25th: King George V today gave a Christmas message to the Commonwealth on the wireless. It was a great success and may be repeated next year.

*New cinemas in Kent this year:
Carlton, Westgate.*

GREAT HITS OF 1932

The Sun Has Got Its Hat On

Love Is The Sweetest Thing

Kent growing rapidly as Britain drifts southwards

January: The new census figures released towards the end of last year shows that people are pouring into Kent's Metropolitan towns at an unbelievable rate. In the ten years since the last census, the population in Bromley, Beckenham and Bexley has each risen by more than 10,000 — an increase of over 10 per cent.

Overall, Kent's population has increased during the past decade by 76,186 to 1,117,929 — a rise of 6.7 per cent. This compares with 5.4 per cent for England and Wales as a whole.

The census shows clearly the southward trend of the population. While the industrial regions of the North and Midlands and Wales have lost population, the South has gained,

Ashford	15,239	Faversham	10,091	Sandwich	3,287
Beckenham	43,834	Folkestone	35,890	Sevenoaks	10,482
Bexley	32,940	Gillingham	60,983	Sheerness	16,721
Broadstairs	12,748	Gravesend	35,490	Sidcup	12,360
Bromley	45,348	Herne Bay	11,244	Sittingbourne	20,175
Canterbury	24,450	Maidstone	42,259	Southborough	7,352
Chatham	42,996	Margate	31,312	Swanscombe	8,541
Chislehurst	9,876	New Romney	1,786	Tenterden	3,473
Crayford	15,887	Northfleet	16,429	Tonbridge	16,332
Dartford	28,928	Penge	27,762	Tunbridge Wells	35,367
Deal	13,680	Queenborough	2,941	Walmer	5,324
Dover	41,095	Ramsgate	33,597	Whitstable	11,201
Erith	32,780	Rochester	31,196	Wrotham	4,510

the most marked increase being in the Home Counties.

Gillingham remains the biggest town in Kent with a population of 60,983, followed by Bromley 45,348, Beckenham 43,834, Chatham 42,996 and Maidstone 42,259.

Detailed figures are shown above.

Poverty and squalor rife in "hungry" Chatham

January: Some areas of Kent may be escaping the worst of the depression but the Medway towns have been hit hard. There is high unemployment in Chatham, families are living on little more than bread and dripping, many children are wearing knitted "hand-me-down" clothes and such luxuries as an evening at the pictures is just a dream.

An office worker at Chatham who faithfully records everyday events in the dockyard's "old red diary" writes this week that the poverty and squalor in the old working class areas of Chatham "has to be seen to be believed".

"To help feed children," he says, "married couples are forced to sell the few sticks of furniture they have fondly called home. In one house, denuded of practically everything but a few bits of crockery and cooking utensils, the several children sleep together in one bed and keep warm covered by old sacks and newspapers. A family living under the same conditions cook their food over a fire made out of oddments of wood and cabbage stalks."

The diarist also writes of a dead baby that was placed in an empty orange crate, with a piece of wire-netting over it to stop a starving cat from climbing in. "Two pennies," he says, "were put over the dead child's eyes but had to be taken away to help buy food."

Those who are out of work euphemistically describe their situation as "being on the big firm". Many of them grimly accept that they cannot spend a penny on a railway fare or omnibus, or purchase a halfpenny newspaper or buy a ticket for a popular concert. It is unwise to write letters for they cannot afford the postage and it is difficult to contribute anything to their church or chapel. Some have declined to join sick clubs or trade unions while others have given up smoking or drinking beer.

Those with a secure job are the lucky ones, although many receive a salary of less than £3 a week. The British Medical Association has estimated that an average man requires 3,400 calories a day to maintain full health and working capacity and that costs 5s 11d a day to provide.

In Maidstone more than 2,000 people (10 per cent of the workforce) are out of work and the figure is rising. The mayor is to set up an employment fund to provide work for the desperate, such as tidying up the parks and municipal cemeteries.

There have been scores of protest meetings in the town. A few months ago a deputation of the unemployed told the council that they had come to the limit of their tether and would rather be in Maidstone gaol and their wives in the workhouse than walking about hungry.

The prospect of increased prosperity and the feeling of buoyancy so enthusiastically reported by the *Kent Messenger* in 1930 has never been realised.

It's still not as bad as the situation in other parts of the country and particularly the north-east but in most areas of industrial Kent engineering is "inactive", several paper mills are on short time, bricklayers are largely without work and the distributive trade is very slack.

June 24th: *Times may be hard as the economic crisis grows but that does not stop fashion designers holding shows for the privileged. Here, on board the Thames showboat today, are mannequins displaying the latest beachwear.*

On the Royal Eagle to Thanet for just 12s 6d

July: The new paddle-steamer, *Royal Eagle*, launched in February is already proving to be one of the most luxurious and best-loved ships on the Thames. Each morning she leaves Tower Pier at nine o'clock and calls at Greenwich, Woolwich and Tilbury before heading for Margate and then on to Ramsgate. On the return journey she docks at Tower Pier by half past eight. The entire journey costs 12/6d. Among her regular passengers are Pearly Kings and Queens and three butchers from Gravesend who say they will never miss their weekly trip.

The *Royal Eagle* was launched on February 24th by Lady Ritchie, wife of the chairman of the Port of London Authority, who was most impressed by four decks, a dining saloon for 310 people and the fact that there are 70 stewards and stewardesses to administer to the passengers' needs.

Captain Bill Braithwaite, a large jovial man, encourages his passengers to sing on their journey to Thanet and back.

Women murdered by deserter who went berserk with gun

June 7th: Three women, enjoying a picnic at King's Wood near the summit of Challock Hill, Charing, who were shot in cold blood on Monday (June 3rd), have been identified as Janie Stemp, her grandaughter Peggy and a friend Janie Swift. The bodies of the women were discovered by the driver of a passing Maidstone and District bus who alerted the police.

The gunman has been named as James Thomas Collins, a private with the 2nd Battalion of the East Kent Regiment (Buffs) who had deserted from his barracks at Shorncliffe, near Folkestone and was attempting to walk to London. Police say he came across the women in the woods, shot them with his rifle, attempted to hide the bodies in the undergrowth and stole the car. He was eventually caught and disarmed by a police motorcyclist on the outskirts of Barnet.

Collins, apparently, is an expert marksmen for whom guns hold an unhealthy fascination. In the autumn of 1931, during a visit to a fairground shooting-gallery, he suddenly turned and shot wildly at the crowds, injuring two people. That incident led to 15 months in prison and he rejoined the Buffs on his release.

He will appear before the autumn session of Maidstone Assizes where his counsel will plead that he is not a sane and rational person.

The Kent cricket team of 1932 (left to right): H.T.W. Hardinge, T.A. Pearce, A.P. Freeman, A.E. Watt, C.S. Marriott, B.H. Valentine, A.P.F Chapman, W.H. Ashdown, L.E.G. Ames, A.M. Crawley, F.E. Woolley.

Lord Harris — the moving spirit behind Kent cricket

March 24th: With the death today of George Robert Harris, the Fourth Baron of Seringapatam and Mysore, and of Belmont, Kent cricket has lost its greatest figure.

Lord Harris was the moving spirit behind the formation of the county club in 1870 and his energy in collecting capable players and encouraging the list of supporters was invaluable. He was appointed captain in 1875, held it until 1889 and during that time was considered one of the best amateur batsmen in England.

He took a side to Australia in 1878-9 and, the follow-ing year, was captain of England in the first Test Match played between the two countries. It took place at the Oval and was attended by more people than had ever watched a game of cricket in England.

After his retirement from playing Harris continued to serve the game. He was a member of the MCC for 60 years and president in 1895. In a speech at the time he said: "Cricket has done more to consolidate the Empire than any other influence."

Alongside his passion for cricket Harris was a great statesman. He served long periods as Under-Secretary for India and for War and handled troubles in some Indian states with tact and vigour.

Lord Harris died at his home, Belmont, near Faversham on March 24th and is succeeded as fifth baron by his only child, George St Vincent. A county memorial fund has been launched and it is hoped to commission a portrait of His Lordship for Canterbury with the funds.

The Gorilla — too terrifying for Beckenham!

April: **More than 5,000 Beckenham residents have signed a petition demanding the Pavilion Cinema be re-opened. The owner has closed it in protest at the Urban Council's decision to ban the film *The Gorilla* because local churchmen and those concerned with public morals believe "it is terrifying, even to adults", even though it carries a U certificate. Beckenham UDC's involvement in film censorship has been a contentious issue for many years and this latest action went ahead even though an angry crowd besieged the council chamber and maintained a barrage of booing and clapping during the censorship debate. Many people believe the Pavilion will never be reopened.**

April: The old man taking supplies to the Dungeness lighthouse finds it's hard work across the shingle. Locals, however, have advised him to wear "backstays" for his next call. These are rectangular pieces of wood with a leather strap into which the foot slips. Locals wear "backstays" to facilitate progress across the shingle, especially children on their way to Dungeness School along the shingle track.

July 19th: Elizabeth, the Duchess of York, today laid the foundation stone for the new Kent and Sussex Hospital at Tunbridge Wells.

Pubs forced to close as beer prices increase

The demand for beer which had increased so dramatically at the end of the Great War has slipped back to its wartime levels, mainly because of the economic climate and the excise duty which has raised beer prices to 7d a pint. Output is now 52 per cent below the level of 1910 and influential parties are taking the opportunity once more to persuade the Government to introduce prohibition. In Kent hundreds of pubs have closed and breweries, feeling the pinch, are amalgamating. Among them is Fremlins, Maidstone's successful family firm of brewers which has joined forces with the Dover company, Alfred Leney and taken a lease on 130 licensed properties, supplying them all from Earl Street, Maidstone. Frank Fremlin, who set up the company with his brothers Ralph, Richard and Walter, has retired and there are new members on the board.

Allington Castle has a fascinating history. It began as a villa, built by the Romans and turned into a stronghold on a moated mound by the Saxons. The Normans replaced the Saxon palisading with a wall which still remains, which is thought to be the work of Gundulf who built the Tower of London for the Conqueror. In the 13th century the manor house was turned into a castle but, by the 16th century, was a complete ruin. Restored as the Tudor home of the Wyatt family, here was born Thomas Wyatt, the poet and Thomas his son. By 1905 it was a roofless ruin — until William Conway transformed it into one of England's noblest homes.

Mountaineer William Conway restores Allington Castle

December: The famous mountaineer, Sir William Conway, who won his knighthood for mapping out 2,000 square miles of the Himalayas in 1892, has completed his second great achievement — the restoration of Allington Castle, Maidstone.

Lord Conway and his American wife, bought the dilapidated 13th century castle in 1905 for £4,500 and set out to make it habitable. After 26 years their task is complete. Allington Castle possesses an authentic mediaeval atmosphere and is full of art treasures from all over the world.

The Great Hall is restored, and the long gallery, and the rooms in which Henry VIII and Cardinal Wolsey slept. There is water in the moat and the tiltyard is visible again.

Born in Rochester in 1856 Conway, in his earlier years, was fascinated by mountains. Following his adventures in the Karakoram (Himalayas), he became President of the Alpine Club and contributed some of the finest descriptive works in Alpine literature. He went on to become Professor of Art at both Liverpool University and the Slade and, as a director of the Imperial War Museum, he presented a collection of 100,000 carefully classified photographs to the Courtauld Institute of Art.

'A war between Poland and Germany by 1940. A world state by 2059' — H.G. Wells in his vision of *The Shape of Things to Come*, published this year.

January 10th: Martial law has been declared in Spain as uprisings take place in Catalonia, Levante and Andalucia.

January 23rd: The future of the MCC tour of Australia is in doubt following England's use of "bodyline tactics". The controversy reached a climax in the Third Test at Adelaide when the Australian wicket-keeper was struck on the head by the English fast bowler Harold Larwood.

January 30th: The German president, von Hindenburg, has appointed Adolf Hitler, the Nazi leader, as Chancellor. The move has been caused by the virtual collapse of democratic government.

February 28th: The Reichstag, headquarters of the German Nazi party, was burned to the ground today. The Communist party has been blamed and a young Dutchman arrested for arson.

March 23rd: Winston Churchill delivered a bitter attack on Mr MacDonald's foreign policy which he said "has brought us nearer to war and made us weaker, poorer and more defenceless."

Against a background of increasing lawlessness in Germany, Storm Troopers armed with revolvers are roaming the streets looking for Jews to beat up. They say that Jewish vampires have heaped up millions of deutschmarks through blackmail and trickery. Jewish businesses have been closed and many are fleeing the country.

April: Special effects technology has been brought to the cinema screen through a giant gorilla called *King Kong* who falls in love with a young girl. It is thrilling audiences in America.

May: More and more traffic lights are being erected in London. Kent County Council has expressed an interest in the new system to control traffic and cut down accidents.

More than 31,000 people have been rehoused at Downham on 400 acres of land between the villages of Grove Park and Southend. Sub-urbanisation, as it is known, is taking place rapidly in the Bromley area. Thousands of new homes have been built at Orpington, Petts Wood and West Wickham. *The Beckenham Journal* has declared that the countryside around has gone. "The change may be regretted but Beckenham has been able to make best use of the change for the roads and houses are well laid out."

June 23rd: News from Germany is that it has become a one-party state. Herr Hitler has banned all opposition parties.

July 3rd: Three new bridges have been opened over the Thames, at Richmond, Chiswick and Hampton Court.

July 10th: Unemployment has fallen to 2.4 million in England and Wales.

July 20th: Jewish people from Kent are among 30,000 in Hyde Park protesting against Nazi anti-semitism.

August 7th: The No 4 hangar at Hawkinge and six Blackburn Darts were destroyed by fire caused by escaping fuel from a Horsley which crash landed on top of the building. The crew scrambled clear.

August 23rd: Mahatma Ghandi has been released from prison hospital in India because doctors say his body cannot stand the strain of fasting. He weighs only 90 pounds after declaring he would "fast unto death".

September 1st: Kenneth Clark, aged 30, has been appointed director of the National Gallery.

September 26th: Beckenham has signed a petition for the grant of a Charter of Incorporation. In a grandiose ceremony today a procession from the City of London with mayors and sheriffs moved through the town to mark Beckenham's corporate status.

October: The London Passenger Transport Board has absorbed many local bus routes, including part of those operated by Maidstone and District.

Under the 1930 Housing Act a massive slum clearance programme has begun in Maidstone with the demolition of homes in Padsole and Upper Stone Street. Displaced families have been allocated council houses. Flats have also been built at Ringlestone and King Street. Those rehoused have suffered the indignity of having their furniture fumigated before moving into council property.

October 14th: In a dramatic announcement from Berlin, Germany says she will take no further part in the Geneva Disarmament Conference.

November 28th: New grounds for divorce are being proposed; these include cruelty, insanity and drunkenness.

December 9th: Fighting continues all over Spain following another attempt by the Communists to seize power.

December 16th: Prohibition in America ends today when Utah becomes the last state to ratify the 21st Amendment. There have been 14 "dry years" in the States.

Obituary: Arthur Drummond Barton, who had died at Hunton won a VC at Lel-el-sher, Palestine in November 1917. Lt-Col Drummond and his men dribbled a football as they went forward and secured a Turkish gun battery. He is interred in St Mary's churchyard.

New cinemas in Kent this year: Odeon, Canterbury; Friars, Canterbury; Regent, Deal; Kinema Royal, Margate.

GREAT HITS OF 1933

Who's Afraid of the Big Bad Wolf
Smoke Gets in Your Eyes

Kent County Council has adopted a new Coat of Arms with the motto Invicta, meaning "unconquered". This owes its origin to the defence put up by Kent against William the Conquerer.

Wicket-keeper Ames back from the "bodyline" tour

February 29th: Leslie Ames, the 28-year-old England wicket-keeper batsman has returned to Kent with an eye-witness account of "the bodyline controversy".

During the Test matches "Down Under" several Australian batsmen were hit on the head and body by short-pitched bowling from Larwood, Voce and Bowes. At one time the crisis reached the point where the tour looked like being abandoned when pandemonium broke out in the crowd. The MCC agreed to bring its players home, the Governments of both countries discussed the affair and, for several weeks, the future of the game was in jeopardy.

Ames, who comes from Elham, near Canterbury, kept wicket brilliantly during the contentious series. He played in every match and, from his vantage point behind the stumps, was able to give his captain Douglas Jardine valuable advice in his adoption of "leg theory" tactics, which so angered the entire Australian continent.

England won the series 4-1 but the usual welcome home has been tempered by the continuing controversy.

Les Ames joined the Kent staff in 1926 and played his first full season in 1928 when he claimed 114 victims behind the stumps and was soon noticed by the England selectors.

He is now looking forward to this year's Test matches against the West Indies.

Civic dignitaries relax after the opening of the Pavilion, Broadstairs today.

Gliding pioneer dies in crash at West Malling

March 13th: Jimmy Lowe-Wylde, who was the first man to design and fly a glider in Britain and went on to become the moving spirit behind the rapid development of this most graceful sport, was tragically killed today in an accident at West Malling aerodrome. While flying a Planette light aircraft it is believed he was taken ill, lost control of the machine and crashed to his death.

It was on February 23rd, 1930 that Lowe-Wylde and his colleagues of the newly-formed Kent Gliding Club made the first flight in a primary glider at Detling aerodrome. It flew only a few yards at a maximum height of 10 feet off the ground and proved a great disappointment to the hundreds of people and press who had gathered to see history made.

But this was a "test flight" and within months the sport had gone from strength to strength. Gliding clubs were formed at Dover, Thanet and Joyce Green.

Lowe-Wylde's first glider was christened Columbus and with members of the Kent Gliding Club he actually worked on the machine in a room at the back of the Nag's Head public house in Maidstone.

This led in time to the establishment of a factory in part of Isherwood-Foster's brewery, Maidstone where Lowe-Wylde developed a series of gliders. He also pioneered the towing of gliders by motor cars and gave many demonstrations during Alan Cobham's flying circus displays.

His death is a tragedy for the sport but he has left it in capable hands and pioneering work will continue in earnest.

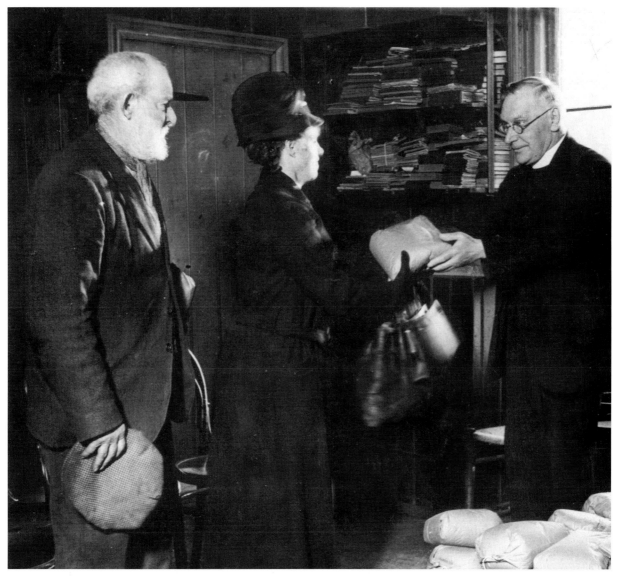

March 30th: *It's Maundy Thursday and two villagers from Sutton-at-Hone, near Dartford each receive a bushel of peas and two bushels of wheat from the rector. This charity dates back to 1572 and the beneficiaries are 20 poor members of the parish. In these days of mass unemployment the depression is biting hard and the existence of these ancient charities — meagre as they are — are helping with morale in some of Kent's poorer parishes.
Long may they continue.*

Anna Neagle almost crushed in the crowds at Gravesend

September 16th: Anna Neagle, the popular British actress, well-known for her comedy roles, was almost crushed today under the feet of several thousand people who came to see her open the Super Cinema at Gravesend — the fourth modern cinema in the town alongside the Plaza, the Gem Picture Theatre and the Majestic.

Anna Neagle, the stage name of Marjorie Robertson, narrowly escaped being hurt but the scenes in New Road were amazing. When the time came for the opening the crowds were so dense that it was only with great difficulty that the police cleared the road.

Miss Neagle, whose new film *Bitter Sweet* will shortly be shown at the Super, was accompanied by Herbert Wilcox, director of productions for the British and Dominion Film Company.

This is the second big event in Gravesend. Earlier this year, Miss Constance Cummings opened The Laughing Water — the large pub on the new road near Singlewell.

The funeral cortege makes its way through Farnborough after the "lying in state".

15,000 people in Farnborough for the funeral of Gipsy Rose Lee

April 28th: Amazing scenes were witnessed at Farnborough on Friday when the funeral of Mrs Urania Boswell, known throughout the land as "Gipsy Rose Lee", took place.

More than 15,000 people poured into the village. The majority stood four deep on the pavement and others climbed buildings and telegraph poles to glimpse the last journey of the great lady they knew as the Queen of the Gipsies.

Every year for 40 years Gipsy Rose spent six happy months in the tiny bungalow at Willow Walk, Farnborough. She was the accepted leader of the great clan of Lees and Boswells, the last great families of the Romany tribe.

Aged 81, she was the daughter of the equally famous Gipsy Rose of Brighton and, like her mother, she had a nationwide reputation as a palmist and fortune-teller. Among her patrons were lords and dukes and many of the privileged classes. Her husband, Levi Boswell, the king of the clan, died in 1924.

She owned property in many places and spent six months of the year at Ramsgate and Margate.

Gipsy Rose had predicted her own death. On Thursday she told her brother that she would say adieu at six or seven o'clock the following day.

She has been buried in Farnborough churchyard.

The boat people at Gravesend. Here are some of the organisers, officials and competitors in this year's annual Gravesend Town Regatta.

Pageant recalls Wat Tyler's great rebellion

August 25th: The Lord Mayor of London, Sir Percy Greenaway today presented Dartford with its Charter of Incorporation. In a magnificent ceremonial occasion, watched by thousands, the mayoral party, in traditional robes, proceeded at a leisurely pace through the streets of Dartford.

In the evening there was the performance of a historical pageant, written by Mr Arthur Botten. Among the characters portrayed was the proletarian rebel Wat Tyler, believed to have been born in Dartford, who led the peasant uprising in 1381 against the poll tax.

Sir Gerrard Tyrwitt Drake, who has been mayor of Maidstone on so many occasions, has reopened his zoo at Cobtree Manor. Admission prices are 7d and 3d for children.

The zoo was originally housed at Sir Gerrard's home at Cobtree but in 1914 the animals were moved to Tovil Court which became the Maidstone Zoological and pleasure gardens and proved a great attraction until it closed.

Housing estate will replace William Pitt's historic home

July: Hayes Place, the final home of the distinguished statesman, the Earl of Chatham and birthplace of his son William Pitt the Younger, has been sold for development and demolished.

This magnificent historic house was originally erected in 1624 and rebuilt in 1756, the year before Pitt the Elder became Prime Minister. His son, destined to become Premier at 24 and a politician of exceptional precocity, was born on May 28th, 1759 and baptised in the parish church.

The family moved to Somerset but the house was re-purchased by the Earl of Chatham who died at Hayes Place in 1778.

Sir E.A. Hambro was the last occupant and, on his death in 1925, the parkland was sold, to the consternation of all who lived in the locality.

The builders have already moved in. Hayes Place will soon be a large housing estate and the quiet little village, north of its yet undefiled common, will become part of Bromley's surburban spread.

Cathedral in danger as fire destroys historic mill

October 17th: Canterbury Cathedral was in danger of burning today as a massive fire in the nearby City Flour Mills threatened to get out of control. In one of the biggest blazes ever seen in the ancient city, the huge six-storey complex, housing Denne's Watermill, was completely destroyed. It took firemen from Canterbury, Bridge, Sturry and Herne Bay most of the day to bring the flames under control.

The fire was first discovered at 8.30 am and tackled with buckets of water which were passed along a chain of employees. By the time the brigade arrived the whole of the upper part of the mill was alight. As flames leapt from roof to roof, setting fire to homes nearby,

one whole street had to be evacuated.

About an hour after the fire was first discovered the roof crashed in and burning beams fell onto more houses. The Miller's Arms Inn was now on fire and, with the mill doomed, firemen concentrated on the secondary outbreaks.

Hundreds of people gathered on the banks of the River Stour to watch the drama on the other side but they were driven away in a hurry when part of the mill fell into the water, causing a great blast of heat.

The corn-grinding watermill was originally built in 1792 as a city granary in case of a Napoleonic invasion.

'I propose to introduce an ability test for all new drivers, a speed limit of 30 mph in built-up areas, experiment with pedestrian crossings and curb the use of horns '— Hore Belisha, Transport Minister

January 9th: The price of butter, at 10d a pound, is the cheapest in living memory. Eggs are between 6d and 9d a dozen.

January 16th: Hermann Goering has ordered the dissolution of all Freemason's lodges in Germany. Police raid the homes of clergy who oppose the Nazi party.

The terrible conditions in Durham's mining villages has prompted many Kent towns to send food parcels. The people of Sevenoaks have raised enough money to redecorate and equip a disused hall for the people of Quebec village.

January 21st: An estimated 10,000 people attended a rally organised by the British Union of Fascists in Birmingham. Supporters gave Sir Oswald Mosley the Fascist salute.

March 1st: In an interview the Prince of Wales says women should be allowed to wear shorts.

March 2nd: Pu Yi, once known as China's Boy Emperor, has been installed by his Japanese masters as puppet Emperor of conquered Manchuria.

March 11th: A clock tower and plaque was unveiled in Gillingham today in memory of Will Adams, the first Englishman to live in Japan.

March 13th: Kent's bigger towns continue to co-operate in the Government's slum clearance plans. Thousands of people are being rehoused.

Maurice McCudden, younger brother of Jimmy McCudden, the flying ace of the Great War has died of colitis aged 33. Maurice, well known as a test pilot, raced his motor bicycles at Brooklands.

March 28th: In the Road Traffic Bill published today, tests will have to be taken by all new drivers. Speed limits will be imposed in towns and crossing schemes may be introduced after experiments in London.

Public house opening times will be extended to 10.30 pm. There

Dean Hewlett Johnson, who is encouraging pilgrims from all over the world, to visit Canterbury Cathedral.

have been many objections from the clergy in Kent.

May 23rd: A Texan couple, Clyde Barrow and Bonnie Parker, have been killed in a police ambush today in Louisiana. The couple have murdered at least 12 people in robbing banks and petrol stations over the last four years.

By swimming the Channel from England to France, Edward Temme, has become the first person to conquer the Channel in both directions.

June 10th: Italy, hosting the World Football Cup in Rome, beat Czecho-slovakia 2-1 in the final. The four British nations were not invited to play.

July 7th: Britain has a tennis champion at last. Fred Perry beat

Jack Crawford in the final today and so becomes the first British men's champion at Wimbledon for 25 years.

Saltwood Castle, near Hythe has been acquired by Lady Conway who is the new wife of Lord Conway of Allington Castle and widow of Reginald Lawson. With the revivalist architect, Sir Philip Tilden she plans to meticulously restore Saltwood.

August 19th: Following the recent death of President Hindenburg, Hitler announced today that the title of President is abolished and he is to be known as Fuehrer and Reich Chancellor. He is also Supreme Commander of Germany's armed forces.

A Neolithic polished axe has been discovered at Headcorn.

August 22nd: Australia won the final Test Match against England by 562 runs to take the series 2-1 and avenge defeat in the "bodyline series". Larwood and Voce did not play but Bradman did and his final aggregate for Australia was 758 runs for an average of 94. Les Ames was again Kent's only representative.

September 26th: The Cunard White Star liner *Queen Mary* was launched today by the Queen. She is the biggest and most powerful ship in the world.

October 12th: Prince George Edward Alexander Edmund, fourth son of King George V and Queen Mary, has been created Duke of Kent.

October 21st: Chinese Communists led by a peasant, Mao Tse-tung, are attempting to break out of encirclement to begin a long march through hostile territory to Yenan, 6,000 miles north. The rebel forces are almost 100,000 strong.

November 12th: Film distributors warned today that Britain has an excess of cinemas and it is likely that many of them will close.

John Cristie has built a small opera house at Glyndebourne, Sussex next to his beautiful country house. The first performance was *The Marriage of Figaro*.

The Association of Men of Kent and Kentish Men have presented a silver bugle to the East Kent Regiment (The Buffs) in recognition of their 150 years association with Kent. The bugle was handed to Colonel of the Regiment, Maj-Gen Sir Arthur Lynden-Bell.

New church: St Augustine's, Bromley

New cinemas in Kent this year: Regal, Margate; Astoria, Margate; Granada, Margate; Royalty, Broadstairs, Ritz, Tunbridge Wells.

GREAT HITS OF 1934

*I Only Have Eyes For You
On The Isle of Capri*

Canterbury pilgrims bring gifts for the poor

July 16th: Thousands of pilgrims from all over Britain, and many other corners of the world, have made their way to Canterbury during the past two weeks in order to leave gifts at the cathedral on behalf of world poverty.

This modern pilgrimage has been masterminded by Dean Hewlett Johnson and it comes as the country struggles with the economic depression.

Affectionately known as the Red Dean because of his support for Soviet Russia and China, Hewlett Johnson has a strong social conscience and unconventional as well as brilliant ideas.

Since his appointment as Dean in 1931 he has travelled far and often but during the pilgrimage he remained in the cathedral, warmly greeting his visitors.

November 29th: The marriage took place in Westminster Abbey today of Prince George, Duke of Kent and Princess Marina of Greece. The bridegroom is the fourth son of King George V and the bride is the daughter of Prince and Princess Nicholas of Greece.

Churchill warns Britain: 'We've never been so defenceless'

October 14th: Winston Churchill, the former Chancellor of the Exchequer and First Lord of the Admiralty during the Great War, is now out of office but not idle. From his home at Chartwell, Westerham he continues to hold press conferences warning that Britain has "never been so defenceless". This week he again emphasised the importance of a strong RAF and suggested the League of Nations was ineffective against dictators.

His remarks are directed at Adolf Hitler, Germany's flamboyant leader who became Chancellor last year and who delivers dramatic speeches which rise to a crescendo bringing audiences to their feet with their arms raised in Nazi salutes.

The Government have made plans to strengthen the RAF with more men, aircraft and airfields. Mr Baldwin told the Commons recently that his aim is to have 1,310 aircraft by 1938 — up to the strength of French and Italian airforces.

Biggin Hill has already undergone a substantial building programme with new hangars, workshops and administrative offices and is earmarked to become one of England's premier fighter stations. Two squadrons are currently based there.

At Manston an Empire Air Day in May attracted more than 6,000 people and that was followed in July by an exercise when three squadrons provided an auxiliary bomber force. They were "opposed" by fighters from Biggin Hill and North Weald.

At Hawkinge there has been a complete station facelift following the disastrous fire in August last year.

Churchill is currently working on a new speech which he will deliver to the Commons. He says there is no reason to feel that Germany will attack but if there was a war with them Britain would be "tortured into absolute subjection with no chance of ever recovering — unless our defences are strengthened".

September 1st: A miniature Brooklands has opened at Dreamland, Margate. To celebrate the innovation thousands of children were invited to receive free rides.

Famous old music hall destroyed by fire

May 18th: Barnard's Palace of Varieties in High Street, Chatham, one of the most famous theatres in England and believed to be the oldest in the world, has been destroyed by fire.

Barely an hour after the curtain had rung down on the last show of last Friday evening and the laughing crowds left the hall, flames were seen pouring from the roof by residents in Medway Street.

The alarm was given at once and Chatham, Rochester and Gillingham fire brigades joined forces to battle with flames that reached heights of 30 feet and lit up the whole of the Medway towns in a lurid glow which was even seen across the Thames.

The old building, the scene of so much entertainment in the past, attracted crowds well in excess of those able to be accommodated inside. Several thousand saw the auditorium become a blazing inferno and then watched the roof collapse.

The Palace of Varieties has a fascinating history. When it was taken over by Mr Dan Barnard more than a century ago, it consisted of a fair-sized public house, The Granby Arms and a skittle alley. But when the brewers went into liquidation, Mr Barnard bought it for a song and transformed the skittle alley into a modest music hall, the first in the world.

It quickly became a favourite place of entertainment for Chatham inhabitants as well as soldiers, sailors and airmen. George Robey appeared there, as did Marie Lloyd, Dan Leno, Little Titch and Charlie Chaplin.

Danger — men at work. The charred remains of Barnard's Palace of Varieties is already being demolished

Dockyard joy at last: Chatham to build more ships

September 4th: The uncertainty in Europe and the spectre of German fascism getting out of hand may be alarming to most people but, for the dockworkers at Chatham, it is, in many ways, really good news.

For more than a year two gangs of shipwrights and hundreds of additional workers have been fully occupied building *The Arethusa*, a name-class cruiser, designed for protecting the trade routes. Today comes further confirmation of Chatham's salvation with the news that the dockyard has won the contract to build *The Euralus*. There will also be a new programme of submarine construction.

After 1926 when the cruiser *HMS Kent* and the submarine *Oberon* were completed, there were no further orders for ships from the Admiralty. Shipwrights found themselves out of work and labourers, desperate to support their families, had to turn to state assistance. Dockyard labour decreased to the unprecedented level of 7,000 by 1933. The depression hit Chatham hard.

It was the contract for *The Arethusa* which sent morale soaring. She displaces 5,000 tons and cost £1,250,000. Now comes *The Euralus* and the submarines.

Further along the River Medway, at the aircraft factory of Shorts Brothers, there has been more frantic activity. The company will soon be launching its Empire Flying Boat one of the finest looking marine aircraft ever designed.

THE WINNERS OF 5 NATIONAL CHAMPIONSHIPS USED **DUNLOP GOLF BALLS** OBTAINABLE FROM ALL PROFESSIONAL AND SPORTS DEALERS

June 29th: This summer's Open Golf Championship was held at the Royal St George's, Sandwich in memorable weather. The winner was Henry Cotton, the 27- year-old British professional, whose last round 79 left him five strokes clear of South Africa's Sid Brews. The conditions on the links were perfect, especially on the second day when Cotton went round in a record-breaking 65.

It was a Scot, Laidlow Purves, who laid out the links before the turn of the century. The long stretch of flat sands which had been the undoing of the commerce in Sandwich were utilised to restore it. Mr Purves founded the Royal St George's Club, bought the freehold of the ground and built a clubhouse. Many of the members today consist of wealthy folk from London but their pilgrimage to Sandwich has brought money and life to the town.

The Royal St George has been one of the regular courses for the Open and was the location in 1894 of the first to be played outside Scotland.

Gravesend's goodbye to Old Man Depression

September 15th: Gravesend is boldly leading the way to prosperity as the greatest depression in history shows signs of fading. Prosperity Week opens in the town on Saturday and the slogan is "spend, spend, spend".

The highlight will be the symbolic burning of a giant guy. Old Man Depression will be towed through the town and publicly set on fire at the Gordon Recreation ground on a 20-ton bonfire.

Gravesend, like all north Kent towns, has suffered badly in the past few years and many inhabitants have come to rely on the dole and outside charity. One Government plan which caused great outcry in the area was the "Means Test" for the unemployed, when officials visited homes of those out of work and ordered the sale of non-essential belongings so that the money gained could be used to support the family.

Now, at last, all this appears to be a thing of the past and this historic town is agog with subdued excitement.

11 killed as two aircraft crash in Kent

October 3rd: Kent has witnessed two aircraft tragedies within three days which have accounted for the lives of eleven people. The first was on September 29th when an Airspeed Envoy crashed at Tiverton Bottom, Shoreham killing the pilot and three passengers. The second was yesterday (Tuesday) when a De Havilland Rapide flew into the sea off Folkestone in rain and low cloud and seven passengers drowned.

The Shoreham incident was heard, rather than seen, by several local people including the local policeman, Reuben Mannering who quickly discovered hot, burning wreckage scattered over a large area.

As he and local people, assisted by a Sevenoaks Chronicle newspaper reporter, undertook the gruesome task of placing the remains of the bodies in one corner, a huge crowd gathered and the entire area had to be cordoned off.

The aircraft belonged to London Scottish and Provincial Airways and it was en route to Croydon airport. The cloud cover forced the pilot to fly low and he became lost and disorientated. Coming even lower he failed to clear a ridge of high ground and crashed.

Few details are known about yesterday's crash at Folkestone except that the Rapide was owned by Hillman's Airways and on its way to the Continent in particularly rough weather.

Kent on the wireless

September 14th: There was great excitement throughout the county yesterday when Kent was the subject of a BBC wireless broadcast.

The programme — about an hour in duration — was planned by a committee consisting of Capt, the Hon W.S.Cornwallis, Mr and Mrs Harold Nicolson, Mr Donald Maxwell. Mr Dudley Le May, Mr B.J. Benson, Mr E.A. Gardner and Mr H.R. Pratt-Boorman.

Among those who featured were the Duke of Kent and Lord Darnley who sang a song. Listeners heard the bells of Canterbury Cathedral, a steam train leaving Dover Marine, the *Golden Eagle* arriving in Margate and regimental marches played by The Buffs and the Royal West Kent Regiments.

The broadcast also swept back to the time when the Men of Kent barred the way to Duke William and challenged his right to enter Kent.

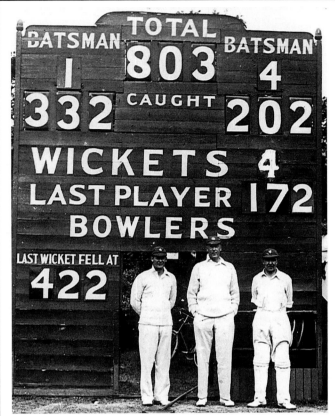

Treble century for Ashdown in Kent's record score

May 31st: How about this for a score? Bill Ashdown 332 — the first treble century ever made for Kent — Frank Woolley 172, and Les Ames 202 not out, guided their team to 803-4 declared, made in just seven hours of the most glorious batting. The match was at Brentwood against Essex, who lost by an innings and 192 runs.

The three batsmen were in good form all season and Arthur Fagg, a 19-year-old from Chartham, showed great promise for the future. The amateur batsmen also played their part and Bryan Valentine completed a 1,000 runs for the season. Woolley also won the Lawrence Trophy for the fastest century, made in 63 minutes, against Northamptonshire at Dover.

There is to be another cricket celebration this summer — the bicentenary of the first match played on the famous Sevenoaks Vine ground in 1734 between the Gentlemen of Kent and the Gentlemen of Sussex.

The Vine is one of the oldest cricket grounds in the country and the anniversary game on July 21st will be staged in the costume of the period. On this occasion the two sides will be The Lord Sackville's XI against The Viscount Gage's XI.

February 23rd: On a bright sunny winter's day the people of Dover turned out in force to greet the new Lord Warden of the Cinque Ports, Rufus Daniel Isaacs, Marquis of Reading, on his way to the installation ceremony. The seven Cinque Ports are Hastings, Winchelsea, Rye, New Romney, Hythe, Dover and Sandwich and their original responsibility was to provide a royal fleet for the defence of the realm. The practical function no longer exists but the ceremonial occasion continues. As Lord Warden, the Marquis of Reading is also the Chief Constable of Dover Castle and has an official residence in Walmer Castle.

Dover welcomes the first train ferry

July 17th: The first train ferry to be introduced by Southern Rail for the new direct service between London and Paris, berthed in the Wellington Dock, Dover today. *The Twickenham* is one of three ships specially-built by Messrs Swann Hunter and Wigham Richardson of Newcastle at a cost of more than £750,000.

The new ferry together with her sisters *Hampton* and *Shepperton* (named after river ferries in the Thames Valley) are designed to carry 12 sleeping cars and two baggage vans. Alternatively they can accommodate forty 25-feet loaded rail wagons on four sets of track on the train deck. Additionally the ferries can carry 25 cars while passengers are accommodated in Ist and 2nd class saloons. The journey between Victoria Station and the Gare du Nord will take just under 11 hours.

A train ferry dock has been designed and a tender of £231,000 approved for the construction near the Marine Station in the Western Docks at Dover.

'The ribbon development between the wars can never be thought beautiful; the contemporary rash of chalets and bungalows is incongruous in colour and feeling '— Kent author Pennethorne Hughes.

January 6th: The railway line from Orpington to Sevenoaks which includes the long tunnel under the North Downs, has been electrified.

February 1st: The BBC has announced plans for a television service to start this year.

February 10th: Gracie Fields of Rochdale has signed a two-year contract with Associated Talking Pictures. The "Lancashire Lass" will receive an unprecedented £150,000.

February 14th: Hitler approves of an Anglo-French-Belgian-Italian air defence pact against would-be aggressors.

March 18th: From midnight tonight a 30 mile-an-hour speed limit will come into force for built-up areas.

March 31st: Anthony Eden, Lord Privy Seal, has flown to Germany to talk with Hitler about his massive rearmament programme. The Führer is demanding an air force parity with Britain, a navy of 400,000 tons and a 500,000-strong conscript army — five times the size permitted under the Treaty of Versailles.

May 19th: T.E. Lawrence, known as "Lawrence of Arabia"has died from injuries sustained in a motor bicycle accident.

May 22nd: The Government announces that the size of the RAF will be trebled to ensure Britain does not lag behind Germany in air power.

May 26th: More than 12,000 young people attended a youth rally at Mote Park, Maidstone. It is the largest ever held in England.

June 7th: Stanley Baldwin has become Prime Minister of the National Government following the resignation of Ramsay MacDonald.

Capt the Hon Stanley Cornwallis, of Linton, has been elected Chairman of Kent County Council.

August 5th: So many people

December: Kent's own Royal Auxiliary Air Force Squadron, No 500, which came into being at Manston more than four years ago, has been converted to a single-engine light bomber unit — its elderly Vickers Virginias (above) replaced with Hawker Harts. 500 Squadron's short life has been enjoyable, hectic and successful but drama has never been far away. In February the crew of a Virginia escaped when the aircraft landed in flames at Manston and two years ago, Flying Officer L.M.Few died in a crash at Weybridge.

Kent is proud of its bomber squadron which was established on a half regular half reserve formula following an extensive recruiting campaign under the initiative of the second commanding officer, Wing Commander Forbes.

With the situation in Europe showing further signs of deterioration, 500 Squadron may have a significant part to play in the defence of the realm.

flocked to the Thanet resorts to take advantage of brilliant sunshine on this Bank Holiday that traffic queues built up in scores of towns. It is said that not an inch of sand was visible between the bodies on Margate and Ramsgate beaches. It was the same story in Folkestone.

The annual Venetian Fete held on the Military Canal at Hythe has never been so popular. Fishing boats, decorated to represent the Cinque Ports, made a stately procession down the canal with the appropriate mayor on board.

A Ramsgate fishing smack, *Provident*, which is one of more than 200 that used to sail out of the harbour, has proved she is still a sturdy lady. Her new American owner took her across the Atlantic with a local crew member Mr R. Powell. All the Ramsgate smacks have now been replaced with steam trawlers.

September 19th: Jewish people

living in Germany have been stripped of their German citizenship and are now "subjects without rights". They have also been excluded from employment in public services.

September 21st: An autumn frost has so devastated this year's apple crop that none can be spared for making Kentish cider.

October 1st: Lord Cornwallis, 71, the first Baron of Linton was buried at the village church today, a farm wagon laden with flowers carrying the coffin across Linton Park. Lord Cornwallis died unexpectedly last week at the home of his son-in-law Major Strang Steel.

October 8th: Clement Attlee has been elected "stop gap" leader of the Labour Party.

October: The *SS Jaguar*, a good-looking touring saloon, has been introduced at the Motor Show. The car is priced at £385.

October 20th: After 20 months of marching and fighting, Mao Tse-Tung's communist army has reached Yenan. There he plans to set up a Soviet state.

November 6th: The prototype of a new Hawker fighter, the Hurricane, today made its maiden flight.

November 16th: The National (or Tory) Government won 432 seats against Labour's 154 and Liberals 20, at the general election.

November 23rd: The Earl of Jellicoe, Admiral of the Fleet and former President of the British Legion, has died. Last year the Earl said Britain does not possess sea power vital for its safety.

New cinemas in Kent:
State, Dartford;
Jubilee, Swanscombe;
Aylsham Cinema, Aylsham;
Palace and Pavilion, Maidstone;
Carlton, Sevenoaks; Dreamland Cinema, Margate;
Argosy, Faversham,;
Astoria, Rochester.

GREAT HITS OF 1935
Red Sails in The Sunset
Blue Moon
Cheek to Cheek

May 7th: It was a day of pageantry and rejoicing all over Kent as King George and Queen Mary celebrated the Silver Jubilee of their great reign. In most towns people came out to enjoy the processions, parades, fireworks and the floodlighting. There was even a thanksgiving service on the lawn outside Tonbridge Castle (see picture).

Many significant events were planned for the great occasion. At Swanscombe, HMS Worcester fired a 21-gun salute at 12 noon. At Dartford there was a carnival procession through the town. At Gravesend the Clock Tower was illuminated in honour of the royal couple. Throughout the county children have been presented with jubilee mugs.

A couple in Sevenoaks have marked the occasion by launching a newspaper and distributing it free of charge across the district. The "Sevenoaks News" is a rival to the well-established opposition papers, Sevenoaks Chronicle and Kent Messenger. The editor/proprietor, Donald Hooper, who has promised that he will always be the first with the news, chose jubilee week to prove his point.

Gravesend or Eynsford for Britain's new airport

Gravesend and Eynsford have been identified by the Government as possible sites for a new national aerodrome, which is necessary because of congestion at Croydon. Gatwick, on the main London to Brighton railway line, will open in October as the most advanced airport in Europe but experts believe the astonishing increase in air traffic over the last few years makes a third aerodrome absolutely imperative.

Gravesend, of course, already has an airfield situated at the top of Thong Lane, Chalk. Opened in 1932 it has accommodated a most successful air taxi service and is used as an emergency runway when conditions make landing at Croydon impossible.

A few months ago, Mr H. Gooding, an airport director told the local Rotary Club that "within five years Gravesend will be the third airport of the United Kingdom. Both the visibility," he said, " and the landing area (eight acres) are better than those at Croydon."

He has the support of Sir Philip Sassoon, Under Secretary for Air who recently said that the "airport will bring great prosperity to Gravesend and all its people".

The green field site at Eynsford is more surprising but workers at Hulberry Farm have seen the land being prospected. It has been known for some time that Dartford Rural Council is planning to build an aerodrome between Lullingstone Park and the Crockenhill-Eynsford road.

Flashback to 1920. Local farmers demonstrated as an Ashford bailiff, Mr Joy, attempted to enter a farm cottage to remove furniture to pay for the unpaid tithes. More demonstrations this week prove that "tithe anger" is still prevalent in southern Kent.

Relic of the dark ages, say tithe-paying farmers

March 14th: The refusal of many farmers to pay tithes — an annual tax imposed by the local church — has caused great distress in Kent for many years. This week, in Ruckinge, the situation came to a head when 30 farmers took part in a hostile demonstration against the rector, the Rev C.P. Newell, who was selling livestock taken from the farms by bailiffs in order to raise sufficient taxes.

The demonstrators gathered on the rectory lawn and banged on the doors and windows while others went to the church and tolled the bell 32 times to denote the number of pounds for which distraint was levied. The police were present but on this occasion took no action.

Kent farmers say the tithe is a relic of the dark ages. It is a tax taken from Kent farmers for which no return is made to payers and diminishes money available for employment and farmsteads.

A few years ago a determined raid was made by bailiffs on farms near Canterbury to collect stock for unpaid tithes. The police, sensing trouble, assembled in quiet country lanes — many of them dressed as labourers. More police were then brought "secretly" into the district in two large furniture vans but one ran out of control down a steep hill, collided with the other and ended up in a ditch. Villagers found 50 policemen piled on top of each other.

The farmers have found a champion in one clergyman. Canon Brocklehurst, rector of Mersham, is in favour of scrapping the system. Giving evidence last week to the Royal Commission on Tithes he said: "Tithes and tithe rent charges have been the cause of irritation, quarrels and lawsuits for hundreds of years. It is affecting the religious life of the English people. It has an ill effect upon the spiritual work and ministrations of the church. The Tithe Act should be scrapped."

It is the farmers in the South Kent area who have led the battle against this ancient law. A few weeks ago farmers at Old Romney refused to pay and were immediately locked out of church. The rectory gates were closed and a party of uniformed police waited inside the grounds. Four farmers were allowed inside to see the rector but came to no satisfactory agreement.

Meanwhile auction sales to raise levies are still being held, demonstrations planned and police time wasted.

Charles Laughton portrays Farningham's Captain Bligh

May: A new film, released this year, is causing immense interest in Kent. It is called *Mutiny On The Bounty* and revolves around the incredible story of Captain William Bligh's command of *HMS Bounty* in the Pacific in 1759, when a mutiny was led by the acting lieutenant Fletcher Christian. Bligh was set adrift in an open boat with 18 men, and, after a hazardous journey of 3,600 miles which he faced with great courage, he reached Timor and safety.

William Bligh lived at the Manor House in Farningham and, on his retirement from the sea and a spell as governor of New South Wales, he settled down to a life of less agitation and excitement in this peaceful corner of Kent.

Mutiny on The Bounty is breaking box office records. It stars Charles Laughton as the betrayed captain and Clark Gable as Mr Christian.

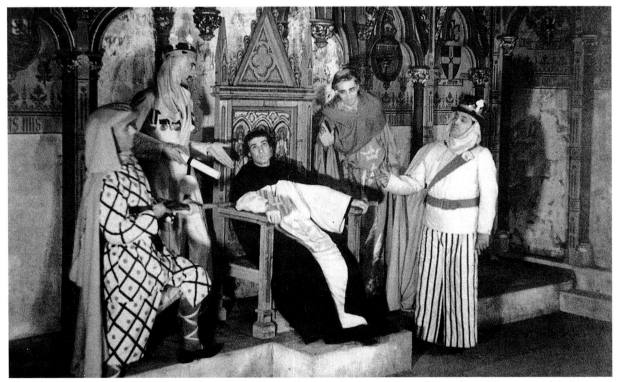

This poignant scene from Eliot's play Murder in the Cathedral, shows Robert Speaight as Thomas and William Stephens, Frank Napier, Philip Hollingsworth and E. Martin Browne as the Knights.

Canterbury salutes the "saint on a bicycle"

June 16th: Hundreds of "Friends of Canterbury Cathedral" packed into the Chapter House yesterday to see the first performance of the play, *Murder in the Cathedral*. Written by the American-born poet, T.S. Eliot, this tragedy in verse about Thomas a Becket is an undoubted masterpiece and is certain to give a renewed impetus to religious drama, despite the controversy that preceded its showing.

It is certainly a triumph for the Canterbury Festival and, in particular, for the ebullient, hard-working steward, Miss Margaret Babington, on whose initiative the play was commissioned. She has worked like a saint. On her ancient bicycle she has toured the city coaxing people into joining the group of "Friends". She has even carried a similar message to America.

The leading role is taken by local actor Robert Speaight, whose family live in St Margaret's Bay. The play will be performed on seven more occasions and then there is a possibility that it will move to London.

July 27th: The most luxurious and up-to-date bathing pool in England was opened at Ramsgate Marina today by the mayor, Alderman E Dye. Costing £50,000 with accommodation for 2,000 bathers at one time, it includes bathing terraces, cafés, car parks and a diving tower believed to be the finest in Europe. Here are some of the bathing beauties.

When the world's 'speed king' was delayed by fog

Sir Malcolm Campbell, surrounded by schoolboys, at Chislehurst Village Hall.

September 3rd: Sir Malcolm Campbell, the "speed king" of Chislehurst, set a new world record today when his car, Bluebird reached an average speed of 301.337 mph along the Bonneville Salt Flats in Utah. That is almost 15mph faster than his own record at Daytona Beach, Florida.

Campbell, who also races on water and has high hopes of setting a double world record, is the son of Mr and Mrs William Campbell, formerly of Bonchester, Chislehurst, where Malcolm was born and later of Manor Park Road, Bromley.

This week, friends recalled seeing the adventurous youth speeding along the local roads when such a sight was still a novelty. Malcolm bought his first machine from Messrs J.Humerston's Vivid Motor Works in 1904. That was a 3°hp Rax motorbike and it was quickly followed by a 20hp German car.

On one occasion he was stranded at Westerham with a broken down motorbike and had to pedal all the way back to Bromley — hard work in such hilly country. The mechanics quickly found the fault. Malcolm hadn't turned the petrol tap on!

A few months ago Sir Malcolm, who was knighted in 1931, gave a lantern lecture at Chislehurst village hall on "The story of the Bluebird". The intrepid driver who thought nothing of wiping his windscreen with one hand while he drove a car at well over three miles a minute with the other, was delayed by an hour — by fog!

When he finally arrived he told his audience that 45 years earlier he had appeared on the same stage as a little oyster in his school performance of *Alice in Wonderland*. He then turned to another "wonderland" — Daytona Beach, Florida where he established his first world record.

Campbell lost the record to Sir Henry Segrave in a Sunbeam but recaptured it on two occasions.

Mr R.F.Anthony, proprietor of Bromley Motor Works, Mason's Hill was Campbell's first mechanic and he remembered reconditioning the first Bluebird in 1909 for the racing at Brooklands.

November 21st: Rochester-born actress Sybil Thorndyke, whose late father was vicar of St Margaret's Church, is seen here with her husband, Lewis Casson and their two daughters Ann and Mary at Waterloo Station yesterday.
Miss Thorndyke made her name at the Old Vic during the Great War when many actors were at the front and her parts included Puck and even Prince Hal.
Many believe her greatest performance was in the title role of Saint Joan, *which followed the inspirational life of Joan of Arc. It was written by George Bernard Shaw and first performed in New York in 1923.*
Dame Sybil, who received her DBE in 1931, has also appeared in the much-acclaimed Othello *alongside Peggy Ashcroft, Ralph Richardson and Paul Robeson.*

Skull bone of Acheulian Man found near Swanscombe

June 30th: Archaeologists are in a state of great excitement this week following the discovery of part of a human skull in river gravels near Swanscombe.

The bone was found at Barnfield pit by a Clapham dentist, Mr Alvin Marston who has been visiting the site since 1933 for the purpose of collecting and studying flint implements.

He is certain that the fragment is the oldest example of Acheulian Man who lived in the area 100,000 years ago.

Mr Marston said this week: "I was alone in the pit when I noticed what appeared to be a piece of bone showing in the face about six feet above the floor. Removing it carefully, I marked the cavity from which it had been taken with a stone wrapped in my handkerchief and set out to find someone to act as a witness. I was fortunate in finding Mr Frank Austen, the pit engineer, working on the crushing plant. He accompanied me to the site. I then took the bone to the nearest chemist, Mr S. Akers of Milton Street, Swanscombe to be packed in cotton wool."

There will be more searches to find the rest of the skull but the first part is well preserved and shows characteristics typical of Neanderthal man.

'I find it impossible to carry the burden of kingship and discharge my duties without the support of the woman I love' — Edward VIII in his abdication speech on December 12th.

January 1st: Thousands of Americans are playing a new board game called Monopoly. It reached the shops before Christmas and sales of 20,000 sets a week were achieved.

January 4th: England have beaten New Zealand in a rugby international for the first time. Among those to score tries for England was Alexander Obolensky, the Russian prince who is studying at Oxford.

January 20th: King George V died today at Sandringham. There will be a service at Sandringham church and he will be laid to rest at Windsor amidst the tombs of his ancestors.

March 5th: A new fighter aeroplane, the Spitfire, made its maiden flight today.

March 25th: Britain, the United States and France have signed a Naval Treaty. Japan has refused.

April 28th: Crown Prince Farouk, aged 16, has been proclaimed King of Egypt.

May 9th: The Royal Air Force has been reorganised into four functional commands — Bomber, Fighter, Coastal and Training. Biggin Hill falls under Group 11 of Fighter Command.

May 18th: The BBC have recruited two women announcers — Jasmine Bligh and Elizabeth Cowell.

Work has started on a pilot bore for a tunnel under the Thames between Dartford and Tilbury.

June: A Kent Crematorium is opened at Charing by Sir Edward Hardy, chairman of the KCC.

Britain's aviation heroine Amy Johnson escapes with bruises when the plane she was flying crashed into a field at Chelsfield. Dense fog has been blamed.

July 3rd: Fred Perry wins the Wimbledon singles title for the third year in succession.

July 14th: Prince George, the Duke of Kent and the Duchess of Kent attended the Tunbridge Wells Agricultural Show today.

July 16th: There is civil war in Spain as the army rises against the Republican government. General Franco is one of the leaders of the insurgent forces. Atrocities are reported all over the country.

July 24th: The GPO has introduced a "speaking clock" service.

August 16th: The Berlin Olympic Games closed today. It was a huge sporting success and efficiently organised by the Nazi regime of Adolf Hitler. Star of the show was America's Jesse Owens who won the 100 metres, 200 metres and long jump. He then took another gold medal in the 400-metres relay. Propaganda minister Josef Goebbels called Owens a "black mercenary".

August 21st: The BBC today makes its first television broadcast from Alexandra Palace. A full public service is expected by November.

August 30th: On her maiden voyage, *Queen Mary*, Britain's new super liner, crossed the Atlantic in the record time of three days, 23 hours and 57 minutes to gain the Blue Riband for Britain.

September 7th: More than 130 million Edward VIII stamps have been sold in the first five days.

September 10th: Queen Mary has paid an informal visit to a housing estate in Folkestone, accompanied by local MP Sir Philip Sassoon. A few weeks ago she opened the new Bethlem Hospital at West Wickham.

October 12th: The new train ferry service between Dover and Dunkirk opens officially today when a train left Victoria at 10 pm and arrived in Paris at 8.55am the following morning. The service allows passengers to travel in the same sleeping car.

October 16th: Lord Beaverbrook has told the King that he will ensure no reports about the King's relationship with Mrs Wallis Simpson are leaked to the press. The lady is seeking a divorce from her husband Ernest.

October 29th: General Franco's advance on Madrid has been halted by Republicans south of the capital. Fierce fighting is taking place. Franco's provisional government has been recognised by both Hitler and Mussolini.

The old picture house at Lydd has been badly damaged by lightning.

December 12th: Edward VIII has abdicated. Today he made the decision to marry the woman he loves and renounce the throne.

December 13th: Prince Albert, better known among his friends and family as Bertie, has been proclaimed King George VI. He and Queen Elizabeth have two children, the Princesses Elizabeth and Margaret Rose. In the Great War the Prince saw action in the Battle of Jutland.

Sir Henry Wellcome, one of two American pharmacists who founded Burroughs Wellcome and Co, has died. In 1921 Wellcome Foundation took over Langley Court, Beckenham, for medical research.

New cinemas in Kent:
Odeon, Ramsgate; Cameo News Theatre, Margate; Argosy, Sheerness; Odeon, Faversham; Majestic, Sevenoaks; Embassy and Palace, Gillingham; Odeon, Deal; New Oxford, Whitstable; Odeon and Casino, Herne Bay; Odeon and The Cinema, Ashford; Canterbury Rep Theatre; Embassy, Petts Wood.

GREAT HITS OF 1936

When I'm Cleaning Windows
The Way You Look Tonight

Viscount Rothermere, who took over the chairmanship of the Daily Mail on the death of his brother Alfred, has signed frequent articles in the newspaper on the need for a strong air force and in praise of Adolf Hitler, with whom he has stayed at Berchtesgaden. He also favours better understanding with the Nazi regime and seems inclined to back Oswald Mosley.

In view of the marriage this year of Miss Diana Mitford to Oswald Mosley, the leader of the British Union of Fascists or Black Shirts, which was attended by Herr Hitler, this is a particularly interesting photograph taken a few years earlier (1928) at Chartwell. Here, left to right, enjoying afternoon tea in the dining room are Mrs Therese Sickert, Diana Mitford, Sir Edward Marsh, Winston Churchill (in foreground), Professor Frederick Lindemann, Randolph Churchill, Diana Churchill, Clementine Churchill and Walter Sickert.

Two of the men in this picture are keen that Churchill should continue to warn the country about the Nazi danger. They are Eddie Marsh, formerly his private secretary, and Professor Freddie Lindemann, Oxford scientist, who provides the former Chancellor with details of all scientific developments at Farnborough and elsewhere.

The other male guest, apart from his son Randolph, is Walter Sickert, the artist who taught Churchill the 'panafieu technique' of painting in oils over an image projected from a photographic plate. Churchill later used this technique to produce his own painting of this wonderful picture.

The nation mourns George V

January 28th: Kings, princes and politicians from 47 nations were among those who attended the funeral today of King George V who died at Sandringham last week after a long illness. He was 70.

The King has been buried at Windsor. A gun carriage, pulled by 124 naval ratings, carried his body through the crowded streets from Westminster Hall, where he had been lying in state, to Paddington Station.

Following behind on foot were the new King, Edward VIII, and his brothers, the Dukes of York, Gloucester and Kent. Queen Mary followed in a carriage.

People from all over the country have been able to listen to a description of the funeral procession, followed by the service from Windsor, on their wireless sets. The medium of broadcasting has been responsible for making King George V the best known monarch in history.

Death of Kipling overshadowed

January 19th: The death of Rudyard Kipling, unofficial poet laureate and one of the most popular authors of our times, has been almost entirely overshadowed by the news of the King's passing and the plans for the royal funeral procession.

Kipling, who has lived at Batemans, Burwash, since 1902, has been secretly cremated at Golders Green and his ashes buried in Westminster Abbey.

The famous author loved his corner of Kent and Sussex and had a particular passion for Romney Marsh and the "puzzling, winding, spindly roads".

Born in Bombay he spent many years travelling before settling down with his wife Carrie at Batemans. His best-known books are *Kim*, *Mandalay*, *The Jungle Books* and the *Just So Stories*. A brilliant prose writer and a distinctly original poet he wrote one of the best loved poems in the English Language, *If*, which was published in 1910. He was awarded the Nobel Prize for Literature in 1907.

'We could be useful so take us seriously' say The Observer Corps

July 18th: The organisation known as The Observer Corps, formed in Cranbrook some 11 years ago by enthusiasts with a penchant for plotting and identifying aircraft, is being taken very seriously by both the Army and the Royal Air Force. This week six more posts have been introduced in Kent and a new recruitment drive introduced.

The establishment of the Corps grew out of the errors of the Great War when it was realised there was no efficient method of aircraft recognition. Responsibility for enemy sightings had rested with the army, policemen on the beat or railway staff and information received usually came too late.

General Ashmore, commander of an artillery division at Ypres, was given the responsibility for London Air Defence and set about creating a workable system for spotting hostile aircraft. In 1925, after a series of successful experiments, he set up temporary controls and operations rooms in Kent and Sussex. Within a few years nearly 30 posts had been established and given plotting and telephone equipment. Staff at control centres were shown how to use grid maps with coloured counters and introduced to sound amplifiers.

The new Observer posts are at Faversham, Whitstable, Sheerness, Deal, Lenham and Canterbury. No longer is it necessary to convince the RAF that the Corps could have a vital role to play in the event of another war.

Twenty new cinemas open in Kent in 12 months

October: There may be an economic depression but that has not stopped people going to the pictures or new cinemas opening. Since October 1935, 20 have opened in Kent alone and the latest is the Odeon, Bromley.

Here the organisers had planned to open with H.G. Wells' famous science fiction film, *The Shape of Things To Come*. However, despite the fact that the famous author was once a resident of Bromley, the Odeon managers feel that gloomy Wellsian prophesies are not appropriate for a light-hearted launch.

Next year even more cinemas will open in Tonbridge, Sheerness, Hythe, Sevenoaks and Chatham.

The picture houses in Kent are packed almost every night. The well-to-do sit in the circle, the unemployed at the front of the stalls. For women the cinema eclipses all other forms of entertainment and for men it is beginning to take precedence over football. Men like the Westerns, women the love stories while the Cecil B de Mille "epics" appeal to everyone.

Most popular film this year — *Anna Karenina* starring Greta Garbo.

One of the most famous buildings in Sevenoaks, the Royal Crown Hotel in London Road, has now been demolished to make way for a super cinema, The Majestic. The Royal Crown has been a popular social centre since it was built and many will remember the heyday of the hotel when gentlemen in tail coats and white ties escorted ladies in full sweeping dresses through the pillared entrance to a variety of celebrations and balls. Sadly, the magnificent gardens are also disappearing — making way for a car park for 1,000 cars.

November 11th: The inhabitants of Sevenoaks are following the Jarrow Crusade with great interest.

Led by Labour MP Helen Wilkinson, the men from this north-east industrial town are marching on London to focus attention on the 67 per cent unemployment level.

Aware of the distress and hardship

Sevenoaks adopts north-east mining village

in the north-east, Sevenoaks has organised its own crusade the other way — travelling from Kent to Durham — to see for themselves the appalling conditions which exist in the mining and shipbuilding communities.

Sevenoaks has "adopted" the village of Quebec, not far from Jarrow, giving both practical and financial support. The marchers are hoping that similar understanding and friendship will be extended to them by Prime Minister Stanley Baldwin when they reach London.

400 firemen fail to save the Crystal Palace

November 30th: The Crystal Palace, built at Hyde Park to house the treasures of the world and moved to Sydenham 84 years ago, was destroyed yesterday in the most colossal blaze ever seen.

The fire which lit up the sky for miles around was watched by thousands who gathered on every prominence in Kent and London. Section by section the glass components shattered and then the iron skeleton, white hot, collapsed in great showers of flames which leapt 300 feet in the air.

Fire brigades from Kent and London could do nothing to check the spread of the conflagration. Almost 400 firemen and 89 engines converged on the site to discharge thousands of gallons of water at the blaze. It had no effect.

It was soon after 8pm that flames were noticed in the main transept and with frightening speed they swept down the nave, into the south-west wing and, urged on by strong winds, fanned out in an unbelievably destructive inferno. People in Sydenham, Penge, Beckenham, Bromley and right across south London stood at their front gates hardly believing their eyes — could all that glass and iron really burn?

Among those who climbed the hill to Crystal Palace Parade was Patrick Beaver. He said: "I found the familiar iron arches silhouetted against the roaring inferno like the bars of a huge furnace and it was obvious that the brass-crested firemen, dwarfed against a backcloth of flaming fabric, were fighting a losing battle."

As great explosions added to the firework show, people started arriving from as far away as Margate and Hythe. Special trains were laid on and mile-long queues of traffic delayed the back-up fire engines.

By 9.30 pm the throng of sightseers was so large that fences and gardens were trampled down. Mounted police arrived to barricade the streets and force back the crowds. As they did so private aeroplanes crossed and recrossed the sky.

When the Great Transept collapsed it was heard from five miles away. Firemen then redoubled their efforts to save the two towers for if they had collapsed the houses below would have been destroyed.

The Crystal Palace was designed by Joseph Paxton for the Great Exhibition of 1851 at Hyde Park and was such a success that it was rebuilt on a more grandiose style at Sydenham , surrounded by fountains and statues and life-sized pre-historic monsters. This unique building survived for 84 years and many believe that its destruction symbolises the passing of an age.

One man who watched the blaze from start to finish was Sir Henry Buckland, the general manager, who spoke to reporters today with tears in his eyes. He said: "The Palace and its contents are insured at Lloyd's through a 'first loss' policy of £110,000. The Great Organ is seperately insured for £10,000".

Today a few smoke-blackened statues remain on the terraces but the Crystal Palace which was 1,850 feet long and 408 feet wide, covering four times the ground area of St.Peter's in Rome, is a twisted, gutted heap of metal.

December 4th: *The Bromley Times* writes today: "For generations the giant glass structure of the Crystal Palace has dominated the whole of south London. It was a landmark for miles around and a lasting monument to the Victorian tradition. It had a place in the affections of thousands. Even those who mocked its appearance, who described it as an architectural monstrosity, had for it, in most of their hearts, a friendly affection born of long acquaintance. It was a home of music, of art, of fireworks, of dog, cat and poultry shows...a glorious place for yesterday's holiday...a meeting ground of a thousand interests and hobbies..."

December 5th: *The central transept of the Crystal Palace soon after the outbreak of fire. All this week letters of sympathy have been pouring in to Sir Henry Buckland and hundreds have written to* The Times *about "the loss of this monumental relic of the golden age". Among the writers is Mr Edward Myerstein, a millionaire who lives at Morants Court, Dunton Green, near Sevenoaks, who suggests that something good could come out of the tragedy. "Since it was built for the Great Exhibition in 1851," he says, "it stood as a link with the Victorian era and the whole world knew the Crystal Palace. Would it not be a wonderful gift for the people of the Empire to erect on the site a convalescent home serving all the great hospitals ?"*

Mr Meyerstein goes on to say: "As a Coronation gift to His Majesty, subscribed for by all his subjects, here and abroad, in sums of a halfpenny upwards it would be an everlasting token of regard. Should His Majesty give approval I am willing to be responsible for the sum of £100,000."

This is the scene at Sydenham Hill two days after the fire. Hundreds of forthcoming events have had to be called off, but the saddest is the cancellation of the concert in honour of the Coronation of King Edward VIII when Miss Gracie Fields, among other singers, was to have entertained 30,000 schoolchildren from all over the country.

Edward VIII renounces the throne for the woman he loves

December 13th: King Edward VIII yesterday chose abdication as the price of freedom to marry the woman he loves. In an act, unprecedented in the history of the monarchy, he has given up the throne to marry American divorcee, Mrs Wallis Simpson. He sails to France, and exile, tonight.

In a dramatic radio broadcast, heard by millions, he said: "I find it impossible to carry the burden of kingship and discharge my duties without the support of the woman I love. The decision is mine alone. The other person most concerned has tried to persuade me to take a different course."

News of the abdication of the King in favour of his brother, the Duke of York, was received by newspapers across Kent via transmission from the Central News Agency. Elsewhere Saturday evening dances stopped and messages were flashed onto cinema screens.

It came after several anxious days of consultation and deliberation between His Majesty and his Ministers. A crowded House of Commons on Thursday heard The Speaker read these momentous words, written by the King: "After long and anxious consideration I have determined to renounce the throne to which I succeeded on the death of my father and I am now communicating this, my final and irrevocable decision."

Among those who have been advising the King in this constitutional drama is Mr Walter Monckton of Ightham, attorney general to the Duchy of Cornwall and one of His Majesty's best friends since their Oxford days.

Monckton is well-known in the Sevenoaks and Borough Green area as President of the Sevenoaks Fat Stock Association, a cricketer with I Zingari and a former officer with the West Kent Regiment.

If the Duke of Windsor, as he is now known, looked to Walter Monckton as a friend, the same could not be said of Dr Cosmo Gordon Lang, the formidable Archbishop of Canterbury, who told Prime Minister Stanley Baldwin that marriage with a divorced woman was incompatible with the King's role as head of the Church of England.

The Proclamation of George VI as King took place on Saturday and the following day, during the evening service at Canterbury, Dr Lang staggered many listeners when he condemned a certain circle of people connected with the Duke of Windsor. Many who heard his words are writing to Parliament alleging a lack of Christian spirit in the Archbishop's address.

Church ministers throughout Kent have taken a

June 3rd 1937: The Duke and Duchess of Windsor pictured after their marriage at The Chateau de Cande in a valley near Tours. There were two simple ceremonies with few witnesses.

different view. The Rector of Sevenoaks, the Rev F.W.Argyle said of the Duke: "He has won deep affection, especially that of the poorer people with his understanding sympathy."

Canon T.C. Bewes of St John's Church, Tunbridge Wells, said: "For 25 years as Prince of Wales and King he has ceaselessly helped many people in different ways, especially in large centres of population as well as in the Colonies."

Other ministers have recalled what an inspiration he was in the terrible days of war "when he was prepared to take the risk of losing his life".

The abdication crisis, the admitted adultery of the King, the conspiracy of silence that followed and the King's love for a divorced woman will continue to be the main talking-point in thousands of factories, homes and offices for weeks to come.

Meanwhile we look forward to the coronation of George VI, provisionally planned for May, next year.

'Nothing this young athlete can do will ever surprise me. He is a wonder — the greatest bit of running I have ever seen' — Guy Butler of The Morning Post on Sydney Wooderson's new world record.

January 1st: It was 40 years ago, in 1897, that trams were introduced in Dover — Kent's first town to go over to the then revolutionary form of transport. The great age of the tram is over and it was with some sadness last night that the people of Dover said goodbye to the last car.

A new law has come into force banning political uniforms. It empowers the police to stop processions and gatherings when there is a risk of disorder. The Government hopes it will stop provocative marches such as those led by Sir Oswald Mosley.

January 10th: The Government has made it illegal for volunteers to fight in Spain. Offenders will be jailed for two years.

February 4th: The Government's education board has unveiled plans for a £2million campaign to make Britons fitter and healthier. They are recommending more playing fields, gymnasiums, swimming pools, camp sites and community centres plus the creation of a national college of physical education.

February 12th: Kent garages today increased the price of petrol by a halfpenny to 1/7d.

March: George Orwell, who wrote about conditions in the Kentish hop fields a few years ago, has moved north. His new book *The Road to Wigan Pier* looks at the life of the unemployed.

March 3rd: Australia has regained The Ashes by three games to two after an exciting series 'down under'. Two Kent players were in the tour party, wicket-keeper/batsman Les Ames and the new opening batsman, Arthur Fagg.

March 20th: England beat Scotland at Rugby at Murrayfield for the first time to capture the Calcutta Cup, International Championship and Triple Crown.

March 24th: Trams in Thanet have been replaced by East Kent diesel omnibuses.

July 21st: Miss Jessie Matthews, the famous film star, crowned 19-year-old Gwenneth Bourne, Ramsgate's Carnival Queen before a crowd of 5,000 at the St Lawrence Cliffs Bandstand on Monday.

April 14th: A new coin comes into circulation today called the "threepenny bit".

April 27th: The cultural home of the Basque Empire, Guernica, was destroyed yesterday by the German Air Force sent to help Franco by Adolf Hitler. Heinkels and Junkers pounded the town with high explosives.

King George VI opened the National Maritime Museum at Greenwich today.

May 6th: More than 30 passengers and crew of the giant German airship *Hindenburg* died today when the airship exploded into flames as she came in to land at New Jersey.

May 12th: The BBC's transmission of the coronation procession is its first television outside broadcast. It has been a great success.

A 2-seater monoplane crashed into Bromley Hill cemetery after stalling and going into a spin. The pilot was killed.

May 28th: Neville Chamberlain is the new Prime Minister following the resignation of Stanley Baldwin. Colleagues say his style of leadership may be less relaxed than his predecessor.

June 3rd: Edward, Duke of Windsor, has married Wallis Simpson in a village chateau near Tours, France. The couple will spend their honeymoon in Austria.

Kent cricketer Arthur Fagg is unable to play this year having contracted rheumatic fever during the winter tour of Australia.

July 9th: Henry Cotton wins the British Open Golf championship for the second time.

July 14th: The Kent and Canterbury Hospital has been opened by the Duke and Duchess of Kent.

August 4th: New locks for the River Medway have been opened at Allington, Maidstone, at a cost of £18,000. They will prevent the flooding which occurs frequently at Maidstone and Tonbridge.

August 20th: Kent have beaten Gloucestershire by eight wickets by scoring 219 runs in 71 minutes. Clean, controlled hitting by Ashdown, Woolley, Ames and Watt gave them this extraordinary victory.

August 29th: As the Japanese bombed Shanghai today, 2,000 British women and children were evacuated aboard a P and O liner.

September 30th: Bexley, Kent's largest borough, has received its Charter of Incorporation from Lord Cornwallis and, in honour of the occasion, schoolchildren have been given the day off.

November 10th: Ramsay MacDonald, Britain's first Labour Prime Minister, has died at sea during a voyage to America.

New cinemas in Kent: Empire, Sandwich; Embassy, Tenterden; Ritz, Chatham; Plaza, Sevenoaks; Ritz, Hythe; Odeon, Sittingbourne; Ritz, Sheerness; Ritz, Tonbridge.

GREAT HITS OF 1937

The Folks Who Live on the Hill

A Nice Cup of Tea

Short Brothers Aircraft Company of Rochester has just completed the most daring aeronautical experiment yet known — a composite aircraft. As shown in the photograph a small, heavily-loaded aircraft sits on the back of a larger, comparatively light and high powered machine and, at a selected height, the pilots of each operate a release and the excess lift of the smaller plane carries her up and away. Here, the upper component is a Mercury — a twin-float high-wing monoplane — and the lower one, a Maia — similar to an Empire flying boat but with larger wings and different hull lines. The composite aircraft has been completed and it is hoped to have the first trial early next year.

Green Belt plan may save Sevenoaks and Dartford

April 8th: An ambitious plan by London County Council to spend £2 million buying open spaces in the home counties in an effort to curb the surburban sprawl is being applauded this week by local councils in Kent

The "green belt", as it is being described, will encircle London. Planning regulations will be introduced to prevent speculative builders offering semi-detached houses for sale between £600 and £800.

When the railways arrived, north-west Kent was immediately absorbed by London. Villages like Eltham, Blackheath, Greenwich and Plumstead became part of Greater London before the turn of the century. Bromley, Beckenham and Orpington are the latest to be swallowed.

The suburban sprawl which has characterised this decade is still spreading and in threatened places like Sevenoaks, Swanley and Dartford the oft-heard cry of "subtopia" fills the readers' columns in the newspapers.

One example of the difficulty facing those who want greater controls comes this week with an offer from the Corporation of the City of London to buy Whitley Forest — a large area of open countryside between Sevenoaks and Riverhead — for building development.

In opposing the sale, Sevenoaks Urban Council has the support of the Council for the Preservation of Rural England. The Green Belt, they say, has to become law.

Coronation street parties have been held all over Kent. This is Swanley in festive mood.

Shy 'Bertie' becomes King George VI

May 12th: King George VI and Queen Elizabeth were crowned at Westminster Abbey today by the Archbishop of Canterbury, Dr Cosmo Lang.

Princes, peers and Prime Ministers from all over the world heard the diffident, shy King, known to his family and friends as "Bertie" take the Coronation Oath in a slightly halting voice.

The procession to the Abbey which proceeded the ceremony was one of pomp and pageantry. Thousands of people lined the route, many more heard heard the commentary on the wireless and a privileged few watched on television. It was the BBC's first televised outside broadcast.

With the nation still slightly shaken from the extraordinary events of the previous year, the coronation came as a wonderful tonic. The excitement, which had built up over several days, reached its climax as the golden coach

with four postillions, six footmen, eight grooms and four Yeomen of the Guard walking alongside left Buckingham Palace for the Abbey.

Among the vessels invited to take part in the Coronation Review on the Thames is the *Medway Queen* paddle steamer built in 1924 at Troon for the Steam Packet Company of Rochester. For years she has been a familiar sight, sailing daily from Strood Pier to Herne Bay and Southend.

Royal order for Lullingstone silk

During the coronation ceremony many eyes were on the King and Queen's two daughters, Princesses Elizabeth and Margaret Rose who wore silk dresses produced by the silkworms of Lullingstone Castle, near Eynsford.

Earlier this year, Queen Mary, the Queen Mother visited the Castle to inquire whether Lady Hart Dyke, who had established her silk farm about five years ago, could produce enough silk for the dresses and also for part of Queen Elizabeth's coronation robe.

The answer was 'yes'. Several young women in the neighbourhood were employed and production of the silk began in earnest.

Zoë Hart Dyke is now in great demand to tell her story of the silk farm and how it started. All you need, she says, is an incubator, a large room, reeling machine and a mulberry plantation — oh yes, and plenty of know-how!

1937

Sydney Wooderson — fastest man in the world

August 30th: Sydney Wooderson of Chart Sutton, near Maidstone — a former Sutton Valence schoolboy — has set a new world record for the mile handicap race. At Motspur Park on Saturday the Blackheath Harrier ran the mile in the unbelievable time of 4 minutes 6.4 seconds — 0.4 seconds faster than America's Glen Cunningham three years ago.

Wooderson is a hero throughout the country. At the aged of 23, this studious-looking, bespectacled youth who stands only five foot six and looks more like an office worker than an athlete, has already entered the realms of legend rather than celebrity.

The Times writes today: "The mile run produced the most inspired effort yet made by the British champion. As the slight figure flashed down the home straight officials and spectators alike found it difficult to contain their excitement and then there were remarkable scenes when the time of the run was announced, the young champion being carried off shoulder high by his admirers."

Sydney Wooderson started running in his home village and was a schoolboy champion at Sutton Valence. Four years ago, in 1933, he won the inter-schools race and the public schools mile in under four minutes 30 seconds. By the following year he was running for England in the Empire Games.

He went to the Berlin Olympics but with little hope of a painful injury recovering in time so that he limped through his heat, only after his return discovering several displacements in his left foot.

This year he set up a new three-quarter mile record at the Glasgow Rangers' meeting before the mile record.
Picture shows Sidney winning the mile on August 2nd at the International athletics meeting at the White City.

Eltham College recalls the fiery brilliance of Eric Liddell

Sydney Wooderson's new world record brings to mind the achievements of another athlete, well-known in Blackheath and Mottingham, where his former schoolteachers still talk with pride — not only of his remarkable all-round sporting ability but his profound Christian principles.

Eric Liddell was born in China but his Scots missionary parents sent him and his brother Rob to Eltham College where their love of sport became evident. In 1918 they were first and second in the long jump, high jump, 100 yards, hurdles, quarter mile and cross country. Eric was captain of cricket and rugby and eventually went on to Edinburgh University to study science.

Eric continued to excel in athletics and in **1923, aged 21, he set up a new British record for the 100 yards in 9.7 seconds. He also played for Scotland at rugby and was in the team which beat Wales at Cardiff Arms Park.**

"The Flying Scotsman" as he became known was chosen for the Paris Olympics in 1924 but refused to run in the 100 yard heats because they were held on a Sunday and that, to him, was the Lord's Day for Christian worship. Instead he took part in the 400 metres and established a new world record of 47.6.

Eric is now a missionary worker like his parents in China but his headmaster, Mr W.B. Hayward stills remembers "the shy, rather weedy boy who grew strong and fiery after plenty of fresh air and several terms of hard rugger".

May 14th: Thousands of busmen all over Kent returned to work today after a three-week strike over pay and conditions. During the stoppage many people had great difficulty in getting to work and traders suffered heavy losses. The busmen also suffered but there has been considerable sympathy shown for their cause. A few bus drivers, who broke the picket lines and went to work, needed police escort. Picture shows the only bus in the Rochester, Chatham and Gillingham district with a police car following as it went through Chatham on April 22nd.

Haven in Tunbridge Wells for 80 refugee children

May 21st: Eighty destitute children from the war-ravaged Spanish provinces around Bilbao arrived in Tunbridge Wells this week as guests of the town. They will live in Rusthall Beacon for at least nine months and longer if the Civil War in Spain continues.

The children were among a party of 4,000 who arrived on the liner *Habana* of Barcelona. It docked at Southampton and from there the children travelled by road, stopping at Eastleigh while doctors checked a suspected case of typhoid.

A 12-year-old girl with her five brothers and sisters, orphaned by the war, were in the party. With the long pilgrimage from their devastated home over, they watched with shining eyes the sun set over the borderlands of Kent and Sussex.

The mayor, Cllr E.J. Strange, has launched an appeal for funds and for volunteers to assist with nursing, teaching and housework.

Allhallows will rival Southend

February 13th: The enterprising development company which promises to transform Allhallows "into another Southend" is pressing ahead with its ambitious scheme despite a few serious setbacks.

The name of the town has already been changed to Allhallows-on-Sea and during the next month work will begin on creating an amusement park with a building of 60,000 square feet. When completed the park will be four times the size of the famous one at Blackpool.

Other features include a zoo, yachting centre, stadium and the largest swimming pool in the world with artificial waves. There will be a holiday camp, 5,000 new homes, up-to-date hotels, restaurants, theatres and cinemas.

The development will take seven years to complete and will cost millions of pounds. It will prove a great convenience to millions of people in London and the Home Counties.

Picture Palace & Oaks Place, Tenterden.

January: Sadness in Tenterden over the demolition of the Picture Theatre (above) which has provided first-class cinema entertainment in Oaks Place since 1912 is somewhat muted by the news that an 800-seat super cinema, The Embassy will be opened on February 11th. Built by the Shipman and King circuit the Embassy will have a first-floor cafe and a series of shops will be opened alongside. It is believed that the first film will be Windbag the Sailor.

Why they are calling Broadstairs 'Little Germany'

There is growing concern about the presence in Broadstairs of the headquarters, at 23 High Street, of the British Union of Fascists. Senior figures in the movement include William Joyce, a former teacher at the Convent School in Kingsgate. Some believe the German foreign secretary, von Ribbentrop has also been a frequent visitor to the town as representative of a German champagne company.

Only a few months ago five Blackshirts were fined a total of £14 by Margate magistrates for Jew-baiting in the town and all were members of the BUF. The magistrate who fined them said: "We don't want this sort of conduct in Margate."

More serious is the case of Dr Hermann Goertz, now serving a four-year sentence in Maidstone prison for spying for Germany.

Goertz, who is 45, rented a bungalow in Stanley Road, Broadstairs and, accompanied by a 19-year-old German girl Marianne Emig, toured the country on his motorbike, stopping at airfields to sketch their layout and defences.

Goertz had booked the bungalow, 'Havelock', for six weeks but moved out shortly before the end of his tenancy. The landlady became suspicious and called the police. They alerted Special Branch officers who found a pair of dungarees and a camera which contained a film showing pictures of airfields and aircraft.

At his trial at the Old Bailey, Dr Goertz said he had come to England to get material for a novel. He was found guilty of committing offences under the Official Secrets Act.

'There has come back from Germany to Downing Street peace with honour. I believe it is peace in our time' — Prime Minister, Neville Chamberlain, September 30th.

January 3rd: The Government has stated that all children must be issued with gasmasks.

January 14th: A full-length feature cartoon, Snow White and the Seven Dwarfs by Walt Disney has captivated audiences all over America. The film is accompanied by Frank William's songs *I'm Wishing* and *Some Day My Prince Will Come.*

February 17th: A large-screen prototype television has been demonstrated by John Logie Baird.

February 21st: Anthony Eden has resigned as Foreign Secretary following differences with the Prime Minister, Mr Chamberlain.

March 14th: Austrians gave the Nazi dictator, Adolf Hitler, a tremendous welcome today as he drove into Vienna, capital of his native land.

March 24th: The Prime Minister told the House of Commons today that Britain will defend France and Belgium against unprovoked aggression. He said that if Czechoslavakia was attacked other countries would immediately be involved.

May 14th: England's football team beat Germany 6-3 in Berlin today. Players of both sides gave the Nazi salute before the game.

June 2nd: A Belgian Fokker airliner crashed into Springfield House at Sellindge and demolished part of the Methodist Chapel.

June 8th: Thousands of Chinese people have been killed as Japanese bombers devastate the city of Canton.

June 11th: An earth tremor in the Bromley area has alarmed many people. It was felt at noon and caused doors to shake and windows to rattle. Mr Arthur Bellringer reported that his stationary car in West Wickham rocked and swayed.

June 14th: Sir John Reith is to leave the BBC to become head of Imperial Airways. There are

1938

September: It has been another remarkable year for Kent cricket club. Frank Woolley retired with 47,000 runs and 1,600 wickets in the bank, Les Ames enjoyed another successful year with England in the Ashes series, a new member Doug Wright, from Chislehurst, made his Test debut against Australia and Arthur Fagg (above) set a new championship record with two double centuries in the same match against Essex at Colchester. The club has a new captain in F.G.H. Chalk and four members of the Kent team, Wright, Fagg, Ames and Brian Valentine have been selected for the MCC South African tour.

considerable fears that the poor record of the Airways is endangering Britain's performance in passenger flight.

June 24th: On the first day of a new recruitment drive by the RAF, more than 1,000 young men have been recruited.

July 3rd: A world record speed of 126 miles an hour for a steam engine was achieved today by *Mallard*, a Gresley A4 Pacific

between Newcastle and London.

August 24th: The Yorkshire batsman Len Hutton scored a record 364 runs against Australia to help England level the series. England declared their first innings closed at a massive 903-7.

September 30th: Agreement on a peaceful solution in Europe has been reached following a conference in Munich between Mr Chamberlain, Monsieur

Daladier, Herr Hitler and Signor Mussolini.

The Streatfeilds have left Chiddingstone Castle the family home since Tudor times.

September 27th: The *Queen Elizabeth,* the largest liner in the world, was launched today at John Brown's shipyard on the Clyde.

Jack Randall has retired after 37 years as golf professional at Sundridge Park Golf Club.

September 28th: Erith is the latest town to be presented with its Charter of Incorporation, the Marquis of Camden officiating at a grand ceremony.

October 1st: Hitler was given a tremendous welcome today as German troops marched into the Sudetenland. Loud speakers in Eger, the capital, announced: "Here comes our liberator."

October 25th: The Duke of Kent has been appointed Governor-General of Australia.

October 27th: Student Tories led by 22-year-old Edward Heath from Broadstairs have been prominent in anti-Chamberlain protests following the Prime Minister's appeasement policy.

November 10th: Jews are given 48 hours to leave Munich or go to a concentration camp.

With more than 100 local authority and volunteer brigades in Kent now under the auspices of the Auxiliary Fire Service, thousands of volunteers have been recruited.

December 25th: Today it snowed heavily in Kent — the first classic White Christmas since 1906.

New churches in Kent:
St Mary's, Gravesend;
St Mary's, Green St Green.

New cinemas in Kent:
Corona, Swanley;
Regal, Cranbrook.

Knife through the heart of Kent's loveliest valley

February 25th: Anger is growing over a Ministry of Transport proposal to build a road from Polhill, Sevenoaks, through the Darenth Valley to the new tunnel beneath the Thames currently under construction between Dartford and Purfleet.

It is significant of the extent of feeling that not a single word has been said in favour of the proposed route and the scheme has been condemned everywhere as "destructive of the most beautiful stretch of countryside, not only in Kent, but England".

The Darenth valley between Otford and Farningham Wood, close to the villages of Shoreham and Eynsford is one of the jewels of the recently-adopted Green Belt.

As shown in the plan (left), the road will give no commensurate public advantage. The white road reaches the Thames in 15 miles. The black road will reach it in 13 miles, thrusting a knife through the heart of this lovely valley.

January 1st: Ministry of Transport officials, 120 feet below the surface of the River Thames, examine the new Dartford to Purfleet tunnel. It is the biggest engineering project under the Thames since the opening of the Rotherhithe Tunnel in 1908. Work is well advanced and the cost is estimated at more than £3 million. Boring on the pilot tunnel has already begun and it is expected that the two halves will meet early next year.

It is now more than a year since the destruction of the Crystal Palace and work on clearing the site and restoring the park has almost finished. Picture shows the Margate Schools' football team visiting the ruins a few months ago.

Student leader Edward Heath leads Chamberlain protest

October 27th: Student Tories at Oxford, led by a 22-year-old Man of Kent, have been prominent in anti-Chamberlain protests following the Prime Minister's appeasement policy.

Edward Heath from Broadstairs, yesterday persuaded his fellow students to campaign vociferously for the Master of Balliol, A.D. Lindsay, who is standing against the Conservative candidate, Quintin Hogg, in the forthcoming Oxford by-election. Hogg is a Chamberlain candidate and supports his policy. Mr Heath's slogan is *"A vote for Hogg is a vote for Hitler"*.

Ted Heath, as he prefers to be known, was born at Albion Villa, St Peter's Road, Broadstairs and attended St Peter's Church of England School before moving on to Chatham House, Ramsgate. He won a music scholarship to Balliol and, unless his other passions — politics, journalism and sailing — get in his way, he is on course for a great musical career. His father is a builder in Kingsgate and his grandfather a railwayman.

The majority of people in Kent, horrified by the prospect of another war, support appeasement but are willingly helping local authorities with the many "air-raid" exercises.

Archbishop Cosmo Lang has instructed the clergy to encourage parishoners to co-operate. "An attack from the air may only be a possibility", he said, "but it is our duty to be ready for it."

Ted Heath says that life at Balliol, under its famous Master, A.D. Lindsay, is a hive of intellectual and artistic activity. The undergraduate from Broadstairs has been awarded an organ scholarship.

Lindbergh seeks solace in Kent village

June: A good-looking 30-year-old American and his wife, who have been living, almost anonymously, in the tiny village of Sevenoaks Weald, have been identified as Charles and Anne Lindbergh.

Lindbergh, who made history in 1927 by completing the first non-stop solo flight between New York and Paris in his monoplane, *The Spirit of St Louis,* has come to England following the murder of his baby son and the most intensive manhunt in history. The little boy was kidnapped from the nursery and then, a few months later, found in a wood, bludgeoned to death.

It was four years later that an unemployed, illegal immigrant, Bruno Hauptmann, was eventually charged with murder but as the sensational news of his trial, then execution, filled the newspapers, Charles and Anne were on their way to Kent.

To escape the attention of the ever-present American press, Charles and Anne Lindbergh flew to England and rented, from Harold and Vita Nicholson, their former home in Sevenoaks Weald. The Nicholsons have only recently moved to Sissinghurst Castle and Long Barn was available.

For the grieving Lindberghs today, this magnificent home in a peaceful village surrounded by lovely wooded countryside is giving them breathing space and peace at last. The few people in the village who know of their identity have jealously guarded the secret of their presence.

Captain Lindbergh became a hero on both sides of the Atlantic following his epic 3,600-mile flight. It was five years later, on March 2, 1932, that the aviator— known as "The Lone Eagle" — made international news again. As he and his wife were dining at their home in New Jersey, kidnappers climbed into the nursery of their 20-month-old son and left a note on the windowsill demanding a $50,000 ransom.

Charles Lindbergh in the garden at Long Barn with his second son Jon who was born after his brother's murder in 1932.

The couple have now been at Long Barn for two years with their second son Jon, and a third son was born last year. Lindbergh says they have been among the happiest, most peaceful days of his life.

They have dined at Sissinghurst and Hever on several occasions and on May 28th were invited to a ball at Hever where the guests included the King and Queen. "I sat with the Queen for about 20 minutes," said Lindbergh later. "She is a very fine woman and very natural. Dignified but not at all stiff and making a tremendous effort to carry her part as Queen of England. She did it beautifully but it is easy to see what a strain she is under."

November 15th: Charles Lindbergh, now living in Paris, having given up the lease on Long Barn, says he would like to settle permanently in Germany. He admires Hitler and was recently decorated, by the Führer, with the Service Cross. Newspapers described him this week as "Hitler's lackey".

A Hawker Demon, on a training flight, high above the Medway at Rochester. 23 Squadron, the only RAF squadron to have flown these two-seater aircraft, became famous for amazing displays of synchronised aerobatics. Sadly, a few years ago, one of the Squadron's most promising young officers, Douglas Bader, suffered a crash and lost both his legs.

Leslie Hope from Eltham a big star in Hollywood

October 5th: A young lad from Eltham, who found stardom in America, has reached the pinnacle of an extraordinary career. This week Leslie Townes Hope, now better known as Bob, is the toast of North East Kent following the release of his movie, *The Big Broadcast of 1938.*

Starring alongside Dorothy Lamour, young Bob — who admits that he is no great shakes as a recording artist — sings *Thanks for The Memory* to Shirley Ross. The song has won an Oscar, the critics are ecstatic and Hope is being hailed as one of Hollywood's great personalities.

The road from Eltham has been a fascinating one. Bob said this week: "I got my first chuckle on May 29th, 1903 when I became the fifth of seven sons born to Avis Townes Hope at 44 Craigton Road, Eltham and I was named Leslie in honour of a local soccer hero. I spent three years there before the family moved to Bristol. The entire Hope clan turned out at Eltham's Well Hall station to see us off."

William, a stone mason, and Avis Hope emigrated to Cleveland, Ohio, where young Leslie learned to dance, developed a passion for the cinema,

August 1939: *Bob keeps his promise. Bob his wife at Waterloo Station. Next stop — Craigton Road, Eltham.*

gained a basic showbiz training and then pounded the provincial vaudeville beat of America night after night looking for work. His big break came in 1928 when he was offered a small part in a comedy at Chicago's West Englewood Theatre.

Leslie T. Hope changed his name to Bob, made several appearances on Broadway and, in 1932, formed a partnership with a like-minded 31-year-old crooner called Harry Lillis Crosby, or Bing as he prefers to be known. Today the pair are working on a film together which will be called *Road to Mandalay.*

Bob Hope is also planning a nostalgic return trip to Eltham.

'Peace in our time' — but Biggin

September 30th: Prime Minister Neville Chamberlain returned to England from an historic meeting with Adolf Hitler yesterday, waved a piece of paper in the air and declared: "I believe it is peace in our time."

The Prime Minister was given a tremendous welcome at Heston aerodrome and later at Buckingham Palace where he appeared on the balcony with the King and Queen. Clutching a copy of the new Anglo-German accord, he said that he, Herr Hitler, Monsieur Daladier and Signor Mussolini had come to an agreement over the future of Czechoslovakia. His mission in Munich had brought peace with honour.

There is no doubt that Mr Chamberlain has played a crucial role in appeasing Hitler and avoiding a world war but many countries are not happy by the agreement in which the Sudeten region of Czechoslovakia will be handed over to Germany.

The terms stress that the region must be evacuated by October 10th. The agreement grants all of Herr Hitler's demands and MPs describe the pact as a "complete sell-out". War, they say, is still a strong possibility.

Since Germany marched illegally into Sudetenland in August, the airfields in Kent have been on "immediate readiness for war". At Biggin Hill, RAF and Army personnel on leave have been recalled, reservists, auxiliaries and territorials called up and the two fighter squadrons, 78 and 32, with their Gloster Gauntlets, put on standby.

At Gravesend, home of the Elementary and Reserve Flying School, more and more pilots are being trained and more aircraft and instructors made available.

At Manston, trench shelters are being dug and machine gun posts put in place for airfield defence. Buildings have been camouflaged. 500 (County of Kent) Squadron has been posted to Detling aerodrome to become part of No 16 (General Reconnaissance) Group.

The worsening situation in Europe has not escaped the attention of the Observer Corps. Group headquarters are at Maidstone and Bromley and they control more than 50 posts in Kent and five RDF (Radio Direction Finding) stations. As the network grows ever larger an appeal has gone out for more recruits and exercises are being organised to unite the RAF with its new partner. Air Chief Marshal Hugh Dowding has placed the Corps on a wartime footing.

Despite Mr Chamberlain's assurances the "Munich crisis" as it is being called has failed to halt the preparation for "possible war".

Air Raid Precaution officers are being appointed, auxiliary firemen recruited and volunteers are coming

forward in droves. Home Office speakers are touring the country and public meetings in Kent are being told about blackout procedures, and the need for air-raid wardens, despatch riders, decontamination teams, rescue parties and those with first-aid experience.

Beckenham, where preparations for "possible war" are more advanced than anywhere in the country, is one of the first towns to be fitted out with gasmasks as a gas attack is likely to be a feature of this modern conflict. Anti-gas drill classes are already being well attended.

Hill remains on readiness for war

Empire Day at Biggin Hill and the crowds who flocked to see the annual air display.

370 bombers in 'aerial war' over Manston

July 22nd: The first aerial war ever seen over England took place in the skies above Manston on Monday night when 370 night and day bombers from three squadrons defended this front-line airfield from repeated attacks by the 'enemy' and attempted to defy the brilliant attention of the searchlights.

This, of course, is one of the many exercises being held in the county in these worrying days. Two months ago the people of the Medway Towns were "on the receiving end" when the Virginias of 500 Squadron "bombed" and "machine-gunned" towns in the Thames Estuary. More than 2,000 people took part in the ARP test and children were given a short holiday so that schools could be used as first-aid centres. There were mock patrols, casualties, sirens, and fires as "bombs" fell on town halls, railway stations and even the Rochester Bridge.

The Munich crisis has produced shock waves throughout Kent. Right across the county buildings are being surveyed for suitability for adaptation as shelters, first-aid posts are being established and trenches dug. Here the children of North Borough School, Maidstone, look quite bemused as ARP trenches are dug in their school grounds.

Dreamland chief loses a fortune as British film industry collapses

December: John Henry Iles, the man who brought Dreamland to Margate and achieved more than any other person in developing the area as one of Britain's more popular tourist resorts, has been struck by financial tragedy.

The entrepreneur staked his entire fortune on the film industry believing that British films could equal, perhaps beat, anything offered by its competitors.

The industry, however, has gone into decline and with the Munich crisis and events in Europe dominating everything, Mr Iles' venture has ended in bankruptcy.

He has now left his Margate interests to his son and resigned all his directorships.

The people of Margate and Birchington, where he has lived for many years, will always be grateful to John Iles. The imposing Dreamland building, the Cliftonville Lido and the greyhound racing stadium stand as monuments to his initiative.

He fell in love with the town in 1915 and by 1919 had purchased Lord George Sanger's famous Hall-by-the-Sea for £40,000. Later he acquired the Clifton Baths estate and spent half-a-million pounds on developing the project — now known as Dreamland. At the same time he was involved in Manchester's famous Bell Vue amusement park.

Until he re-establishes himself, Mr Iles, 66, will concentrate on writing, which is one of his many interests. He is also a musician, a champion of working men's brass bands. He built the first British scenic railway at Blackpool and erected 'luna' parks in many big cities around the world.

Gillingham may disband: out of Football League

May 30th: Total disbelief and sadness among thousands of people in the Medway Towns accompanies the news that Gillingham F.C. has been voted out of the Football League.

The club finished bottom last season and was forced to seek re-election to Third Division (South) for the fifth time. Then the unthinkable happened. In a ballot among member clubs this week, newcomers Ipswich were given the vital vote.

Although an application has been made to join the Southern League many people feel the club will go into liquidation.

Gillingham has spent 18 years in Division Three (S), mainly in the lower reaches. Recent average crowds have been in excess of 7,000.

'I have to tell you that no such undertaking has been received and that consequently this country is at war with Germany' — Mr Chamberlain at 11 pm, Sunday September 3rd.

January 1st: It is believed that Germany is producing up to 600 new aeroplanes a month. Britain is not far behind. The aim is to have 2,840 aircraft by March next year. The RAF now has almost 6,000 pilots.

The railway line from London to Maidstone has been electrified.

February 9th: Steel-built, tunnel, shaped Anderson shelters will be distributed to all homes where air raids are likely. The Government made the decision today that families earning less than £250 a year will get their shelters free of charge.

February 20th: A new type of stocking is on sale in America. It is made of nylon and costs about $1.15 a pair (five shillings).

March 15th: Two days after presenting a set of ultimatums, Germany has marched into Prague. The Prime Minister, Mr Chamberlain, said that Hitler's coup was a shock to confidence.

March 28th: The civil war in Spain ended today with victory for the Nationalist forces. General Franco is in control in Madrid.

March 29th: The Territorial Army is to be doubled in strength to 340,000. The Government has also ordered more weapons and the building of more army camps.

March 31st: Britain and France have signed a pledge to defend Poland against attack.

April 5th: The Civil Defence Bill passed today includes plans for the evacuation of 2,500,000 children should hostilities begin.

April 27th: Men aged 20 or over will be conscripted for military service. They will face six months of intensive training before being transferred to the Territorials or Special Reserves.

May 3rd: The Government fears that food imports will be in short supply in the event of war so farmers have been told to plough up pasture areas.

May 22nd: Herr Hitler and

Police in Thanet are baffled by the mysterious disappearance of Dr Albert Tester, believed to be German, who has been living for some months in this mansion, Naldera, Broadstairs (on the left) close to the North Foreland lighthouse. His wife and five children left earlier in the year. Local people say that Tester is a spy and they believe he escaped by rowing out to a submarine before the police could arrest him.

Signor Mussolini have signed a military alliance known as the "pact of steel".

June 2nd: A Women's Auxiliary Air Force is formed.

June 16th: The seaside town of Littlehampton, on the mouth of the River Adur in Sussex, has been offered for sale by Lord Norfolk. 850 acres of land have been earmarked for new building.

Philip Sassoon, MP for Folkestone and Hythe since 1912 and Under Secretary of State for Air from 1924 to 1937, has died. He has left his beautiful property, Port Lympne, motor cars and aeroplanes to Mrs Hannah Gubbay. His sister Lady Cholmondeley will receive the

residue to the MP's wealth. Sassoon was very popular. During a recent speech to Folkestone Rotary Club he said: "God made my constituency the most beautiful in England. It remains for man to make it the most popular."

July 8-9th: Kent is one of 15 counties to take part in a test "blackout". It is a great success.

August 18th: Frank Baum's classic book, *The Wizard of Oz*, has been made into a technicolour film, starring Judy Garland.

August 23rd: Germany and the Soviet Union sign a non-aggression pact.

August 25th: Richard Church, a

well-known writer, has moved to Curtisden Green, near Goudhurst, and converted an oasthouse. His writing study is high up in the cone, reached only by ladder.

August 31st: With name labels on their coats and clutching their personal possessions and gas masks, the children of Britain's cities today began to leave their homes. The evacuation will continue for the rest of the week.

September 1st: German troops today invaded Poland. With six armoured divisions and 1.5 million men they swept across the frontier in the wake of furious aerial bombardments.

September 3rd: Britain is at war with Germany. The Prime Minister made a statement from the House of Commons. Tonight the King will speak to the Commonwealth.

September 4th: Winston Churchill is appointed First Lord of the Admiralty, the post he held at the outbreak of the Great War.

September 18th: Three Shorts' Sunderlands attended the torpedoeing of the SS *Kesning Court*, one aircraft picking up 21 men, the second rescuing 12 and the third remaining on guard in the air. The Rochester aircraft were among the first to come into contact with the enemy.

September 27th: Income tax is raised to 7s 6d in the pound — its highest-ever figure.

October 12th: Thousands of Kent men are among the 158,000 British Expeditionary Force now in France. The troop movements are considered a great success.

October 16th: The battleship *Royal Oak* has been hit by a German torpedo. It is believed that 800 have died.

GREAT HITS OF 1939

Hang out Your Washing on
The Siegfried Line
Over the Rainbow

Chiddingstone Village, famous for one of the most beautiful streets in Kent, has been taken over by the National Trust which now has the responsibility for looking after the unspoiled row of sixteenth and seventeenth century houses, half-timbered inn and shops and fourteenth century church with its lofty tower and crockety pinnacles. Chiddingstone is one of many fine places recently acquired by the Trust. The architect, Sir Herbert Baker, has left his own home, Owletts, and the yeoman's house he restored at Sole Street, near Cobham, to the National Trust. Another charming bit of Tudor England soon to be in Trust hands is the Ellen Terry house at Smallhythe.

Hurricane pilots killed as aircraft hits hillside

August 11th: The bodies of two Hurricane pilots, who crashed onto the North Downs at Tatsfield, have been discovered less than 100 yards from each other.

The first to die was Flying Officer Olding who had been sent up from Biggin Hill to observe the result of a trial blackout of the London area. It was a wild and stormy night and, in the blackness, Olding hit the hillside.

The Biggin Hill commanding officer, Group Captain Dick Grice, ordered the crash tender out immediately but first instructed Flying Officer Woolaston to drop a marker flare on the spot. He, too, hit the hillside.

The loss of these two pilots is among many aircraft tragedies in Kent. In May Flying Officer J.F. Spanton died when two Tiger Moths collided on the approach to Gravesend aerodrome. Sergeant J.E. Morgan was killed when his aircraft crashed into Rowhill Woods,

Wilmington and three died in July when a Hawker Hind, piloted by D.C. Lewis, collided with a Gipsy Moth at Tilmanstone.

As the possibility of war gets ever closer the Kent airfields are making the final preparations for the expected assault from the Luftwaffe. There are 13 RAF squadrons based in the county — at Biggin Hill, Manston, Lympne, Hawkinge, Detling and Gravesend. Fighter Command controls seven, Coastal Command three, Bomber Command one and Fleet Air Arm two. There are two Elementary and Reserve Flying Schools at Eastchurch.

Hurricanes, Spitfires, Blenheims, Ansons and Lysanders are in a state of readiness. So is No 11 Group which controls the Kent airfields and feeds information to the Sector Station at Biggin Hill using RDF (Radio Direction Finding) and data supplied by the Observer Corps.

The children of St Joseph's School, St Mary Cray try out their gas masks.

Mustard gas — the horrors are still very vivid

July: Thousands of crippled ex-servicemen, some still living in special homes in Kent, are a living reminder of the horrors of the gas attacks on the Western Front during the 1914-18 war and, as hope for peace deteriorates every day, the fear of gas attack is very real.

Everybody has now been issued with a gasmask. There are special Micky Mouse masks for children and a gas helmet has been issued for babies — a small airtight chamber into which filtered air is pumped by means of hand bellows.

In Kent there are gas exercises almost every day. Last week in Sevenoaks mythical enemy bombers wrecked hundreds of homes and sprayed the district with mustard gas. This air-raid demonstration was designed to test the air-raid precaution service and those who had been 'burned' were rushed to the first-aid station next to the hospital. There 'contaminated' clothing was removed.

A nurseryman from Hextable, near Swanley, Mr E.W.

Mills, has invented a gas-proof perambulator. Built of wood it has a triplex glass window, air valve, filter from a gasmask and a large bulb at the rear to pump out the air. It has been approved by the local ARP.

The provision of the gasmask is affecting people in different ways. Some children feel this macabre precaution against gas attacks is really just a game. Others hate the smell of rubber and disinfectant. Many people, though, are panicking. In East Kent there has been a spate of hasty marriages, in Maidstone a boom in the sale of wills and in south London it is believed that many people are hoarding sugar and petrol.

The Anderson shelter, named after its designer, Dr David Anderson, is also being distributed free of charge to all those earning less than £250 a year. It consists of 14 sheets of corrugated iron and forms a shell about six-foot high. It is then buried in the garden to a depth of four feet and covered with soil. It can accommodate up to six people.

September 2nd: *This little girl from Chatham is one of many children who doesn't want to leave home. With a name label attached to her coat, gasmask holder strung from her shoulder and a few belongings in a well-labelled suitcase she is taking part in the great evacuation which began yesterday. Along with the children of London, the boys and girls from the Medway towns are being taken to reception areas considered safe from air attack — and then on to homes to adapt to a new life in the country. The Medway evacuation is taking place over two days. The children have no idea where they are going and their train tickets are blank but the allocations include the following — Folkestone will receive 13,000, Ashford and Malling 7,000 each and Tunbridge Wells 5,000.*

Gravesend children aboard the boat that was to take them "somewhere in England". Actually they were going to another town in Kent, earmarked as an evacuation reception area and considered safe from possible air attack.

August: *Films and exhibitions are being held all over Kent to prepare people for the possibility of war with Germany. Here at the State Cinema in Dartford is* The Warning and Heed It - *a documentary showing German bombers over Britain and the reaction of our air defences. While people queue to see the film, anti-aircraft gunners hold their own recruiting drive.*

Jewish refugees pour into Richborough camp

August: Thousands of Jewish people, driven out of Nazi Germany, Austria and Czechoslovakia in a reign of terror almost without precedent, are now living in a special transit camp set up for them at Richborough. The numbers are rising almost daily and this week it was estimated that almost 3,500 — more than the population of nearby Sandwich — will remain until a permanent home can be found.

The men have harrowing stories to tell. Some say they were beaten senseless by Nazi youths with lead piping and others told how their shops were looted, then set on fire. The men described how synagogues were burned down, money confiscated — all, it appears with the blessing of Dr Josef Goebbels, the Minister of Propaganda.

Richborough, the entrance port to the Roman province of Britain, and later occupied by Saxons and Normans, is once again in the hands of Europeans, many of whom were rescued or escaped from concentration camps. Among the refugees are skilled plumbers, electricians and carpenters who have worked hard to introduce some amenities into the huts used during the Great War.

The two camps at Richborough are both alongside the Sandwich-Ramsgate Road on the west side. Many of the refugees are keen to find work locally on the farms or in Sandwich or Canterbury. Many have been helping to fill sandbags for the protection of Sandwich and the rest — over a thousand — have volunteered for National Service.

The Jewish people — who include Christian non-Aryans and political fugitives — are proving to be kind and helpful and several English families are engaging the wives of the men in camp as domestic servants.

No-one knows how long it will be necessary for the camp to remain open but they are preparing for a long stay. There is talk of a film theatre being opened and many have expressed a wish to learn English.

Lord Cornwallis calls for the "spirit" of Francis Drake

September: As Kent assumes the responsibility as Guardian (rather than Garden) of England, there have been many rallying speeches on the subject of the role the county will play during the difficult months ahead.

Lord Cornwallis, president of the County Society and chairman of the Kent War Agricultural Committee, has spoken frequently about the "spirit of Kent". In his address to Sittingbourne Chamber of Commerce recently he referred to Francis Drake's campaign against the Armada. "Did you know," he asked, "that Drake played bowls at Milton having anchored in the Creek. I believe he introduced the game of Crown and Anchor into the country."

Winston Churchill's concern about Chamberlain's policy of appeasement has been fully vindicated and after many years in the political wilderness he has joined the War Cabinet as First Lord of the Admiralty, the job he had between 1911 and 1915.

Churchill's home at Chartwell, Westerham is in darkness but many people in Kent have been prosecuted for breaking the blackout law. Arthur Nash of Park Road, Ramsgate, one of the first, was fined £15 for "failing to obscure lights at his residence". Mr Nash, a millionaire, was not too concerned about the fine. What worried him more was the hostile crowd, armed with stones, which had gathered outside his house on the day of his offence.

Sandbags in Cathedral as war is declared

September 3rd: The formal declaration of war, which everybody expected but hoped would never happen, came at 11 am yesterday (Sunday) when Mr Chamberlain announced that Britain's ultimatum to Germany had expired.

Many Kentish people were in church at the time and others were in their homes. Dowding's pilots at Biggin Hill, Manston, Hawkinge and the other stations heard the Prime Minister's grim voice as they gathered around their wireless sets.

Most families in the county immediately checked their blackout screens, gas masks and shelters. A nervous tension was discernible in the eyes and gait of everyone. Hitler's deadly air force, its powers amply demonstrated in Poland, would soon be threatening their lives.

The first air raid warning came minutes after Chamberlain's broadcast, but it was a false alarm. A French transport aeroplane bringing staff officers to London had been seen by the vigilant men of the Observer Corps. The Hurricanes of 32 Squadron at Biggin Hill were scrambled but the "suspect bandit" had landed peacefully at Croydon.

The people of Kent have been preparing for this war for three years. ARP services have been mobilised, cellars and basements requisitioned for shelters, town halls converted into control rooms, decontamination centres opened and air raid exercises held in every town from Westgate to Westerham.

Sandbags piled around doors and windows of public buildings are commonplace throughout the county. To the alarm of many people they are even inside Canterbury Cathedral. Soon after the priceless thirteenth and fourteenth century stained-glass windows were removed, Dean Hewlett Johnson allowed lorries loaded with sand to drive through the Great West Door to drop thousands of tons of earth and sand in the Nave. The idea is that they cushion the Crypt roof from falling masonry in the event of an air attack.

October: As restrictions are slackened football is being played again and here Gravesend and Northfleet are in action in the Southern League. Spectators, however, must carry their gasmasks.

Blackout blamed for the first casualties

December: The war is less than four months old but already many lives have been lost, mainly on the road and all attributable to the blackout.

Motor-cyclist Eric Dixon and his pillion passenger Joan Humphrey died at Watling Street, Strood, on September 2nd. A man of 74 was killed while crossing the A20 at Hothfield, near Ashford, shortly before 9 pm on December 15th when he was knocked down by one car and run over by another.

Another tragic incident also occurred on September 3rd when a 67-year-old woman from Newberry Road, Bromley, collapsed and died of heart failure when the false alarm sounded.

The blackout restrictions, the panic-buying which accompanied petrol rationing, the evacuation of children, the flurry of activity around the airfields, the digging of trenches across the county, the shortage of material in the shops, the frantic recruitment of Civil Defence workers, the gasmasks, the air-raid warnings (all false alarms), the sight of policemen in steel helmets, the barrage balloons and the sadness of saying goodbye to husbands and fathers as they join their units has brought a strange atmosphere of abnormality and tension to Kent.

As the lights go out right across the county everything associated with the lifestyle of the Thirties has gone with them. How long will it before it returns?

'Never in the field of human conflict was so much owed by so many to so few' — Winston Churchill, on August 20th, in his tribute to the RAF pilots in the Battle of Britain.

January: The Ministry of Home Security, convinced that mass bombing with gas is imminent, has created Civil Defence administrative regions. The south-east headquarters is at Tunbridge Wells.

January: This is one of the coldest months ever known. Piercing winds have whipped snow into huge drifts and many Kent villages are marooned with supplies dangerously low.

February: The snow has severely hampered work on a new concrete runway at Biggin Hill and the excavation of deep shelters. Lord Haw Haw on *Germany Calling* announced this week: "The Luftwaffe has inspected Biggin Hill's new runway and will shortly finish it off."

April 10th: Germany's blitzkrieg of the low countries; parachutists and heavy panzer divisions have swept through Holland and Belgium whose resistance was soon overwhelmed.

May 15th: A new long-range high speed bomber, the Stirling, has finally come off the Shorts' production line at Rochester. Designed by Arthur Gouge of Northfleet the Stirling is powered by four Hercules engines.

June 5th: *Operation Dynamo*, the evacuation of the British Expeditionary Force along with a great number of French and Belgians, has been completed.

June 10th: Benito Mussolini, Italy's fascist dictator, has joined Hitler's victorious panzers and declared war on the Allies.

France has surrendered and the armistice has been signed in the same railway carriage at Compiegne in which the Germans were forced to surrender at the end of the Great War.

July 1st: Corporal Daphne Joan Pearson, a WAAF medical orderly has become the first woman to win the George Cross for bravery. On May 31st she risked her life in rescuing an injured pilot from a burning Anson loaded with

August 12th: Pilot Officer Douglas Shepley and Miss Frances Linscott, a local nurse pictured on the occasion of their marriage at Sidcup in June. Today Mrs Shepley received the tragic news that her husband is missing, presumed dead after an attack on Junker 88s south of the Isle of Wight. His Spitfire crashed into the sea. Born at Lindrick in 1918, PO Shepley entered RAF College, Cranwell as a flight cadet in 1938. He was flying with 152 Squadron when the tragedy occurred.

bombs, which had crash-landed at Detling.

July 10th: Following intense raids on Channel shipping a new name has been given to the section of Kent between the North Foreland and Folkestone — Hellfire Corner.

July 13th: Hitler has announced his plans for the invasion of Britain. An essential requirement is that the Luftwaffe should gain superiority over the RAF.

Lord Beaverbrook, Minister of Aircraft Production, has appealed for aluminium which can be turned into fighter aircraft.

August 14th: Military medals

have been recommended for Corporal Josephine Roberts and WAAF Sergeant Youle of Detling who carried on "with coolness and efficiency" when a dug-out by the Operations Room received a fatal hit yesterday. Several men died.

August 22nd: German batteries today shelled Dover from cross-Channel guns. Many people took refuge in caves in the cliffs.

August 23rd: Flight Lieutenant Roderick Alistair Learoyd of New Romney has been awarded the Victoria Cross — the nation's highest award for valour. On August 12th he single-handedly successfully attacked a target in the Dortmund-Ems Canal by taking

his aircraft through a lane of anti-aircraft guns and through the glare of searchlights.

August 31st: Hitler has ordered the invasion of Britain to go ahead. He plans a landing on a 200-mile front from Ramsgate to Lyme Regis. The invasion, code-named *Operation Sealion*, is fixed for mid-September.

September 7th: German raiders today switched their attack from the Kent airfields to the London docks.

HMS Kent has been torpedoed in the Eastern Mediterranean. It is planned to tow her home via the Cape of Good Hope.

There are rumours in Kent that the invasion is imminent. Church bells have been pealing and the Home Guard is on standby. Most units are confident of repelling the raiders.

December 18th: Hitler has ordered his generals to prepare for the invasion of Russia under the code name *Operation Barbarossa*.

Most Kent towns have exceeded their targets for War Weapons Week. They include Maidstone (£1 million), Tunbridge Wells (£510,000 and Sevenoaks (£250,000).

Kent recipients of the George Cross are: Flying Officer Anthony Tollemache of the Auxiliary Air Force who tried to save his passenger when crash-landing at Manston, Squadron Leader Eric Moxey who was killed as he attempted to defuse an unexploded bomb at Biggin Hill and Sub-Lt John Babington of the Royal Navy Volunteer Reserve, who tackled a bomb with a new type of fuse knowing a similar device had recently killed a colleague.

Chief Officer Albert Twyman and Fireman Frederick Watson of the Margate Fire Brigade have been awarded the George Medal.

GREAT HITS OF 1940

We'll Meet Again

A Nightingale Sang in Berkeley Square

February 6th: *The central structure of the old pier at Deal collapsed today after being heavily buffeted by the Dutch cargo ship* Nora. *Mined while at anchor a mile out at sea, the 350-ton vessel was towed towards the pier where salvage tugs managed to beach her. She was completely submerged for some time but, last night,* Nora *was lifted by the rising tide and hurled several times against the side of the pier which finally collapsed.*
No-one seems to worry about the fate of the pier; it was one of the few left intact in south-east England. Others have been purposely divided so that Germans cannot use them as landing stages if and when they invade.

Trouble at sea but peaceful at home

January 8th: Food rationing is introduced today. Butter, sugar, bacon and ham can be bought only on production of ration books.

January 9th: The Union Castle liner *Dunbar Castle* has been sunk by a mine off Ramsgate and 152 people are feared dead, including many children. The mine, dropped by parachute is one of hundreds that have been laid in sea lanes in the Straits of Dover.

January 15th: *Ajax,* the cruiser which played such a prominent part in the Battle of the River Plate, sailed into Chatham dockyard today for essential repairs. The *Ajax*

helped in the sinking of the pocket battleship, *Graf Spee* — pride of the German fleet. She was scuttled off Montevideo.

January 20th: Many of Kent's cinemas and music halls which were closed on the outbreak of war have re-opened and are doing a brisk trade.

January 29th: It is believed that the voice behind the programme *Germany Calling* is that of William Joyce, a former member of the British Union of Fascists. Joyce, nicknamed Lord Haw Haw because of his superior nasal drawl, lived in Chatham before the war and was a regular customer at the Lord Raglan on Chatham Hill.

AIR RAID WARNINGS

The following instructions have been issued in the event of a threatened air raid:

In urban areas warnings will be given by means of siren or hooters which will be sounded in some places by short intermittent blasts and in other places by a warbling note changing every few seconds. The warning may also be given by short blasts on police whistles. No hooter or siren may be sounded except on instructions of the police. When you hear any of these — take shelter.

Keep of the streets as much as possible. Carry a gas mask with you always. Make sure that you and every member of your household, especially children, have on them their names and addresses clearly written.

All cinemas, theatres and places of entertainment are to be closed immediately until further notice.

A strange array of objects, designed to interrupt Hitler's invaders, litter towns and villages throughout Kent. Steam rollers, water carts, concrete blocks, barbed wire etc have been placed in the way. Here, not far from Churchill's home at Chartwell, a line of old cars are blocking what could make an ideal landing strip.

Churchill takes over as the Germans advance

April 11th: The resignation of Chamberlain and the appointment of Winston Churchill as Prime Minister is accompanied by the news today that Hitler has followed up his occupation of Norway and Denmark by attacking Holland and Belgium.

What has been called the Phoney War is over. Every day wireless sets in Kent crackle with the news from the Continent where thousands of local men are serving with the BEF. The German advance is so awesome it is now certain that the small Belgian army will be surrounded and France may fall.

The invasion of Britain can be only months away. Road blocks are being constructed on all main roads in Kent, bridges mined and signposts removed. Wardens throughout the country are distributing new instructions for invasion precautions, car owners have been ordered to immobilise cars at night and wardens' posts and town halls are staffed day and night.

Most newspaper commentators are relieved that Churchill is now in charge. The new PM has written: "At last I have the authority to give directions over the whole scene. I feel as if I am walking with destiny."

Schoolboys and Great War veterans stand side by side in Kent's new army

May 15th: Kent has never seen such a display of patriotism and enthusiasm. Yesterday evening, as Anthony Eden, the new War Secretary, was talking on the wireless, volunteers from all corners of Kent were arriving at their local police stations saying: "We want to sign on, now."

The police were confused. In fact one bobby saw what he thought was a mob of illegally armed civilians marching on his police station. He demanded they hand over their weapons only to be told that they were for "parashooting".

Within minutes it all became clear. Mr Eden, in his broadcast, was requesting that men "not presently engaged in military service between the ages of 17 and 65 should come forward and offer their services".

"Holland and Belgium have fallen," he said, "and an invasion of France is imminent." He then spoke about the threat of German parachutists landing in Britain, unaware that many men were already volunteering to shoot them down!

"The name of the new Force which is now to be raised will be the Local Defence Volunteers", he said. "This is a part-time job. You will not be paid but you will receive a uniform and will be armed."

May 23rd: In less than a week more than 2,000 men have enrolled in the LDV. Several groups have been established, a Zone Commander appointed and boundaries drawn out, roughly in line with police divisions. With no further instructions on which to work beyond the wireless announcement, there is considerable confusion but with help from volunteer drivers, group organisers have borrowed private cars and found temporary storage space for rifles and other weapons. The LDV headquarters in Kent is 67 College Road, Maidstone — the TA Centre.

May 27th: Weapons for the LDV are proving hard to come by. Apart from rifles issued just over a week ago the only weapons available are those handed in to police stations — and that is a odd assortment.

Col Stagant in conversation with Provost Sgt K. Woodward of Cobham Home Guard. Sgt Woodward served with the Royal Flying Corps in the Great War.

The elderly Lee-Enfield .303 rifles make up the greatest number but they are in short supply. There are a few revolvers and Browning automatics. Some shotguns have been supplied with a cartridge which contains a single solid ball as opposed to pellets. The volunteers have been told that this will kill at 200 yards or more.

There is a rumour that the units will soon be supplied with petrol bombs made from a pint bottle containing petrol, tar, creosote with a simple fuse and known as a Molotov Cocktail and was used in the Spanish Civil War.

Enthusiasm among the volunteers is evident by the way that the men have provided their own weapons. They include aged rifles, cutlasses and broomsticks converted into pikes. No steel helmets are available.

June 1st: Kent's great citizen's army is growing every day. The only uniform is army denim with field service caps but officers of 1914-18 vintage are now standing shoulder to shoulder with bank managers, bishops, schoolboys and former privates, many of whom are disabled. The spirit of defiance is astonishing. Hitler is going to have a shock.

May 25th: *As the troops of the British Expeditionary Force and the French First Army are pulled back into a diminishing pocket of land centred on Dunkirk, the Government has ordered the immediate evacuation of as many men as possible. Vice-Admiral Bertram Ramsay has been put in charge and he has less than a week to prepare. His headquarters, within the cliffs of Dover, held an electrical plant during the last war. For this reason Ramsay is codenaming his plan for the evacuation,* Operation Dynamo. *It is believed the Vice-Admiral has about two days before the Germans overrun the beach head. He has to clear the Channel of mines, bombard the German batteries at Calais, drive off U-Boats and hold back the Luftwaffe. Passengers ferries are already steaming to Dover and more are available at Southampton. Destroyers, minesweepers, coasters and pleasure steamers will all help. The situation is desperate.*

Kent's 'little ships' are the heroines of Dunkirk

June 4th: As the last men are picked up from the beaches of Dunkirk in an operation which began on the night of May 27th-28th, warmest congratulations are being showered on the men who manned the "Little Ships".

Motor launches, pleasure boats, lifeboats, yachts, trawlers, drifters, tugs and paddle steamers sailed from Kent through wrecks and minefields to help the Royal Navy snatch some 338,000 troops from the tiny pocket of land in Dunkirk where they were trapped.

The *Dail Mirror* yesterday greeted the successful completion of *Operation Dynamo,* as it was called, with the headline "Bloody Marvellous". Churchill today told the House of Commons that wars are not won by evacuations but it was, he said, "a miracle of deliverance".

It was on May 20th that the formidable German war machine, having thrust through the Ardennes and crossed the River Meuse, reached the Channel. As the Panzer Divisions rolled on Boulogne fell, followed by Calais, and the British and French troops found themselves pushed back into a 30-mile stretch of coastline.

The Government ordered the immediate evacuation of as many men as possible and Vice-Admiral Bertram Ramsay drew up contingency plans from his underground bunker, deep within the cliffs of Dover.

The Royal Navy destroyers and passenger ferries sailed on May 26th. With the combined hazards of shallow waters, minefields and shelling from the German batteries on the coast, they found the going painfully slow. Ramsay immediately appealed for more ships and the response was astonishing.

A mudhopper skipper was the first to offer his services followed by the *Medway Queen*, now converted to a minesweeper. Armed with a 12-pounder on her bows, the paddle steamer was one of the first to reach Dunkirk. She picked up her first cargo of hungry, exhausted troops and returned for more. Day after day the *Medway Queen* refuelled and turned back for Dunkirk picking up a total of 7,000 British and Allied servicemen.

On one occasion she saw the *Brighton Belle* in trouble. Her Sussex companion had struck a wreck and was sinking

Single file and keep cool. Another batch of men are rescued from the Dunkirk beach. The evacuation took six days to complete. All told, 222 naval vessels and 800 civilian craft joined the operation. Six destroyers and 243 ships were sunk. The killed, missing or wounded numbered 68,000.

but the *Medway Queen* picked up 800 men floundering in the water. All the time she was under relentless enemy attack but her luck held out until the final trip when she was badly damaged. Somehow she made it back to Dover to receive the simple signal "well done *Medway Queen*".

The *Queen of the Channel*, another Medway pleasure steamer, was less fortunate. Hit by a bomb, she broke her back and sank. The *Royal Sovereign* made six voyages to the Dunkirk beach and picked up more than 11,000 men while the *Queen of Thanet* returned twice. On the first trip she went to the aid of a crippled mail-steamer *Prague* and took 2,000 troops on board.

June 6th: The final batch of men arrived at Dover today and received a great welcome. These French marines and a handful of British Tommies fought a brave rearguard action against overwhelming odds but managed eventually to escape.

June 12th: It has been revealed that a Kentish man played a major role in the events leading up to the great Dunkirk evacuation.

Prior to the operation, former Royal Flying Corps airman Group Captain Victor Goddard of Brasted made a dramatic flight from France with a message from General Viscount Gort, Commander-in-Chief of the British Expeditionary Forces, that the Germans were closing in and more ships were needed quickly to help get the men off the beaches.

Goddard actually interrupted a meeting of the Chiefs of Staff with an impassioned plea for pleasure steamers, fishing boats and others to help with the rescue.

Vice-Admiral Ramsay was told immediately and the unique naval manoeuvre, unprecedented in history, swung dramatically into operation.

Eight hours a day for nine days and nights cutting sandwiches for the troops. That was the task which faced the ladies of Headcorn — one of the food stops for the train from Dover.

Sardines and bully beef for the starving troops

June 5th: When the full story of *Operation Dynamo* is told a special tribute will be paid to the ladies who made the sandwiches for the troops. At Headcorn, for example, 50 local girls have been working in eight-hour shifts for nine days and nights cutting up to 2,500 loaves each day. When the train from Dover pulled up at this special food stop the men found 19 stoves on the go. Alongside, in open trenches, beef was being roasted on spits. On one evening 5,000 meat pies, 5,000 sausages and 5,000 rolls were made and delivered to be eaten by the starving men from the Dunkirk beach.

It has been the same at Tonbridge, Paddock Wood and Redhill. Soldiers covered in bandages, exhausted by their ordeal, now surrounded by sardines and bully beef, found the energy to cheer the ladies of the WVS, Rotary wives, Salvation Army, YMCA and other civilian volunteers.

Details are also emerging of the part played by Southern Railway in *Operation Dynamo*. A total of 620 trains pulling 7,000 coaches moved 319,056 troops. The first special train left Dover at 4 am on May 27th and the last at 4 pm yesterday.

Dover had 327 trains and moved 180,982 men, Ramsgate carried 783 men on 82 trains, 64 trains were supplied at Folkestone, 75 at Margate and 17 at Sheerness. Margate's Dreamland was a first aid and casualty station and, at Dover, battalions were marched along Snargate Street to waiting East Kent buses.

Along the line many soldiers threw slips of paper, containing their name and address, out of the carriage windows hoping someone would pick them up and inform their next of kin that all was well. As the trains pulled in to the food stops, people clambered down the embankments to hand postcards and pencils to the men so they could send messages to their loved ones. Those trainloads of courageous men, snatched from the hell of Dunkirk, epitomise the realities of war.

The story of Dunkirk, the bravery, the tragic scenes of drowning soldiers, the moments when those little ships edged their way alongside the Prince of Wales Pier and many more images of grief and triumph will be forever etched on the subconscious memory of a grateful nation.

The spirit of camaraderie and defiance is best summed up by Mr Churchill's speech yesterday. "We shall go on to the end," he said. "We shall fight in France, we shall fight on the seas and oceans, we shall fight with growing confidence and growing strength in the air. We shall defend our island whatever the cost may be; we shall fight on the beaches, we shall fight on the landing grounds, we shall fight in the fields and the streets, we shall fight in the hills. We shall never surrender."

Just room for the buses between the road blocks in Maidstone. Hitler's tanks will have far more trouble.

■　An MBE has been awarded to Mrs Collard, wife of the stationmaster at Tonbridge, for her work in the Dunkirk rescue. When she heard there was to be a food stop at Tonbridge she organised relief teams of volunteers on the platforms and worked four days and nights without sleep. Schoolgirls at Tonbridge handed out postcards supplied by the local printing firms for men to tell their families that they were safe.

■　Another stirring Dunkirk story has come to light. The Ramsgate lifeboat, *Prudential*, with coxswain Harry Knight at the helm, towed eight small craft to Dunkirk, manned by 18 volunteers.

The small flotilla arrived at night and slipped quietly towards the beach. A voice from the blackness called out: "I cannot see who you are. Are you a naval party?"

"No sir," said Harry, "we are the crew of the Ramsgate Lifeboat."

"Thank God for such men as you," came the reply. "There's a party of 50 grateful Highlanders coming aboard."

■　The number of beds at the Royal Sea Bathing Hospital, Margate was increased from 324 to 520 for the Dunkirk men. This was achieved by putting extra beds into wards with veranda accommodation and by removing pews from the chapel.

Triple murder at Matfield

September: Florence Ransom, better known as Julie, has been sentenced to death at the Old Bailey for the murder of her lover's wife, Mrs Freda Fisher, 46, her 20-year-old daughter, Freda and their maid Mrs Charlotte Saunders, aged 48.

The triple murder which took place on July 9th had baffled police for many weeks but Julie Ransom was eventually arrested and the gruesome story unfolded.

Ransom, aged 35, lived with Walter Fisher. His wife also had a lover and so condoned the liaison but Julie wanted to be the real Mrs Fisher.

She borrowed a shotgun, hitched a lift to Tonbridge, made her way to Crittenden, Matfield, the Fisher family's cottage and there in an orchard brutally shot the two Freda's and then the maid who had run out to see what was happening.

Julie Ransom tried to cover her tracks but left behind a white hogskin glove which detectives later found fitted her hand perfectly.

The defendant will appeal against her sentence. Because of her disturbed mind there is a chance it will be commuted to life imprisonment.

September 26th: **The poet William Henry Davies has died at 69.** It was Davies who gave us the oft-quoted lines "What is this life if, full of care, we have no time to stand and stare?"

He was born in 1871 and, at the age of 22, went to New York with 10 dollars, worked as a fruit picker and cattleman and learned the hobo's art of getting about by train-jumping. Unfortunately at Renfrew, Ontario, he slipped and his right leg was severed at the ankle.

He returned to England and made a living by singing in the street. Living in a doss house in Lambeth, Davies was

'Supertramp' and poet dies at 69

"rescued" by the poet Edward Thomas and came to live in Eggpie Lane, Sevenoaks Weald, near to Thomas' home at Else's Farm. Here he wrote the *Autobiography of a Super Tramp* in 1907/8. G.B. Shaw wrote the preface, and it was this book which made him famous.

Davies also wrote poems of delicacy and perfection with the appearance of effortless ease and, in 1923, 636 pieces were published in his *Collected Poems.*

Churchill's stirring words precede the Battle

July 20th: For several weeks since the great rescue of the British Expeditionary Forces from Dunkirk, the fighting in the air and over the Channel has been relentless. But it appears that Hitler still nurses hopes of a British surrender. Yesterday, addressing the Reichstag, he said: "I consider myself in a position to make this appeal since I am not the vanquished begging favours but the victor speaking in the name of reason." The BBC has already replied, on behalf of the Government, rejecting his overtures.

Winston Churchill has said that Hitler knows he will have to break us in this island or lose the war. Describing it as the Battle of Britain, he said: "Upon this battle depends the survival of Christian civilisation. Upon it depends our own British life and the might of the enemy must very soon be turned on us...If we can stand up to him, all Europe may be free and the life of the world may move forward into broad, sunlit uplands. But if we fail, then the whole world, including the United States, including all that we have known and cared for, will sink into the abyss of a new Dark Age...Let us therefore brace ourselves to our duties, and so bear ourselves that, if the British Empire and its Commonwealth last for a thousand years, men will still say: 'This was their finest hour' "

These stirring words were delivered in June, after Dunkirk. It is now July and the battle, as forecast by the Prime Minister, has slipped into a higher gear. On August 10th, says Hitler, the Luftwaffe will systematically knock the RAF out of the skies. *Adler Tag* is Eagle Day.

Meanwhile the Hurricanes and Spitfires of Biggin Hill, Manston, Hawkinge and Gravesend are flying hundreds of sorties in an effort to protect harbours, naval bases, airfields and coastal shipping.

Last week BBC reporter Charles Gardner gave a vivid description of what he called a "dogfight" over East Kent. "There's one coming down in flames," he said. "There, somebody's hit a German and he's coming down. There's a long streak. He's coming down, completely out of control. A long streak of smoke. Ah, the man's baled out by parachute - the pilot's baled out by parachute. He's a Junkers and he's going slap into the sea and there he goes - SMASH. Oh boy, I've never seen anything so good as this. The RAF fighters have really got these boys taped."

July 15th: Three cheers for the RAF. A rousing thankyou today from the children of Chelsfield School who emerged from their air raid shelter unscathed.

Battle of Britain diary: July 10th-Sept 15th

Here is a diary of the Battle of Britain as it has affected the fighter stations in Kent and the people of this front-line county. Because of the enormous scale of the battle — the squadrons, sightings, scrambles, bombing, casualties — it is only possible to give a brief outline of the action.

July 10th: First dogfight of over 100 aircraft. Main target Channel convoy. Losses: Luftwaffe 13 - RAF 6.

July 14th: More attacks on merchant shipping off Dover by Stuka dive bombers. *HMS Vanessa* hit and towed into Dover by tug *Lady Duncannon.*

July 19th: Tragic day for Defiants of 141 Squadron, West Malling. Six aircraft lost, four pilots and five gunners killed. Remainder of Squadron released from operation. Defiants unmanoeuverable and at a hopeless disadvantage.

July 22nd: Twelve high explosive bombs dropped on Margate. Buildings damaged but only one casualty. More attacks on shipping. German peace offer rejected by Britain.

July 25th: Scores of people on Abbot's Cliff, Dover see merchant ships and destroyers attacked by dive bombers. 11 ships sunk including the *Corhaven, Polgrange, Leo, Henry Moon* and *Portslade.* Six Spitfires and two Hurricanes lost in the sea.

July 27th: Two destroyers sunk and one damaged off Dover. Royal Navy supply ship *Sandhurst* also crippled and sunk.

July 31st: Dover balloon barrage attacked by Messerschmitts. Runaway and damaged balloons cause havoc to roads and railways around Dover.

August 12th: Several Kent airfields are attacked including Manston, Lympne and Hawkinge and radar stations at Dover, Rye and Dunkirk. Damage at Hawkinge is appalling, with hangars, workshops and domestic buildings flattened. Airfield put out of commission. Twenty high explosives dropped at Ramsgate, Sarre and Monckton. Margate Lifeboat picks up Pilot Officer

Survivors of a Nazi U-boat swim from their raft to a British warship. The U Boat had been attacking a British convoy in the Channel

Geoffrey Page who was trying to swim with severely burned hands. Since early July the Luftwaffe have attacked shipping on most days and laid mines on most nights but sunk only 30,000 tons out of the nearly five million tons which passed around the coasts. It has lost 286 aircraft against Fighter Command's 148.

August 13th: This was *Adler Tag* (Eagle Day), the day when Goering was to open the great *Adlerangriff* intended to crush all RAF opposition and clear the way for *Sealion,* the invasion of Great Britain. Great armadas of German bombers swarm over Kent.

August 15th: The Luftwaffe's biggest assault so far — more than 500 bombers escorted by 1,250 fighters. Eastchurch, Manston, Rochester, Hawkinge and West Malling airfields are damaged.

August 18th: Low level attack on Biggin Hill by Dorniers. In an extraordinary act of bravery WAAF sergeant Elizabeth Mortimer plants red flags to mark unexploded bombs. She has been recommended for the Military Medal. Medway Towns bombed. 59 casualties. Three killed at Sevenoaks.

August 24th: More than 250 high explosives dropped on Ramsgate killing 31 people and destroying 1,200 homes. Most of the town's population below ground in shelters under the town. Manston evacuated

as front-line fighter station.

August 27th: Luftwaffe bomb hits Maidstone and District bus depot at Gillingham, destroying 50 buses. Town centre also hit. 20 people killed.

August 30th: Biggin Hill attacked again by small formation of Junkers. 39 killed in shelter including many WAAFs; others entombed as concrete walls cave in. Airfield devastated. Hornchurch takes control until communications are restored.

September 1st: The wave of bombers and fighter escorts flying over Dover is five miles long. Main targets are Biggin Hill, Detling, Eastchurch and London Docks.

September 7th: The greatest attacking force yet. 348 bombers and 617 fighters cross the Kent coast between Ramsgate and Deal. 21 squadrons are scrambled to meet them. Great confusion in Kent as deciphered codeword indicated that an invasion is imminent. Church bells are rung, country roadblocks closed and road bridges demolished in many places. It turns out to be a false alarm.

September 9th: Canterbury bombed. Nine people killed, many homes demolished. Three Hurricane pilots crash and die — at Lime Trees Farm and Bockingfold Farm, Goudhurst and at Mount Ephraim, Cranbrook. On this day the Luftwaffe lose 27 aircraft and many pilots are captured or killed.

1940

August 31st: When word was received that a bomb had hit a shelter at Biggin Hill yesterday these nurses were among those who had the task of administering morphia to the living who were within reach. The damage was caused by a small formation of Junkers who flew low over the airfield. The shelter, crammed with airmen, received a direct hit and was reduced to a yawning crater, full of rubble and mangled bodies. The death toll is 39.

October 31st: A naval officer and his wife had a miraculous escape today when a bomb landed in front of the car he was driving along Mill Street, Maidstone. A crater opened in front of them and the car plunged into the wreckage. Fourteen people have been injured in this raid. There are no reports of fatalities.

Countryside littered with burning wrecks as the Luftwaffe is 'cut to rags and tatters'

September 15th: This has probably been the most crucial day in the Battle of Britain. Field Marshal Hermann Goering's promise that he would finally sweep aside the few remaining Spitfires and Hurricanes and clear the way for Germany's invasion of Britain — code-named *Operation Sealion* — has been a dismal failure, thanks to the pilots of the RAF.

Soon after dawn on this sunny morning the RDF sets showed that an attacking force of some 100 Dornier bombers with a massive fighter escort was crossing the coast. Tonight the countryside of Kent is littered with the burning wrecks of Heinkels, Junkers, Dorniers and Messerschmitts — 61 enemy aircraft shot down and many others harried and chased across the Channel.

Fighter Command believes that today's classic battle may prove to be the turning point. Churchill, due to address the House tomorrow, has already told colleagues that the British pilots, aided by squadrons of their Polish and Czech colleagues, "cut to rags and tatters three separate waves of murderous assault upon the civil population".

The morning raid brought Biggin Hill into action. Air Vice-Marshal Keith Park, commanding 11 Group, ordered 92 and 72 Squadrons to join 10 other squadrons from Northolt, Kenley, Duxford, Hornchurch and Middle Wallop. At first they patrolled the heavens at altitudes ranging from 15,000 to 25,000 feet but within minutes the sky was a whirling mêlée, like a dense swarm of insects.

Flight Lieutenant Brian Kingcome, commanding 92 Squadron, knew it was "going to be a big day". His Spitfire pilots met the German bombers head on breaking their formation so that bombs were scattered over a wide area. The fight raged all the way from the coast and back again with British pilots chasing crippled bombers and Messerschmitts short of fuel.

In this battle and others that followed the Biggin Hill squadrons are claiming "a bag of nine" destroyed and 12 damaged. Two Spitfires are damaged but repairable. One is lost. Bob Holland of 92 baled out and is now believed to be safe in the hands of nurses at East Grinstead hospital.

Many families in Kent on this sunny September Sunday took lunch out of doors and watched the battle. They heard the explosions in the distance and the ripping sound of machine gun fire but whenever the battle moved above their heads they wisely took to the shelters.

There has been just one civilian death. Earlier today a German fighter crashed in flames on a building at Bilsington. A house is gutted, a small shop wrecked and wreckage is scattered over a wide area. This evening a widow living close to the scene found a German machine gun on her bed.

It is also believed that a number of British fighters have been shot down in Kent. Reports coming in say that Pilot Officer G.L.J. Doutrepont of 229 Squadron crashed on Staplehurst railway station and Sergeant L. Pidd of 238 Squadron died when he smashed into an oak tree at Kent College, Pembury.

Flying Officer A. Pease of 603 Squadron has died in his Spitfire at Chartway Street, Kingswood. Polish Sergeant M. Brzezowski of 303 Squadron is lost in the Thames and the famous Belgian pilot, Albert van der Hove d'Erstenrijct died when his machine exploded over Chilham and fell into the River Stour. Other fatalities, it is believed, are Pilot Officer J. Gurteen of 504 Squadron who dived full throttle into a house at Hartley and Flying Officer M. Jebb who died shortly after admission to Dartford Hospital.

September 17th: Sunday's huge aircraft losses have so alarmed the Luftwaffe Commanders that the decision has been made to postpone the invasion of Britain "until further notice". Yesterday the weather was too poor for large-scale fighting but bitter inquests have been held in Pas de Calais where concern has been expressed about the German airforce "bleeding to death".

September 18th: Excitement in Maidstone reached fever pitch yesterday when a Junkers 88 was shot down by the pilots of a Defiant night fighter following a chase that was plotted on the school blackboard at Biggin Hill, where the Operations Room is temporarily housed. "Stuffy" Dowding, Commander-in-Chief of Fighter Command, was a guest observer. The successful Defiant pilots were Sgts George Lawrence and Wilfred Chard. The fuselage crashed on a house in St Andrew's Road, Maidstone. The pilot and his crew will be buried with full military honours.

September 27th: What is believed to be the first battle on British soil since 1797 occurred today when the crew of a Junkers 88, brought down on the Graveney marshes near Faversham, opened fire on troops of the London Irish Rifles billeted in the nearby Sportsman Inn, who confronted them. No-one was killed and the Germans were eventually arrested.

Land girls keep an eye on the skies as they gather the harvest above the white cliffs of Dover.

Darts match at the Star ends in tragedy

November 11th: A darts match at The Star, Swanscombe, came to an abrupt and tragic end last night when a German bomb scored a direct hit on the pub, killing 27 customers and seriously injuring another six. Villagers, many of whom were in the shelters, said the explosion was deafening and they found the building had just fallen apart. All that was left was a heap of smouldering debris and twisted timbers. Inside victims were yelling hysterically and trying to claw their way to safety. Firemen and rescue squads removed the bodies one by one while their families stood by the street corner waiting for the official casualty list to be posted.

Secret army will sabotage German tanks

November 26th: In an operation surrounded by the utmost secrecy a small but growing army of guerillas has been planning ways of sabotaging tanks and hassling the enemy should the German invasion take place.

The man who formed the resistance patrols is Captain Peter Fleming. He has been replaced by Lt-Col Norman Field, whose hideaway is at Bilting, Ashford. It is part of a national movement with HQ at Swindon.

Fleming began with a number of soldiers, drivers, batmen and a platoon of Lovat Scouts but most of his members were civilians, armed with pistols, truncheons, rifles, grenades and plastic explosives.

Nobody knows of the men's dual role and a protective air of secrecy surrounds the exact whereabouts of 25 hideouts all over Kent, including an enormous underground chamber believed to be in the vicinity of Godmersham Park.

Should Hitler have any success with his landing tactics, Kent's secret army will work in much the same way as the resistance movement in France.

Lt-Col Field has identified many more useful hideouts in the county, thought to be near Challock, Badlesmere, Wickhambreaux, Rolvenden, Minster and Ash. In the meantime the guerillas are being taught how to kill silently.

Be wary: sterner trials lie ahead

December 24th: In a Christmas message to the people of Kent Sir Auckland Geddes, southeast regional commissioner for the Civil Defence, said today:

"Since we welcomed back the men from Dunkirk and the women of Kent were proud to feed the 338,000 who came home, more than 4,000 air raids have been delivered by Germans and Italians on this county alone. Thousands of homes have been destroyed..."

"To all of you, to the police, fire services, wardens, rescue squads, decontamination squads, WVS and to all the men and women who, by their gallant fortitude, have kept life and work going on the farms, in the villages, in the seaside resorts and in the towns, I say well done. Sterner trials lie ahead. Be vigilant and don't talk to strangers."

'I award these badges for sustained courage under dangerous conditions. I don't think we could have carried on without you' — Lord Cornwallis at a Kent Land Girls rally at Maidstone in July.

January 1st: Royston Newman of Tonbridge has been awarded the silver medal of gallantry. The 10-year-old threw himself across his younger brother's pram as a raider raked his street with gunfire and Royston received a bullet wound in the back.

January 20th: Men and women between the ages of 16 and 60 have been ordered to register for part-time Civil Defence work.

February 6th: Adolf Hitler says that bombing is to be intensified on shipping and the ports in order to inflict "the greatest possible damage to the British economy".

February 13th: A German long-range shell yesterday wrecked a bungalow in Whitehall Road, Ramsgate. It is the first time a shell has reached Thanet.

March 1st: Heinrich Himmler visited the Auschwitz concentration camp today and announced a big programme of expansion.

March 9th: An appeal for 100,000 women to sign up for munitions work was made yesterday by Ernest Bevin, Minister of Labour.

April 5th: General Erwin Rommel has launched his African offensive by driving the depleted British forces back along the desert roads to the east of Benghazi.

April 8th: More than 200 RAF bombers yesterday attacked the German shipping port of Kiel.

April 17th: Among those killed in the air raid on Bromley last night was Josiah Charles Stamp, his wife Olive and son Wilfred. Mr Stamp, first Baron of Shortlands, was an economist and taxation expert and chairman of the Bank of England.

April 20th: The Luftwaffe has introduced a new terrifying offensive — landmines which fall to their targets by parachute.

April 27th: As the German army advances into Athens, Allied troops have evacuated Greece.

May 5th: Emperor Haile Selassie has returned to Ethiopia after years in exile.

A volunteer fire watcher in Old Farm Avenue, Sidcup raises the alarm.

June 5th: A British Restaurant will open this week in the Parry Hall, King's School, Canterbury. A three course meal will cost 9d. It is planned to open such restaurants in every town in Kent.

June 12th: Fifteen people were killed yesterday when a parachute mine exploded on Randolph Road, Dover, while the occupants slept. Four complete familes were among those who died. Scores of people were dug from the rubble badly injured.

June 22nd: Germany has attacked Russia along an 1,800-mile front from the Baltic Sea to the Black Sea.

July 21st: Churchill yesterday launched his "V" for Victory campaign.

August 16th: Five members of Broadstairs fire brigade were killed today when a raider dropped a string of bombs on the town.

September 8th: The landlady of the West Cliff Tavern, Ramsgate, Edith Evans, was among eight people killed at Ramsgate last night when two Junkers bombed Townley Street and Adelaide Gardens.

The city of Leningrad is now completely encircled by German and Finnish troops.

September 17th: In a campaign to encourage Britons to eat more vegetables, mashed potato sandwiches and potato pastry have been recommended.

October 1st: Four Belgian men and one woman have been rescued by the Dover launch, after drifting in the mined waters of the Channel for three nights and two days in a tiny motor dinghy.

October 15th: Prime Minister Winston Churchill has been appointed Lord Warden of the Cinque Ports.

October 20th: In an effort to stiffen the resolve of the Red Army, Stalin, the Soviet leader, has declared a state of siege in Moscow.

October 21st: A Dornier bomber is today in the hands of British Intelligence having run out of fuel and landed at Lydd. The crew had got lost when navigational beams guiding them to France were blotted out by the RAF.

November 14th: Britain's great carrier, the *Ark Royal,* has been sunk by a U Boat off Gibraltar with the loss, it is believed, of just one crew member.

December 4th: Unmarried women between the ages of 20 and 30 must now serve in the police, fire service or armed forces.

December 8th: President Roosevelt has signed America's declaration of war on Japan following yesterday's devastating air attack on Pearl Harbour.

December 25th: Hong Kong today surrendered to the Japanese.

After repairs at Davenport, *HMS Kent* has been recommissioned and will serve on convoy duties in northern waters.

GREAT HITS OF 1941

White Cliffs of Dover

Boogie Woogie Bugle Boy

Beat 'FIREBOMB FRITZ'

BRITAIN SHALL NOT BURN

BRITAIN'S FIRE GUARD IS BRITAIN'S DEFENCE

Amy Johnson drowns in the Thames

January 5th: Amy Johnson, the famous aviator who made history with her 10,000-mile solo flight to Australia in 1931, was killed today when her plane ditched in the Thames. Miss Johnson, 38, had been flying aircraft for the Air Transport Auxiliary from factories to RAF bases and she was on one such trip when her engine cut out over the estuary and crashed into the sea. Amy baled out and the captain of a naval trawler attempted to rescue her. He is now seriously ill in hospital with hypothermia and not expected to live.

Fire bombs destroy Kent's "city church"

January 1st: Among London's most cherished buildings which were gutted in last weekend's incendiary raids on the capital was the Church of St Andrew-by-the-Wardrobe in Queen Victoria Street — used by thousands of Kentish people.

It was in 1932 that the County Association set up a permanent link with the church on behalf of the people who travelled daily to the City. A service has been held on a day in November ever since.

Sadly, this will no longer be. The fire blitz on Sunday gutted the church and with it went the Kent Corner where the arms of the diocese of Rochester and Canterbury were on display together with two wrought-iron candlesticks made by Kent craftsmen and other memorabilia from the county.

The attack on London is the most devastating yet. More than 22,000 fire bombs were dropped by 136 planes and the blaze damaged eight Wren churches and the Guildhall.

January 18th: Houses at Palmerston Road, Chatham were badly damaged in another air raid yesterday — the seventh since the start of the year.

Already four people have died at Ramsgate, one at Folkestone, three at Chatham and two at Dartford. There have been serious raids at Stone and Gravesend.

The people of north Kent are under fully aware that Chatham Dockyard and the Shorts seaplane works on the Esplanade remain prime targets for the Luftwaffe

February: Barbed wire is now everywhere in Kent. There is certainly no access to the beaches as these girls have discovered.

■ With the war now costing Britain more than £11 million a day, every town and village has been asked to make a big effort to raise money for official national funds. The response to the first big appeal — War Weapons Week — has been astonishing and most towns have exceeded their targets. Recent figures, for example, show that Maidstone has raised £1 million, Tunbridge Wells £510,000 and Sevenoaks £250,000.

■ One fire fighter who has died in action is Stinker, a stray mongrel dog attached to Canterbury. Left behind at the station when a call was received from the South Eastern Tar Distillery at Broad Oak, Stinker raced at full speed to the scene of the fire and right into the flaming tar. He was buried with all the honours due to a good fireman and friend.

■ The largest railway gun in England, an 18" Mk1 90-ton Howitzer named "Boche Buster", has been stationed on the Elham Valley railway line and will be fired in the event of a Channel invasion. The monster is attached to the 2nd Super Heavy Regiment of the Royal Artillery from Yorkshire.

74 killed in massive raid on Bromley

April 17th: In a big raid on the Bromley area last night 74 people were killed and more than 1,500 made homeless. It is believed the German raiders dropped almost 200 bombs. Many fires are still smouldering today, including the wreckage of St Peter and St Paul Church.

Last week (April 8th) a parachute mine and a thousand incendiary bombs were dropped on Rochester. Eleven people died, including two members of the Auxiliary Fire Service, when their sub-station received a direct hit.

There was drama of a different kind north of Bromley yesterday, Wednesday, when the remaining great north tower of the Crystal Palace was demolished by explosives. Visible for many miles around it was presumed to be a helpful landmark for the Luftwaffe bombers as they approached the centre of London.

Last night provided the heaviest raid of the war to date when 728 long-range bombers caused extensive damage and loss of life in 66 London boroughs.

Martyred in the cause of liberty

April 26th: **The funeral took place today of the 19 members of the Beckenham Auxiliary Fire Service who died in London last week during a bombing raid. In one of the saddest occasions in the town's history, the men were buried in Elmers End cemetery where an inscription records: "We remember proudly the heroic men martyred in the cause of liberty." Fire brigades from all areas of Greater London were represented.**

March 19th: Residents of Winstanley Crescent, Ramsgate managed to crawl from the wreckage of their homes in nightwear when a high explosive fell in their road yesterday. The only casualty was Albert Wood, a warden.

April 16th: Down comes the north tower of the Crystal Palace, demolished at midday by explosives. Now there is no landmark for the German bombers.

May 1st: These may be busy days for wardens all over Kent but the vigilant men of the Gordon Recreation post at Gravesend still have time to pose for this picture. From the time the Luftwaffe stepped up its night bombing raids Gravesend has been continually under fire with fatalities every month since November.

May 15th: The Queen knows all about the bombs. On March 15th a stick of high explosives fell across the courtyard of Buckingham Palace and there was considerable damage to the house. The King and Queen, however, refuse to leave London and have opted to remain "in the front line". Photograph right shows the Queen this week on her first official visit to the WRNS stationed at Chatham Naval Barracks.

A challenge by the Kent Messenger newspaper urging the people of Kent to raise enough money to buy a squadron of Spitfires has become a reality. A cheque for £108,000 has been handed to Colonel Moore-Brabazon, Minister of Aircraft Production and 131 (County of Kent) Fighter Squadron created with 22 aircraft. Each plane bears the name of a town which contributed and the squadron has adopted the motto "Invicta" Here are some of the pilots.

Nazi airman surrendered his trousers!

May 10th: Since the Battle of Britain began early last year, followed by the indiscriminate bombing of Kentish towns and villages, it has been commonplace to see Nazi airmen parachuting out of the sky.

Last week on Romney Marsh, a lone shepherd working with his lambs saw a bomber crash and then, a few minutes later, a young German airman striding towards him.

The Kentish Express tells what happened next: "The shepherd made the German hold up his hands in surrender and, although he was armed, the Nazi decided to obey.

"Now came the problem. Some ewes needed attention — so did the airman. He must not be allowed to make a getaway. The shepherd solved the quandary. 'I'm too busy to worry about you — take your trousers off'.

"Meekly the Nazi did as he was told and sat watching the shepherd tend his sheep. When the last ewe was comfortable, his trousers were returned to him and with his wary escort he set off for captivity."

Recently a Nazi airman crashed into a Weald village and was invited to have a cup of tea with a lady who then 'phoned the police.

July: It has been revealed that the Air Ministry Experimental stations at Dover and Dunkirk, played a vital part in winning the Battle of Britain. Tributes were paid this week to Robert Watson-Watt, the scientist who pioneered Radio Direction Finding or RDF in which an aircraft entering a system of rays immediately sends back a signal to the detecting station. In America it is called radar. The Luftwaffe bombed the stations on several occasions but they were never out of action for long.

The courageous land girls of 'hellfire corner'

July 15th: Nine land girls from East Kent have been awarded the Invicta badge for "sustained courage under dangerous conditions". The awards were presented by Lord Cornwallis during a rally at Maidstone Zoo Park attended by almost 1,000 land girls.

They included former library assistants, children's nurses, hairdressers and schoolgirls who continued working despite machine gun fire, bombing and shelling.

Among the bravest was Miss T. Ledger who carried on working when the cowsheds were hit, Miss R.Lloyd-Evans who set an example of courage throughout the Battle of Britain and three girls — Miss A. Eke, Miss L.M. Gardner and Miss B. Gimbert, who dodged bombs, bullets, shells and craters on their respective farms near Dover in Hellfire Corner.

The girls said they were disappointed there are so few opportunities to wear pretty frocks but the countryside is making them gloriously fit and doing wonders for their complexion.

A safe haven in Kent's 'underground cities'

August: The bravery of the land girls and farmers is clearly demonstrated by the fact that thousands of people in Kent try to avoid coming "above ground" during these terrifying nights.

Tunnels, caves, cliffs and lime pits provide shelter all over the county but among the best known is the "underground cave city" of Chislehurst.

During the recent aerial onslaught there were more than 8,000 people living there. Hitler knows about them and so does Lord Haw Haw who recently announced that the time would come for the "rats of Chislehurst".

At first conditions were bleak but thanks to the hard work of many

Mrs Shepherd with her seven children in a double Anderson shelter. Gas masks in their boxes are at the ready. The family live on the Downham Estate, near Bromley.

there is now lighting, entertainment, evening classes, a medical centre, cinema, WVS canteen, church, telephone kiosk, bank and shops.

Ramsgate, which has suffered so much during the attacks on Manston, also has extensive tunnels 70 feet under the town which have been adapted from the former railway tunnels. Three miles long they provide shelter for thousands of people and have become permanent homes for the bombed-out.

Abandoned lime pits in Swanscombe are in regular use and, in the village of Borstal, near Shorts flying boat works, a flint-lined tunnel links two monstrous caves which come "alive" during the blitz.

A nightly procession of families are sleeping on old mattresses on the hard earth floor. Whenever there is a raid they receive a running commentary from a man who bravely insists on standing by the entrance.

The people of Kent's most-bombed town are living in the tunnels under the cliffs of Dover. Most of the cave dwellers here come from Athol Terrace which directly faces Occupied France and the shells of Calais.

Several children have been born in the Dover caves and it will be a long time before they know what it is like to have a bedroom of their own.

May 1st: General Bernard Montgomery has taken command of the 12th Army Corps, responsible for the defence of Kent and Sussex. His underground headquarters is on the southern outskirts of Tunbridge Wells.

Two compressors laying idle in the abandoned Dartford Tunnel works have been loaned to Joseph Lucas Ltd of Birmingham who are helping engineer Frank Whittle develop a jet engine.

May 7th: Three children were among nine killed yesterday when Aylesham County School was bombed by a low-flying raider. 600 people in the village are being accommodated in rest centres.

May 30th: The people of Folkestone are mourning the death of their charismatic mayor, Alderman George Gurr and his wife who were among 13 killed in yesterday's air raid on the town.

The entrance to the huge shelter below the cliffs at Ramsgate.

Parachute mines tear the heart out of Sturry

November 19th: The two parachute mines which were dropped on Sturry yesterday evening have completely wrecked the village centre. Shops are still burning and every building in the street is damaged. 15 people are dead and many injured.

The mines fell within yards of each other, one directly in the main street outside the Red Lion pub and the other near the allotments. Rescue parties made up of soldiers, Home Guard personnel and villagers were formed immediately to begin the work of extracting bodies from homes and the massive crater in the street. Among those dead are a married couple, their two children and a visitor. Another woman was found lying across her two children as if she were trying to protect them. Milner Court, a large house near the centre of the village, has been turned into a first-aid post.

Miners with lamps and floodlights arrived from Chislet and a local doctor gave priority to children who were trapped in the debris.

January 6th: America is to enter the war. Land, sea and air forces will be sent to Britain immediately, President Roosevelt has announced.

January 20th: 50 people have died in a Japanese air raid on Singapore.

February 9th: Kent housewives will be allowed 2 oz of toilet soap per person per month as soap rationing is introduced.

February 15th: Britain's great naval base Singapore has surrendered to Japanese forces. In a broadcast to the nation Churchill has described the loss of this "once impregnable fortress" as a far-reaching military defeat.

February 23rd: Sir Arthur Harris has taken over as head of RAF Bomber Command.

February 28th: The news has just been received that Wing Commander Bob Stanford Tuck, one of Biggin Hill's best loved pilots, is a prisoner of war in Germany. He was shot down attacking a distillery near Le Touquet.

March 3rd: The Board of Trade has introduced a new standard cloth for both men and women. Hemlines will rise again and men will wear trousers with no turn-ups.

March 14th: Mr George Hicks, Minister of Works, has appealed to the people of Kent to collect as much metal as possible for the munitions factories. Bedsteads, redundant threshing machines, and pre-war automobiles are among the objects already handed in.

March 23rd: 16 people were killed today when German bombers dropped 20 high explosives on Dover. One fell on the air raid shelter belonging to the East Kent Road Car Company and another hit the Carlton Club.

March 29th: 200 aircraft of RAF Bomber Command yesterday launched a raid on the Baltic shipbuilding centre of Lubeck.

April: There are not many postmen left in Kent because women have now been officially registered to fill positions normally occupied by men. The majority of women have taken jobs in munition and shell-filling factories.

April 3rd: An air raid shelter in Union Road, Dover has been hit by a German bomb. It is believed that nine have died. Nearby two houses in Park Gate Road have collapsed. Eight people are still trapped in the wreckage.

April 25th: William Temple has been installed as Archbishop of Canterbury following the resignation last month of Cosmo Lang.

April 25th: Princess Elizabeth today registered for war service. She is just 16.

April 26th: Rescuers have reached the Betteshanger miners who have been trapped at the pit face for several hours after a bomb fell on

the powerhouse. It is believed that some men are badly injured.

May 9th: Raiders returning for the second time in 48 hours have killed three people in Deal. On May 6th seven people died when bombs were dropped in the Park Lane and Alfred Square areas of the town.

May 14th: Women have now been asked not to wear stockings in the summer so as to conserve supplies for the winter.

May 18th: A bomb which fell on Christ Church, Folkestone yesterday completely destroyed the building—just minutes before Matins. The congregation moved to the church hall.

May 20th: Japanese troops have completed their capture of Burma.

June 1st: Cologne was devastated last night by RAF bombers. It is being described as the largest raid in the history of aerial warfare.

June 21st: Rommel has captured Tobruk.

June 24th: Prisoners of war from the Kent regiments are among Allied POWs building the 294-mile Singapore to Bangkok railway line through the jungle to Rangoon.

June 25th: American General Dwight D. Eisenhower has been appointed Commander of US forces in Europe.

July 4th: The Duke and Duchess of Kent have announced the birth of a son, Prince Michael George Charles Franklin.

July 26th: From today, sweets and chocolates will be rationed. The allowance is half a pound per person every four weeks.

August 12th: Field Marshal Bernard Montgomery has taken command of the Eighth Army in North Africa.

August 20th: Allied forces today suffered defeat in Dieppe. It is believed that the death toll is more than 4,000, and most of them are Canadians.

November 3rd: "Good old Monty" is being hailed as a hero following Rommel's retreat at El Alamein. The offensive was launched less than two weeks ago.

November 15th: This Sunday, church bells across Kent are ringing in celebration of Monty's desert victory. Churchill said yesterday: "If not the beginning of the end, it is at least the end of the beginning."

GREAT HITS OF 1942

White Christmas

We'll Meet Again

Court jails Betteshanger's striking miners

January 26th: Three senior officials of the Kent Mineworkers' Association have been jailed for terms ranging between one and two months for inciting their colleagues at the newly-opened Betteshanger Colliery to go on strike. A further 1,000 underground workers have been fined.

The sentences have brought strong protests from miners all over the country. Although it is illegal to strike during war years, there is considerable sympathy for the men who, they say, have been treated badly by the owners of Betteshanger, Messrs Pearson and Dorman Long.

The trouble stems over conditions at the pitface. A bad seam full of rubble and flood water combined with intense heat caused production to fall dramatically and the men were accused by the management of 'ca-canny' (malingering).

This caused great resentment among the miners who claimed they were making great efforts to beat the rogue seam despite the fact that they could not earn their usual bonuses.

Sir Charles Doughty, an arbitrator, whom, the miners claim, "knows as much about mining as a pet dog", came out on the side of the owners, who immediately cut the men's basic wage. At a mass meeting the miners voted to strike and the Government retaliated by prosecuting the men.

The hearing at Canterbury on Friday (January 23rd) attracted miners from all over the country. Colliery bands played in the street outside the court and, fearing a national strike, the Secretary for Mines issued petrol coupons for the journey to Canterbury.

The three men jailed are Tudor Davis, Betteshanger branch chairman, Joe Methuen, vice-chairman and William Powell, branch secretary.

February 2nd: In a dramatic about-turn the Home Secretary has released the three Betteshanger officials from Maidstone Gaol and the colliery owners have agreed to pay miners the full rate with back pay. In return 1,600 miners will return to work and enforcement notices for the payment of fines will not be issued.

This is a great victory for the miners who say they will attempt to meet production levels of 8,000 tons of coal a week.

Posthumous VC for Manston's Swordfish hero

February 14th: The recovery of the body of Lieutenant Commander Eugene Esmonde from the mouth of the River Medway today brings to a tragic conclusion one of the bravest and most audacious acts of the war. The hero,

who has already been recommended for a posthumous VC, will be buried in Gillingham Cemetery.

Two days ago Esmonde was killed along with his entire Swordfish Squadron while attempting to prevent the German battle cruisers *Scharnhorst* and *Gneisenau* from finding a safer port near Calais. The battleships, along with the cruiser *Prinz Eugen*, had "broken cover" at Brest but were accompanied by destroyers, torpedo boats, E boats, minesweepers and a massive fighter escort.

It did not seem to bother Esmonde or his crews that their torpedo-carrying Swordfish bi-planes of 825 Squadron were far too slow and hopelessly outdated to compete with the biggest fighter escort ever seen

over a naval force. They simply knew that if the battleships could be sunk the German navy would be in total disarray.

It was not to be. Despite the presence of a small fighter escort the confrontation was a disaster for the Manston Swordfish. Esmonde himself was the first to die. As he led the first three aircraft just above the waves his crews heard the final orders. "We're going to deal with them now. Fly 50 feet, close line astern. Individual attacks. Find your own way home. Good luck". A brutal barrage of shells, fragments and tracer bullets sent him spinning into the sea, followed, in turn, by each of the other six aircraft.

In all 13 men perished in this inferno of fire and the seven Swordfish lie at the bottom of the sea.

Eugene Esmonde was 33. He will be the first member of the Fleet Air Arm to win the Victoria Cross and his colleagues who responded so bravely to his orders will also be recognised for their great courage.

These provocative ladies with their frilly knickers, black "utility" stockings and fetching hats are, in fact, ferocious anti-aircraft gunners of the Royal Artillery, whose battery is positioned on the banks of the Thames at Gravesend. Some weeks ago, during rehearsal for their troop's Christmas pantomime, they were required to man positions on the guns as a formidable formation of German bombers was seen droning towards the capital. The cumbersome dresses proved a little bit of a handicap as they raced from the army hall to the battery but they were soon able to show that their shooting ability was on a par with their dancing skill as a barrage of fire crippled at least three enemy planes.

Grim news for Kent families as Singapore falls

February 28th: For several days now families in Kent have been receiving the grim news about the fate of their loved ones who were in Singapore when the island fell earlier this month.

Many were killed during the invasion by Japanese assault troops including those bayoneted to death in Singapore general hospital.

Others are in Changi Jail where 50,000 British POWs have been squeezed into four barracks. Among them is a young cricketer and journalist, Acting Major E.W. Swanton, who is better known as Jim.

The attack on Singapore was decisive. So invincible were the enemy divisions that the British commander Lt-Gen Arthur Percival chose not to counterattack despite orders to do so.

March 23rd: Nine staff members of the East Kent Road Car Company were killed today when bombs fell in St James Street, Dover. Most of those who died were in the air raid shelter. The Carlton Club next door was also hit and among those killed were former deputy mayor William Austen and Donald McKenzie, manager of the Co-op Bakery.

Volunteers have been helping soldiers to search for survivors while ambulances ran shuttle services to the hospital. It is believed the death toll will be about 16.

April 2nd: Thousands of Kent's single girls between the ages of 20 and 30 are now undertaking military service. Many have joined the RAF and ATS and some are working alongside anti-aircraft crews. Other conscripted women are in the police and fire service. Meanwhile married woman are taking essential jobs.

Canterbury welcomes Archbishop Temple

April 25th: Canterbury's new Archbishop, Dr William Temple, 96th Primate in direct line from St Augustine, came to the ancient city on Wednesday and received a warm welcome in the Guildhall. The following day, with all the traditional ecclesiastical ritual, he was enthroned in the Mother Church of the British Empire. Despite the grim reminders of war, the blinded windows and sandbagged monuments, the service lost little of its pageantry.

Dr Temple is the son of Dr Frederick Temple who was himself Archbishop from 1897-1903 and author of the controversial book which advocated the disestablishment of the Irish Church.

Fireguards save the Cathedral as an ancient city burns

June 2nd: Historic Canterbury stands no longer. Last night's devastating reprisal raid by German bombers has reduced much of this once-proud, ageless city to a heap of rubble. Vast craters surround the Cathedral, St George's Church is a smouldering shell, the birthplace of the playwright Marlowe has been destroyed and the scene today is an unbroken vista of desolation.

Among the still-smouldering rubble, crowds of people are walking and staring — dazed and aimlessly — at the unreal scene before them. Others are sitting outside the wreckage of their home. Fire pumps and hoses are trailed against the side of open cellars. Masonry is constantly falling and everywhere there is the smell of burning.

The cathedral, surrounded by mountains of wreckage, has escaped the worst of the damage but the walls and windows bear scars. Mrs Catherine Williamson, former mayor, says the desecration is as vile as when Becket fell beneath his murderers' swordblades.

The raid, which occurred in the early hours of the morning, was preceded by the dropping of parachute flares which illuminated the city and picked out every brilliant detail of its mediaeval architecture. The bombers, wave after wave, came from the direction of Herne Bay.

For more than an hour a mixture of high explosive and incendiary bombs dropped onto the city. Some clattered onto the roof of the cathedral but fireguards were waiting and pushed the sizzling incendiaries onto the grass below.

The ancient city buildings did not escape. As dive bombers zoomed in, homes, shops, offices and churches became engulfed in flames. When the all-clear finally sounded and people ventured from the safety of their shelters, a great smokescreen hung over the city. Then, as it faded to reveal the light of more than 100 fires, the cry went up: " The Cathedral is still standing."

One enormous bomb, believed to be four tons, fell near the entrance to

continued

Warriors Chapel and caused considerable damage.

Firemen from all over Kent are today converging on Canterbury, although many have been in the city for most of the night. Members of the Civil Defence and troops are helping with the rescue operation for many people are still trapped in collapsed buildings. Rest centres have already been established and first aid posts set up. The British Restaurant is handing out emergency food supplies.

Dazed, confused, desperate and homeless. The people of Canterbury head out of the still-smouldering city in search of shelter. The harrowing ordeal of June 1st will remain with them for the rest of their lives.

The Deanery is badly damaged. Dr Hewlett Johnson was sheltering in a passage during the raid and had a narrow escape. The old Palace survived as did Archbishop William Temple who sat with his wife under the old stone stairs. The homes of Canon Shirley, Canon Macnutt and Lady Davidson were completely destroyed.

November 2nd: In another massive raid on Canterbury last night, German bombers dropped almost 50 high explosives, killing 32 people including six children. It is believed that a further 250 people are now homeless.

Many of the bombed homes were not occupied. Terrified of further raids many had left the city to stay with relatives and others were sleeping in open fields, against haystacks and hedges. The most popular shelter is the Tyler Hill railway tunnel.

Among the many visitors to Canterbury in the last few weeks have been Mrs Roosevelt and Mrs Churchill who toured the city and saw the anti-aircraft defences. They also met some of the fire watchers who had crawled around the parapets of the cathedral, throwing off burning incendiaries while the June raid was at its height. Bravery awards await many of those men.

Time and time again the raiders have returned to Canterbury. Five were killed on June 6th when the electricity grid system was destroyed and by the end of the month the June death toll was 49 dead, 46 seriously injured, 310 homes destroyed and almost 3,000 buildings wrecked or damaged. Nearly 700 people were made homeless.

Canterbury's plight was still not over. Two days ago (October 31st) German aircraft came skimming over the city at rooftop height. One of their bombs hit a bus on the Sturry road. The conductress and eight passengers were killed and the bus was tilted on its end by the blast.

Canterbury, the cradle of English Christianity, will never be the same. The city is in mourning. But the Union Jacks which drape so defiantly from the ruined buildings convey a message which is crystal clear: We shall pick up the pieces and carry on.

The only building to survive in this part of St George's Street, Canterbury is the tower of St George's Church, which can be seen covered in scaffolding. Below: The same street earlier this century.

August 20th: Pilots of the five squadrons of the Biggin Hill Wing who gave cover for yesterday's Operation Jubilee — *the Allied attempt to seize the French port of Dieppe — have now learned that at least six Spitfires were shot down in the intensive, confused fighting over the French coast.*

In all Fighter Command have lost 106 aircraft but, on the ground, the tragedy is even greater. Of the 6,000 British and Canadian commandos who took part in the raid, more than 4,000 have been killed, wounded or are missing.

Photograph shows some of the lucky ones returning to Kent.

Duke of Kent dies in flying accident

August 26th: Air Commodore HRH the Duke of Kent was killed on active service last night when his Sunderland flying boat crashed in the north of Scotland. His Royal Highness, who was attached to the staff of the Inspector General of the RAF, was flying to Iceland on duty.

This latest tragedy comes when morale in Kent is low. Prince George, the Duke of Kent was Colonel in Chief of the Royal West Kents, patron of the Association of Kentish Men and Men of Kent and he had built up a loyal following in the county.

He was quickly on the scene after the Baedeker raid on Canterbury in June and during the same month also visited King's School, Canterbury at its wartime home in Cornwall.

Today flags are flying at half mast and thoughts go out to Princess Marina and her three young children, Alexandra, Edward and Michael.

August 12th: With machine guns crackling and bombs falling, raiders flew low over Deal yesterday. People ran for cover or threw themselves on the ground but there were several casualties. A 16-year-old, who was trying to escape on his bicycle, was among the eight killed. Many buildings were damaged including the Odeon cinema.

November 27th: The pilot of a Focke Wulf 190 was killed today when his aircraft clipped the steam dome of the railway engine he was attempting to destroy. The train was at the Caldecot level crossing on the branch line to New Romney. The fireman, Albert Hills, was scalded by steam but Mr Gilbert, the driver, escaped injury.

December 26th: Lord Cornwallis was delighted to learn today that a new branch of the County Association has been formed — in Stalag 383! Kentish POWs in the Austrian camp have told their president that 161 members have already enrolled but they all badly miss the Garden of England. "Will you please send us some literature on Kent?" they ask. "We want to show the other lads what a marvellous place it is."

The Duke, as Colonel-in-Chief of the Royal West Kents, inspects a Bren gun carrier. His death is deeply felt by the Regiment.

'The latest threat to Kent is the inevitable widespread disruption between Ashford and the coast if plans for the Channel Tunnel materialise' — Kent author, Arthur Mee, who died this year.

1943

January 23rd: Allied troops have captured Tripoli. It is the Italians' last remaining city in their former African "empire".

January 26th: Two women died in Ramsgate today when bombs fell on their houses in Coleman Crescent.

February 2nd: The siege of Stalingrad is over. The last pockets of German resistance surrendered today. It is believed that some 100,000 German troops have been killed or died from starvation.

February 7th: Shoes are to be rationed to just three pairs a year to save shoe leather.

March 3rd: 178 people were crushed to death today at Bethnal Green underground station. The disaster occurred when a mother carrying her baby slipped and fell down the flight of steps. Hundreds of people, seeking refuge from an air raid, fell on top of each other.

March 4th: A badly-crippled Junkers bomber jettisoned its cargo over Chatham today and killed six people before crashing in flames at Boxley Abbey, Maidstone. Two of the crew died.

March 5th: The Gloster Meteor, Britain's first jet fighter, will make its maiden flight today.

March 20th: Kent members of Equity have voted in favour of opening theatres on Sundays.

April 5th: St James' Church, Dover, has been hit by a German shell for the second time and is virtually destroyed.

May 8th: Part-time war work has become compulsory for women between the ages of 18 and 45, except for mothers with children under 14.

May 13th: General Alexander, Commander-in-Chief, today said the Allies were now masters of all North African shores.

May 14th: Some days ago the intelligence service left a corpse off the coast of Spain with briefcase and papers implying that

CHALK, KENT.

February 18th: Flight-Lieutenant F.G.H. Chalk, Spitfire pilot with 124 Squadron and perhaps better known as captain of Kent Cricket Club, was shot down and killed over the Channel yesterday. Gerry Chalk, 32, was one of cricket's finest pre-war captains. In his short first-class career he made 6,732 runs with a highest score of 198 against Sussex at Tonbridge. He will be badly missed.

the Allies were intending to invade Greece. It is believed the Germans have been successfully hoodwinked.

June 1st: Leslie Howard, the film actor, is one of 13 people missing on a civil airliner shot down by the Germans in the Bay of Biscay.

June 5th: Thousands of pounds have been raised in Kent for Wings for Victory Week. Faversham has raised enough to buy three Sunderland Flying Boats and Cranbrook 20 Typhoon aircraft.

June 25th: RAF and USAF bombers have continued to bombard towns in the Ruhr valley. The town of Wupperthal now lies in ruins.

June 28th: The gasholder at

Ramsgate was set alight today for the third time in three years by a long-range shell from the French coast. Another shell exploded in St Luke's Avenue killing 70-year-old Alice Miller.

June 30th: Now that the danger of invasion has receded signposts are to be re-erected in some rural areas of Britain.

July 1st: Poland's Prime Minister in exile, General Wladislaw Sikorski and his military adviser, Victor Cazalet of Fairlawne, Shipbourne died today in an air crash in Gibraltar. Sikorski lived at Great Swifts, Cranbrook.

July 12th: The UK birthrate has reached its highest level for 17 years, despite the fact that most men

are away from home.

July 31st: The city of Hamburg has been razed to the ground.

September 6th: A full-scale amphibious exercise, code-named *Harlequin*, will take place today in Kent. The idea is to convince Hitler and his generals that an invasion of the Continent is planned from south-east England.

September 8th: Italy has unconditionally surrendered.

October 15th: Three members of the crew of a new Junkers 188 were killed when the bomber was shot down by a Mosquito of 85 Squadron. It crashed at Great Brooks End Farm, Birchington and disintegrated.

October 18th: A B17 American Flying Fortress crashed today near the Halfway House on the A2 Canterbury to Dover Road, just missing a moving car. The bomber veered through a hedge and ploughed into a field. The crew survived the impact.

December 2nd: One out of every ten men called up between the ages of 18 and 25 will now be ordered to work in the coalmines instead of going into the forces. The scheme has been introduced by Mr Ernest Bevin, Minister of Labour.

December 19th: Leading West End variety artistes will entertain the people of Dover today at the Royal Hippodrome in aid of the RAF Prisoners of War Fund. Among the cast will be Tommy Trinder, Sonnie Hale, Tessie O'Shea, Cherry Lind, Morton Frazer and the Jerry Allen Trio.

Squadron Leader H.E.Bates,the novelist from Little Chart, near Ashford is currently employed by the Air Ministry.He will be writing a new novel about a bomber crew shot down in occupied France. It is to be called *Fair Stood the Wind for France*.

GREAT HITS OF 1943

You'll Never Know
My Heart and I

The search for children buried under tons of masonry at Sandhurst School, Catford.

38 children die as bomb hits Catford school

January 21st: Thirty-eight children and six teachers were killed yesterday when German raiders dropped a 500 kg bomb on Sandhurst Road School, Catford.

The majority of those who died were taking their midday dinner break when the bomb blew out the whole central part of the LCC school. As the dust and smoke subsided the scene was appalling. Children, with terrible wounds, lay strewn about the dining room. Others died on the staircase and the second floor. The blast reached the staff room where three teachers died while another was killed in the science room.

This fiendish onslaught is attracting enormous publicity and everyone wants to know why there was no warning.

Frantic parents joined Civil Defence workers in a rescue operation that continued throughout the night. One of the first workers to reach the scene said: "There were no balloons up and the air raid warning had not gone...there was a terrific explosion and the school just fell to pieces. It seemed a never-ending job passing the dead and injured children out from the wreckage."

Margaret Clarke, the headmistress, heard a tearing, rending sound and the hall, six yards from where she was standing, fell away. "The children were magnificent", she said. They took three younger ones home and even tore up their clothing to bandage the youngsters who were wounded."

The children will be buried in a communal grave at Hither Green next week, preceded by an address from the Bishop of Southwark. An inquiry will open at Lewisham Town Hall later next month.

Under these flags they fought for you

NOW HELP THEM

FORCES DAY

WEDNESDAY **APRIL 23RD**

SOLDIERS, SAILORS & AIRMENS

HELP SOCIETY

The hunt continues for survivors of the Ashford raid

Luftwaffe ace killed in terror raid on Ashford

March 25th: In the last few weeks Kent has suffered badly from reprisal raids caused by RAF Bomber Command's increased activity over Germany. Yesterday it was Ashford's turn.

The raid lasted just three minutes but in that time 50 people were killed and 77 seriously injured, many by the machine guns which strafed the streets as people fled for safety.

One bomb fell on the Victoria Road Primary School but the 300 children were already in the shelters.

They were not so lucky at the Ashford Railway Works where five were killed and 50-ton locomotives in the erecting shed totally mangled.

The worst damage was at Milton Road, New Street, where two died in Hayward's Garage, Dover Place, New Rents, Star Road, Hardinge Road and Kent Avenue, where five were killed in a baker's shop.

In terms of lives lost in a single raid this was Kent's worst blow of the war. It is believed the attacking Focke-Wulf 190s belonged to Staffel JG26 from St Omer and were led by Paul Keller, nicknamed "Bombenkeller".

To the satisfaction of the Ashford gunners, Keller did not survive the raid. His Focke-Wulf was hit by Ack Ack fire and crashed in Godinton Road.

The hunt continues for survivors of the Ashford raid

March: The South African fighter ace, Sailor Malan who has a reputation as one of the most fearless and skilful pilots in Fighter Command, is the new CO of Britain's "Number One" station, RAF Biggin Hill. He has drawn up new rules for air fighting which he calls his Ten Commandments.

April 25th: Two houses in Bromley were destroyed by fire today when a Junkers 88 was shot down by the pilots of a Mosquito night fighter. It crashed near Homefield Road and Widmore Road with a series of thuds. Wheels, guns, engines and other parts of the Junkers were spread over a large area of the town.

Following the astonishing successes of the big appeals — for fighters in 1940, war weapons in 1941, warships in 1942 — which had raised millions of pounds, Kent has been asked to contribute in a big way once more. Wings For Victory Week opens this Spring with a variety of attractive events. Here, on display outside the Half Moon pub at Hildenborough, is a Heinkel III.

Trials at Reculver for the bomb that 'bounces'

May 17th: Some weeks ago a few Lancaster bombers appeared over the north Kent coast between Herne Bay and Margate and dropped an experimental bomb into the sea. The bomb bounced once on the surface and then exploded into tiny fragments. The aircraft then flew away and the top brass RAF observers, accompanied by a well-known British scientist, left in their cars. They returned again and again. On each occasion police cordoned off the area leaving nearby residents puzzling over the "secret trials".

With yesterday's breaching of the heavily defended Möhne and Eder Dams in the Ruhr valley, all can now be revealed. The Lancasters were from 617 Squadron, their leader was Wing Commander Guy Gibson, the scientist was Barnes Wallis and the trials at Reculver were testing Dr Wallis's theory that his latest prototype could skip along the water several times before exploding.

It appears that the bouncing bomb idea was successful. Reports coming in indicate that the heavily reinforced concrete dams were attacked by 19 Lancasters and breached. It is believed that 300 million tons of water are now pouring into the western Ruhr valleys killing hundreds of people and destroying factories, bridges, farming land and even coalmines.

Tragically there are also reports of heavy casualties among the Lancaster crews with only eight aircraft returning.

Luftwaffe lands at West Malling

April 17th: **There was a dramatic incident at West Malling last night when three Focke-Wulf 190s lost their way in the darkness after a raid on Essex towns and landed at the Kent airfield. The pilot of a fourth 190, realising he was in hostile territory, abandoned his aircraft but was too low for his parachute to deploy and died at Staplehurst.**

The other pilots were arrested and taken into custody where it transpired that they had each experienced navigational difficulties because of mist and assumed they were landing in France.

The pilot of the second Focke-Wulf tried to take off again but was hit by a burst of fire from a nearby Vickers gun. With his clothing on fire, the German leapt free and ran for his life — straight into the arms of the CO at West Malling, Wing Commander Peter Townsend. He was taken to the sick bay.

May 15th: *French fighter pilot, René Mouchotte and Jack Charles, a Canadian, yesterday shot down two Focke-Wulf 190s to bring the number of aircraft destroyed by the Biggin Hill Wing to 1001. The station, by far the top-scoring in Fighter Command, now plans to celebrate the feat with a party, possibly at Grosvenor House, London. The victorious pilots are delighted with the station's success. They share the proceeds of a sweepstake believed to be in excess of £300. Gilbert Harding, the well-known BBC commentator, was at Biggin Hill to cover the occasion. Photograph shows the two pilots celebrating with colleagues.*

Civilians die in surprise raid on Margate

June 1st: A surprise attack on Margate was carried out yesterday by a dozen Focke-Wulfs who came low over the rooftops and dropped 14 high explosives on an unsuspecting town. There was no air raid warning and the raid lasted one minute but in that time nine civilians were killed and four seriously hurt. Bombs fell on a number of roads including St Peter's Road, Thanet Road and the High Street.

The attackers were chased by Hawker Typhoons of 609 Squadron based at Manston and two were shot down by Flight Lt Wells. One German pilot baled out too low and his parachute failed to open.

Most of the civilian victims were in the town centre. An ARP warden died at the bar of the King's Head when the roof caved in, three were killed at 13 High Street and a butcher's errand boy was cycling past a house when he was thrown off his bike by the bomb blast. He died in hospital.

More people died in Milton Square and Arnold Road where the bodies of Elizabeth and Robert Denchfield were never found — the bomb penetrated the actual room where they had been.

Holy Trinity Church, Margate, also suffered a direct hit and it is believed that several soldiers may have died in Warrior House, Dalby Square, where they were billeted. No details of military casualties are being released.

August 13th: Holcombe Fire Station, Chatham, is run entirely by women. This week they took part in a large scale exercise code-named Harlequin *to test their readiness for action when the invasion of France takes place.*

Kent loses a literary legend

May 27th: One of Kent's best-loved and most prolific authors, Arthur Henry Mee, died in his lovely village of Eynsford today. He was 68.

Born in Nottinghamshire at Staplefield, the son of a railway fireman, Arthur Mee will be best remembered for compiling, in 1908, an encyclopaedia for children which sold thousands of copies, translated into six languages and made him famous.

He also helped to write 38 beautifully produced county guides entitled *The King's England.*

By profession Arthur Mee was a journalist who left school at 16 and became editor of the *Nottingham Evening News* in his early 20s. He joined the *Daily Mail* as literary editor and launched a successful children's newspaper in 1919.

It was during this period he came to live in Kent. Writing for the *Kentish Times* just before the war he said: *"I stole upon Eynsford, that fairest of villages, like a thief in the night. No mortal was aware of my coming. Yet there was a certain shade that hovered as perpetually it hovers, about beloved ground, which did me the honour of welcome. 'Come', it said. 'If you would see your Eynsford — my Eynsford — I will be your guide".*

Arthur was referring to the shade of Mr Elliott Downs Till, a famous local benefactor who introduced him to the village and its inhabitants.

Miss Ruth Dewe, volunteer fire watcher of Old Farm Avenue, Sidcup

Sikorski and Cazalet killed in air crash

July 4th: Poland's Prime Minister in exile, General Wladyslaw Sikorski who has been living at Great Swifts, Cranbrook and his military advisor, Major Victor Cazalet, were killed today when their Liberator bomber crashed in the sea off Gibraltar.

Cazalet, owner of Great Swifts and proprietor of the racing stables at Fairlawne, Shipbourne, and Sikorski were on their way to the Middle East to inspect Polish forces. There were 17 passengers in the Liberator and the only survivor is the pilot.

Victor Cazalet was also an officer during the 1914-18 war, a friend of the Royal family and a Member of Parliament who spoke out strongly against the growth of the Nazi regime in the thirties.

When war broke out he was offered command of the 16th Light Anti-Aircraft battery, then forming in the Sevenoaks area and he personally recruited the first members. His battery became known as "Cazalet's Cuties" because of the high proportion of actors in the ranks. By 1941 some 80 per cent of the Cuties' gunners had been commissioned and Cazalet was appointed as military adviser to Sikorski.

The Hollywood actor Leslie Howard, best known for his portrayal of Ashley Wilkes in the film *Gone With The Wind*, has also died in an air crash. He was one of 13 to die when a civil aircraft was attacked by enemy raiders over the Bay of Biscay.

Howard, who was a frequent visitor to Kent, lived with his wife and family at Stowe Maries, near Dorking Surrey.

Boys come home in prisoner exchange

September 3rd: Hundreds of Kentish families are delighted by the news coming from Italy this week. Allied troops are on the toe of the country, Mussolini has been sacked, the country has been plunged into political chaos and the armistice is expected to be signed soon. More important is the immediate repatriation of POWs.

There is also to be an exchange between Britain and Germany of sick and seriously wounded prisoners captured in 1940 at Dunkirk or in the abortive raid on Dieppe last year, or in later battles.

Hungry work, this war! The Pioneer Corps, stationed at Deal, wait outside the Clarendon Hotel for the signal that lunch is ready.

Members of the 20th Kent Battalion of the Home Guard take part in an exercise in woods near Tonbridge.

Prime Minister inspects shell damage in Dover

August 4th: Complaints by the people of Dover that constant shelling by the German long-range guns in Pas de Calais are only reprisals for the Dover guns have reached the Prime Minister's office. Winston Churchill, accompanied by the US Secretary of State for War, H.L. Stimson, will visit the town today to see if "artillery duels" are really taking place.

It was on Monday August 12th, 1940, that the German guns fired the first shells onto British shores. Since then the people of "Hellfire Corner", in particular Dover, Folkestone, Ramsgate and Deal have endured an almost constant barrage. At first the shells were fired from railway-mounted guns operating on the French rail track but now there is a network of batteries along the Pas de Calais coast, under the control of the German Navy.

The shells take, on average, about a minute to cross the Channel. There is no warning until after the first shell has

fallen, but then a double siren indicates that the guns are in action. Of the 73 guns, 11 are long-range and the largest is Batterie Lindeman whose three 406mm guns can reach 34 miles.

There have been terrible tragedies all around Hellfire Corner. On June 27th this year 11 servicemen were killed in Biggin Street, Dover and the next day a salvo of shells hit the GPO building in Priory Street, killing three telephone operators.

Buildings have been destroyed or gasholders set alight all along the coast. It is estimated that more than 4,000 shells have landed and a further 1,000 have fallen in the sea.

Churchill will view the damage in Dover and make his recommendations to Parliament with the knowledge that the ordeal will not end until the German guns are silenced.

January 4th: Hitler has ordered the mobilisation of all children over the age of 10.

January 27th: After a German siege lasting 872 days Leningrad has been freed by the Red Army. More than a million people have died.

February 1st: Restrictions on pleats and buttons on women's clothes have been lifted. Men may now also wear trousers with pockets and turn-ups.

February 5th: Michel Hollard, the French resistance leader who passed information to the British on the development of launching sites for the V1 flying bomb, has been arrested by the Gestapo.

February 12th: Reports are coming in that residents of the Channel Islands are near to starvation, some existing on root vegetables.

March 8th: Britain at last has a fighter to match the speedy Focke Wulf 190. The Spitfire Mark XIV was introduced today.

March 26th: After two years of preparation and digging, 76 Allied POWs have escaped through a tunnel from Stalag Luft III. The man who masterminded the escape was "Big X", better known at Biggin Hill as Flight Lt Roger Bushell.

March 31st: The Battle of Berlin is over. The Allies have called off the bombardment having lost more than a thousand bombers in less than six months.

April 30th: The first prefabricated house has been erected in London. The two-bedroom single storey factory-made home cost £550 and took two days to build.

June 6th: Allied invasion of Europe.

June 13th: A pilotless plane, or flying bomb, crashed today at Swanscombe. No damage was caused but more are expected.

June 23rd: Australian Flying Officer Ken Collier, flying from West Malling, today tipped a flying bomb with the wing of his Spitfire

1944

Nowhere is Kent's defiance better illustrated than here at The Hippodrome, Dover. Despite the air raids and the shelling the old 580-seater music hall remains open and the 11 girl attendants and four barmaids continue to turn up every evening. Because of the danger, many artistes have refused to appear at the Hippodrome and others charge big fees but a programme has always been made up, usually from the local service units.

when his ammunition ran out.

Rather than take children into shelters, schools in Kent are posting "doodlebug spotters" outside the classroom. Wearing tin hats, children take turns, with their eyes trained on the skies and their ears tuned to the ghastly roar.

July 20th: There has been an unsuccessful attempt to assassinate Hitler with a bomb at his "Wolf's Lair" headquarters.

July 28th: 59 people died today when a flying bomb crashed on the market place at Lewisham. Many of the dead and injured were in the basement cafe of Woolworths.

August 4th: The twin-engine Gloster Meteor, a high performance jet fighter has joined

the battle against the flying bomb.

August 30th: The Freedom of Maidstone has been conferred on the Queen's Own Royal West Kent Regiment.

September 1st: As the battle of the doodlebug drew to a conclusion, so the shelling of coastal towns began with a new intensity. Just after midnight last night the German batteries at Cap Gris Nez fired more than 100 shells on Dover and the harbour. Four were killed in the Lagoon Cave shelter in the High Street and two died near Tower Hamlets.

September 1st: A Junkers 88 was shot down at Hothfield, near Ashford yesterday.

September 17th: The blackout

has been replaced by a dimout — but only for the towns of West Kent. In Hellfire Corner there is no sign yet of the war ending.

September 27th: Allied troops have failed in their attempt to capture Arnhem.

October 15th: 3,000 officers and members of the Home Guard attended a stand-down service in Canterbury Cathedral today. The men, representing 60,000 colleagues, marched through the city past cheering crowds.

December 16th: The bandleader Glenn Miller is missing. His plane apparently disappeared today en route from England to Paris.

Henry Eric Harden, aged 33 of Colyer Road, Northfleet, has been awarded a posthumous Victoria Cross. A Lance Corporal with the Army Medical Corps, Harden risked enemy fire to bring in wounded colleagues near Arnhem. Twice he made the trip and was wounded. On the third occasion he tried to reach a wounded officer who was fully exposed to enemy fire. Harden fell with a sniper's bullet through his head.

A second Arnhem Victoria Cross has been awarded to Lionel Ernest Queripel of Warwick Place, Tunbridge Wells. Wounded on three occasions and trapped with his unit of the Royal Sussex Regiment, Captain Queripel decided to cover his men's withdrawal. He was last seen alone with a pistol in one hand and a grenade in the other. The VC and citation will be presented to his family.

Another Victoria Cross hero to die this year is Thomas Byrne of Canterbury. His award, however, belongs to a different era — the 21st Lancers' famous charge against the Dervishes at Omdurman, Sudan, in September 1898, when he saved the life of an officer. Winston Churchill, who was also in the charge, said it was the bravest thing he had ever seen.

GREAT HITS OF 1944

Mairzy Doats

There Goes That Song Again

145

Kent towns suffer in the "baby blitz"

May 30th: The bombing raids on English towns, code-named *Operation Steinbock,* have caused enormous damage and loss of life in Kent but it is believed that the Luftwaffe have suffered far worse. Reports from agents suggest that 300 aircraft have been lost in five months and scores of newly-trained young pilots and their crews killed. There is every possibility that this is the end of bomber operations over Britain.

The "Baby Blitz", as *Steinbock* has been described, began in January when bombs fell on Erith and Bexley, damaging the mental hospital and killing 13 people.

During that eventful night enemy aircraft were shot down and crashed at Dungeness, Western Heights, Dover (Junkers), Horton Priory, Sellindge (Junkers), Lydd Ranges (Messerschmitt), Hop Pocket, Paddock Wood (Junkers) and Lower Chantry Lane, Canterbury (Junkers).

At Gravesend on February 4th, eight were killed when a high explosive fell at the junction of Wrotham Road and Cross Lane. A huge crater was caused by the explosion and buildings all around collapsed into the chasm.

One of the worst incidents was on Tuesday March 2nd at Strood when bombs fell in the Grove Road/Station Road area and killed 18 people. Almost 40 people were buried under masses of debris and 300 others were left homeless.

September 26th: Here in the middle of Dover, in Castle Street, is written the last grim sentence of the noble town's Shellfire story. Here, after 1,510 days, the ordeal ended with a deafening crack. Photograph shows workmen getting on with the task of clearing the debris.

One of the bravest. After three years of convoying supplies to Russia under constant enemy attack, HMS Kent comes home to Chatham dockyard where she was built. The cruiser spend much of the early war years in the China Station and was never far away from the action. It is believed she will now be transferred to the Reserve Fleet and eventually broken up.

Invasion imminent, Monty tells the troops

February 3rd: With the tightening of security precautions in Kent, the presence of hundreds more American soldiers, and the establishment of decoy airfields all over the county, it is clear that an Allied invasion of France is imminent.

Yesterday Field Marshal Bernard Montgomery, fresh from his great victory at Alamein, was at Mote Park, Maidstone — part of his tour of the South East. There, surrounded by more than a 1,000 soldiers, he stood on his jeep and told them they would be under his command for the Second Front. It was the message every soldier wanted to hear.

He gave no specific details but the men know that a liberation army is being prepared. Troops have been recalled from North Africa, Sicily and Italy, long lines of vehicles under camouflage netting are appearing all over the county and troop exercises include wading in rough water in full kit and how to assemble a folding bicycle in seconds.

It is the presence of the Americans which is causing the greatest stir. Known as GI's, named after the words "Government Issue" on their equipment, they are making a hit with the local girls, who are intrigued by their brash, carefree attitude and simply love the gifts of nylons and cigarettes.

The Yanks may take the girls to local

dances but the seaside will soon be out of bounds to anyone but those who live there. For reasons of "operational security" the Secretary of State for War has introduced a coastal ban from The Wash to Lands End. It comes into effect on April 1st and anyone who breaches the

regulations will be fined £100.

March 10th: A new type of Spitfire, the Mark XIV, has been seen in the skies of Kent. The Merlin engine has been replaced by the Griffon which enables the aircraft to reach speeds of almost 450 mph as well as improving the rate of climb. A good match for the Focke-Wulf 190.

May 18th: The Kent boys involved in the Italian campaign have helped to open the road to Rome, it was reported this week. Units of the Buffs and the Royal West Kents held vital positions under a hail of fire, then helped to breach the German lines before taking the town of Monte Cassino.

May 22nd: Eight airman died today when a 1,000 bomb fell in their tented RAF camp in Coleman's Wood, Chilmington.

Grenade explosion kills 22 soldiers

June 3rd: Twenty-one infantrymen and an instructor have been killed in an explosion at Dymchurch.

It is believed the accident occurred when a lieutenant instructor was demonstrating how to light a grenade. Soldiers were gathered around him on the steps of the sea wall.

The instructor lit a match which

appeared to blow out. He lit a second and three boxes of anti-tank grenades immediately exploded, blowing the instructor in the air and killing all those close to him.

Like all military personnel in the south-east the men knew that *Operation Overlord* was just a few days away from reality.

How 500 Kentish Men helped to save India

May 24th: Extraordinary heroism by the 4th Battalion of the Royal West Kent Regiment in defending the small town of Kohima, Burma, a month ago is being hailed as one of the greatest rearguard actions in the history of warfare.

For 16 days — between April 5th and 21st — 500 men, all wearing the famous white horse cap badge, held out against a furious assault by an entire Japanese division which needed possession of the Kohima Pass and entry through it to Assam, their intended route into India.

The Kentish Men refused to submit. Attacked ceaselessly day and night, often with furious hand-to-hand fighting with butt and bayonet, and peppered with grenades, they held their ground before the second British Division were flown in to relieve them.

By that time 200 men had died and many others were suffering badly from sickness. Their ammunition was almost spent and one man, Lance Corporal John Harman, had been recommended for a posthumous Victoria Cross.

The 4th Battalion have had a tough war. Many of these young men who learned their skills at drill halls in Maidstone, Tunbridge Wells, Tonbridge and Sevenoaks,

April 22nd: The burial service has been held and the men of the fourth battalion of the Royal West Kent Regiment stand for a few moments' silence in memory of their colleagues killed in the defence of Kohima. In the foreground is the grave of Lance-Corporal John Harman.

were in action with the BEF in France and later in the Western Desert. They arrived in the Far East in October 1943 and were soon in action. By the end of March this year the Japanese army was moving through Burma towards India. The all-weather road across the mountains, through Kohima was their only route to India, and in their way were British and Indian troops.

The 4th Battalion, a mixture of Territorials and conscripts called up at 21, were sent by lorry to Kohima on April 5th to reinforce the small Indian garrison but within hours the Japanese had virtually surrounded them.

Lance Corporal Harman's actions typified the bravery

of the men. The Japanese had established a machine-gun post within 50 yards of his company but the 29-year-old Beckenham soldier went forward on his own and lobbed a grenade which annihilated the post. The next morning, with fixed bayonet, he charged a party of Japanese who were digging in and killed five of them. He was mortally wounded on return to his position.

The Defence of Kohima should always be remembered as an action of extreme heroism. In this jungle country miles away from home, the "forgotten army" as many of the men see themselves have made a stand that could well mark the turning point in the war against Japan. It is believed that plans for the invasion of India have been postponed.

Allies land in Normandy as Kent helps to deceive the enemy. This is D Day

June 6th: "It is with a long, pent-up sigh of relief that Kent, proud dauntless bastion of England heard that the Allied invasion for the liberation of Europe has been launched. For months, for years — ever since Dunkirk, in fact — Kent has yearned for this glorious moment, prayed for it, toiled for it, sacrificed her blood and beauty for it."

So wrote the Kent Messenger this morning as *Operation Overlord* got under way at last. As the county slept, a vast armada of more than 6,000 ships was on its way — not to Pas de Calais as the Germans expected — but to Normandy. Fifty miles wide and protected by scores of fast-moving torpedo boats the invasion fleet carried 185,000 men and 20,000 vehicles.

News of the landings early this morning and the securing of substantial bridgeheads has excited tremendous elation. Ministry of Information vans are driving through town centres broadcasting the great news, people are shaking each other's hand, members of the forces here in Kent are being hero-worshipped. Women are weeping with joy.

It is too early to celebrate the end of the war. There is a long way to go. As England's front-line county, Kent has too many memories of blackouts and airraids and shell warnings and the whistling shrieks of explosions. But the tension that has existed during the great military build-up has suddenly been lifted. "Invasion services" are even being planned in churches throughout the county.

It is also too early to give full details of *Operation Fortitude,* the giant hoax designed to make the Germans think the Allied force would take the shortest route to France. But right across Kent, mingled with the real equipment for the real invasion, have been elaborate clues designed to mislead the enemy.

Planned in 1943 by the Chief of Staff to the Supreme Allied Commander (Designate) the deception included a fuel pipe line at Dover, camps, depots, railway sidings, extra port facilities. Under branches of oak trees, in farmyards and fields stood fake equipment for the Second Front — guns, tanks, landing barges, bulldozers, cranes, pontoons and gliders. Many of them were inflated dummies made at Shepperton film studios.

Omaha Beach after a rough crossing. "Get the hell out of here quickly", the colonel shouted.

It is not known whether Field Marshal Rommel and his army have completely fallen for the deception but there are reports of massive troop movements in Pas de Calais. Valuable German divisions remain in the area.

Part of the deception includes many new airfields in Kent. Advance landing grounds have been established at Ashford, Kingsnorth, Brenzett, Egerton, High Halden, Headcorn, Lydd, New Romney, Newchurch, Staplehurst, Swingfield and Woodchurch. There are enough airfields for fifty squadrons but half that number have been deployed.

As the real invasion force was on its way last night, an attack was made against beaches near Boulogne by six harbour-defence motor launches of the Dover Command and a squadron of Bomber Command. Using special equipment and smoke they towed balloons with reflectors while the aircraft dropped radar-deceiving foil. It was hoped to emulate the echoes received by radar from large ships that an approaching convoy was on its way.

Meanwhile the real convoy has landed, official confirmation coming at 9.32 this morning. Under the command of General Dwight Eisenhower the Allies are in France again. This is D Day.

As the Phoenixes (concrete pontoons) are laid in line, a soldier makes a hazardous crossing on a wire rope. This is the moment the prefabricated floating port, known as Mulberry, arrived at Arromanches where the advance party were already waiting. It had been towed across the Channel by the paddle steamer HMS Aristocrat.

Mulberry harbour built in Kent by 20,000 men

June 12th: Another great innovation of the whole *Overlord Operation* came into use today. A floating dock called the Mulberry Harbour is now in place, enabling supply ships to unload onto the landing beaches instead of waiting until the Allies capture a French port from the Germans.

Work on building Mulberry on the banks of the Medway, the Thames and at Richborough has been proceeding for more than a year in complete secrecy. So secret, in fact, that many of the 20,000 men employed in its construction had no idea of the intended use. The harbour consists of a rigid breakwater made by sunken blockships and an outer wall made up of concrete pontoons known as 'Phoenixes'.

Two Mulberries are now in place at Arromanches and St Laurent and a port the size of Dover is able to float up and down with the tide. Other parts include a "Swiss Roll", a floating trackway strong enough for heavy lorries, with a pier at the seaward end.

Kent newspaper reporters are among the 558 journalists in Normandy covering the *Overlord* landings. Many of their reports have been heavily censored but they have been able to tell us that Allied air forces have absolute superiority in the skies and that French resistance fighters have been magnificent in paralysing the rail network, blocking roads and disrupting the military phone system. 326,000 troops have already been brought ashore.

'Doodlebug' terror weapon puts Kent in the front line again

July 31st: Kent has been under attack now for six weeks. 120 people have been killed and hundreds more injured. Homes in scores of towns and villages have been destroyed or damaged. Once more the children have been evacuated to safer areas and, in their place, have come the builders, the volunteers to work alongside firemen, Civil Defence and the good ladies of the WVS. Courage, endurance, tragedy have again become a part of daily life.

The weapon with which Hitler is indulging in his latest orgy of terror is the flying bomb or VI (V stands for *vergeltung*, meaning revenge). The noise of its flight is hideous, like the harshness of a gigantic motorbike. From below it looks like a black cross, spitting red flames from its tail. From the side it has the appearance of a giant rifle with a telescopic sight. Among many names, it is perhaps most often called a doodlebug.

Launched from ramps in France, the VI is a pilotless mid-wing monoplane, constructed of plywood and sheet steel and propelled by a pulse-jet engine with a ton of explosive in its nose. An air log measures the pre-set distance and when the engine cuts out the missile falls silently to earth, followed by a shattering explosion.

After a brief range-finding affair on June 13th, the real onslaught against Kent began on June 17th when three people were killed at Benenden. One week later 47 soldiers died when a flying bomb was shot down onto Newlands Military Camp at Charing Heath.

Anti-aircraft gunners were also responsible for the next big tragedy. A battery stationed on the North Downs scored a direct hit against a missile which crashed onto Weald House, Crockham Hill, where 22 children and eight domestic staff were killed. The little ones, all under five, had just been evacuated from London.

The slaughter continued. 11 died when one fell on the army camp at Pattenden Lane, Marden. AA fire was again responsible. There were fatalities at Sevenoaks, Rolvenden, Lympne, Old Romney, Maidstone, Capel and Brabourne. And yesterday (July 30th) 13 were killed at Swanscombe.

For several weeks the fighters which chased the monsters across the skies and the formidable gunners on the Downs frequently got in each other's way. So, in early July, the defences were redeployed. Fighters were instructed to patrol the area between Beachy Head and Dover and they are the first line of defence. The second is an enormous barrage of anti-aircraft guns ranged along the coast and on the coastal slopes of the Kent Downs. The third is more fighters, roaming the area inland above the Weald and the fourth are barrage balloons — a great, glistening, formidable wall of some 2,000 glowing in the southern sun — all anchored on higher ground.

The doodlebugs are launched from ramps in Pas de Calais and Picardy, set up in woods and villages. The busiest route is between Hythe and Dungeness so the greatest emphasis on air defence is placed there.

In the air, the battle is led by a Tempest Wing, established on a small air strip at Newchurch on Romney Marsh and commanded by Wing Commander Roland Beamont. The Mustangs of 129 Squadron and 315 (Polish) Squadron are operating from Brenzett and, further inland at West Malling, 316 flies the Mustang alongside the Spitfires of 91 and 96.

At night radar-controlled fighters take over, brilliantly aided by the searchlight units sited alongside the coast. Control of the defences is in the hands of RAF Biggin Hill. The airfield is also Balloon HQ and operations are situated in a large house at Towerfields, Keston.

In a tribute to all those who are fighting the flying bomb, Churchill said: "Whatever capacity, be it intelligence, fighters, bombers, guns, balloons, scientists or Civil Defence, it is a great and concerted defence."

Churchill also mentioned the great body of men, both civilian and Service, who have been drafted in to repair and make safe, damaged property. By the end of June, more than 20,000 houses were being damaged every 24 hours and the backlog was increasing by 12,000 a day.

Squadron Leader H.E. Bates of the Air Ministry who is preparing the official documentation of the flying bomb says that the people of "doodlebug alley" are seeing the monuments and landmarks of centuries go down in dust. "They say goodbye to their children as they go to school in the morning and never know if they will see them again."

August 7th: Twelve people were killed when a flying bomb, shot down by a fighter, crashed in Malling Road, Snodland on Saturday (August 5th). The bomb fell near a surgery and two doctors, who were both badly injured, continued to treat others who had been hurt. Among those killed was a nine-year-old girl, a police sergeant, his wife and two girls who were staying with the doctors.

All over, says Sandys, except for a few last shots

September 8th: Duncan Sandys who was appointed by his father-in-law, Winston Churchill, as Britain's supremo in the hunt for flying bomb launching sites, told a crowded press conference yesterday that the battle of the doodlebug is over "except for possibly a few last shots".

He said that during the 80 days of the bombardment the Germans had sent over some 8,000 flying bombs of which 2,300 had got through to London. He also said that the understanding and restraint of the people living in Kent is deserving of great praise. "By their readiness to accept a share of London's dangers, the people of Bomb Alley played a notable part in keeping down overall casualties."

The people of Kent certainly displayed defiance against this indiscriminate weapon but, as the casualties in August continued to rise, there was little understanding. Maidstone suffered on August 3rd when a bomb exploded in the goods yard at Maidstone West railway station. Five were killed, five seriously injured, gas and electricity supplies wrecked and more than 1,000 homes damaged.

A few days later a doodlebug crashed in Malling Road, Snodland, demolishing ten houses. On this occasion 12 were killed including a nine-year-old girl in a doctor's surgery, a police sergeant, his wife and two daughters who were staying with the doctor and several neighbours.

That was on August 5th. The following day it was the people of East Hill, Dartford, who suffered when 10 were killed and 700 people made homeless. Hythe's turn came on August 15th when five people living near the Military Canal died.

The men manning the guns became more accurate as the campaign continued but to those who lived in this part of Kent anti-aircraft fire became as great a trial as the doodlebugs, the jagged fragments of lethal shrapnel ruining many homes.

There was an unusual tragedy at Newington when a Spitfire pilot succeeded in his frantic attempts to destroy a flying bomb only to see it crash and destroy a railway bridge. Round the corner came the Margate Express, crammed with passengers. The engine jumped the chasm caused by the explosion but the first two carriages ploughed into the wreckage of the bridge. More than 600 people were on that train, mostly soldiers. Eight were killed.

By the beginning of September the Allied armies were closing in on the launching sites, giving Duncan Sandys an opportunity to say the battle is virtually over. He issued one warning. The missiles might be launched from aircraft. "I have firm evidence," he said, " that Heinkels are being converted for this purpose. The attack will come from the east."

Bomb damage in Park Avenue, Northfleet

Cargo of bombs lies on a sandbank

August 21st: Residents of Sheerness may be unaware that an American ship carrying more than 3,000 assorted bombs lies wrecked on a sandbank in the Thames Estuary and could easily wipe the town off the map of Kent if the whole cargo goes up!

The drama began two days ago when the *Richard Montgomery* sailed into the Estuary with her explosive cargo for the US air force. She anchored two miles off Sheerness to wait for a convoy to lead her safely to Cherbourg. With such a lethal freight it would have been a perilous journey, so great care would have been required.

It wasn't necessary. After being tossed about by those rough Estuary waters, the American ship swung onto a sandbank, split in two and sank with her masts sticking out of the water.

Salvage experts will attempt to transfer the cargo to another ship but it won't be easy. Sheerness waits with bated breath.

Citizens' Army told: 'You are no longer required'

October 17th: Battalion. Dismiss. These two words echoed around Kent on Sunday as the various units of the Kent Home Guard were told officially there is no longer a risk of invasion and so their services are not required.

From the shambles of 1940 the KHG has grown into a well armed, well disciplined, well trained professional outfit consisting of 60,000 men from 52 battalions, three transport columns and two AA batteries.

They can look back on a record of service unsurpassed by any other fighting unit. Bank managers, Great War veterans, teenagers stood together guarding the front line county, willingly, cheerfully and efficiently. There is even disappointment among some that Hitler never actually made it across the Channel — for his reception would have been very hot.

All round Kent there were parades and hundreds of people in each town saw their Home Guard proudly march past for the last time. The official stand down was at Canterbury Cathedral where the Lord Lieutenant, Lord Cornwallis took the salute. He said: ..."We will remember with pride that when our tired Armies were retreating from Dunkirk, a citizens' army was rising in the south-east, ready to fight on the beaches, in the fields and in the streets to secure the breathing space the nation so urgently required. That citizens' army was you. the Home Guard of Kent."

Americans to hang for the rape and murder of a girl, 15

October 6th: Two American GI's have been sentenced "to hang by the neck until they are dead" for the rape and murder of a 15-year-old girl, whose body was found at the Old Cricket Ground, Black Path, Ashford.

Private Augustine Guerra, 20 and Corporal Ernest Lee Clark of the USSAF appeared separately before court martials at Ashford.

The trial heard the men had been drinking heavily on the night of August 22nd at The Smith's Arms. The girl, who had been to a fair, met the men at the end of Black Path.

Guerra, in a statement, said he held the girl down while Clark had sex with her. Thinking she had fainted they felt her heart before leaving. It was still beating.

A plea by the defence that the charge of murder be reduced to manslaughter was lost.

'Enjoy your stroll on the front, we have captured all of Jerry's Big Berthas!'

October 30th: The official confirmation that the big guns at Cap Gris Nez and Calais have been silenced at last came yesterday evening when Alderman Cairns, Mayor of Dover, received this telegram from the commander of the 9th Canadian Infantry Regiment.

"To the citizens of Dover. Greetings from the Brigade and may you enjoy your pint of beer and stroll on the front from now on. We have all of Jerry's Big Berthas."

Dover's reply came immediately: *"Thank you for your message just received and most grateful appreciation of the gallantry and skill of you and your officers in capture of Jerry's Big Berthas. We shall not enjoy our beer and stroll on the front to the full until you can join us in it. We wish you Godspeed."*

The final blitz on Hellfire Corner was more menacing than ever. As the Allies in France moved closer to the German stronghold, the 406mm guns of Batterie Lindemann and the 380mm guns of Batterie Todt opened up. Shells fell from Ramsgate to Hythe. Between September 1st and 26th, 54 people were killed — 40 in Dover. The town was shattered and desolate.

It was on Tuesday September 26th

Shell damage at Dover Marine Station

that the Canadians moved in for the final kill but, as a parting salvo, 50 shells were fired at Dover. One actually bored it way through 40 feet of chalk and several inches of concrete before exploding in the entrance of Barwick's Cave where a woman was killed. Others fells in Valley Road, River, Victoria Park, Tower Hamlets Street, Castle Street, Barton Road and Beaconsfield Avenue.

They still kept coming. Mayfield Avenue, St James Street, Castle Avenue, Green Lane, Queen's Street, the Ferry Dock, Biggin Street, Penchester Road.

At 7.15 a shell demolished two unoccupied shops at the corner of Castle Street and the Market Square. A policeman reported it and it was given a number — 67857.

That was the last German shell. Across the water, British and Canadian soldiers were making their final assault upon the cross-Channel guns. Just under 30,000 were taken prisoner.

'The Socialist Government hates freedom. I dare say it would suit them to keep rationing for ever.'
— Major J. Baker White, MP for Canterbury, speaking in the Corn Exchange, Maidstone.

January 5th: A B17 bomber returning from Central Germany crash-landed at Hawkinge today killing four of the crew. During the raid the port-inner engine had been shot away and the pilot killed. The navigator took over for the flight back to England but could not close the throttles fully and crabbed as he overshot Hawkinge. He and the tail-gunner have both survived.

January 4th: Geoffrey Fisher has been appointed Archbishop of Canterbury to succeed William Temple who died last year.

January 15th: The first boat train for five years today left Dover for the Continent.

January 27th: The Russians today entered Auschwitz and discovered the horrors of the Nazis' biggest extermination camp.

February 14th: The Royal Marines have been awarded the Freedom of Deal.

February 16th: There has been great criticism over the bombing of Dresden which was totally devastated by RAF bombers two days ago.

February 19th: A woman was killed in her bedroom when a V2 rocket fell near the church at Stoke, Isle of Grain. Yesterday, three people died when a rocket exploded at Rede Court, Strood.

March 27th: Ivy Millichamp, a 34-year-old housewife from Kynaston Road, Orpington, was killed today by a rocket launched in Holland. It may be the last one, for the rocket troops near The Hague are cornered.

April 12th: President Franklin D. Roosevelt died today aged 63. He is succeeded by Harry S. Truman.

April 28th: Mussolini has been killed by partisans in Italy.

April 30th: After a nine-day battle the Allies have captured Berlin. Hitler and his mistress Eva Braun are reported to have committed suicide.

The Conservative politician, Harold Macmillan, who lost his seat at Stockton-on-Tees in the general election, is the new MP for Bromley. In a by-election which followed the death of Sir Edward Campbell, Macmillan was an easy victor. An outspoken opponent of appeasement in the 1930s he was given a Government post in 1940 in the Ministry of Supply. Bromley's new member, who is 49, is also closely involved in the Macmillan publishing firm founded by his grandfather.

The Victoria Pier, Folkestone, has been destroyed by fire.

May 28th: William Joyce (Lord Haw Haw) has been captured. He once lived in Chatham and was well-known in Thanet.

July 15th: Britain is ablaze with light once more. After more than 2,000 nights of blackout and dim-out the great switch-on came last night.

June 18th: The demobilisation of British troops has begun. Each man may have a "demob" suit.

July 28th: 1,700 Kent Land Girls filled the nave of Canterbury Cathedral today in the presence of the Duchess of Kent for their official stand-down.

July 29th: The streets of Canterbury echoed to the rhythm of marching veterans today when the Kent British Legion revived their annual festival in the Cathedral. The parade was headed by the Buffs and the nave was massed with their standards.

August 11th: England's only remaining Quintain was restored to Offham Green today. Standing on a post 10 feet high with a cross-beam mounted on an iron spindle, it was once used by knights who would ride full gallop attempting to strike the cross beam and avoid being thrown from their horse by a blow from a sandbag swinging at the other end.

September 9th: Reports are coming in of atrocities by Japanese captors to Allied prisoners of war. Thousands of British prisoners have been killed or died from starvation. Returning prisoners are talking of executions and frequent beatings.

November 7th: An RAF Gloster Meteor today flew at 606 mph at Herne Bay. It is the fastest man has ever travelled.

November 20th: German leaders today go on trial at Nuremberg to answer for their crimes. Hitler's associates will sit before a tribunal formed by Britain, America, Russia and France.

Eltham Palace, where Henry V spent his first night as King and used as a family home by a succession of monarchs, has become headquarters of the Royal Army Educational Corps.

GREAT HITS OF 1945

We'll Gather Lilacs
in the Spring

Cruising Down the River

When the Lights go
on in London

July 30th: A vigilante group who operate from Brighton are helping homeless families in Kent to secure homes by just "taking over" unoccupied property.

Among those to benefit is L/Cpl Albert Simpkins of the RASC, who served his country well during the war years.

Simkins, his wife and two children had nowhere to live, having been evicted, and approached Tunbridge Wells council who said they had a long waiting list and couldn't help.

The Vigilantes took over and put L/Cpl Simkins and his family in a house in Upper Grosvenor Road, almost opposite High Brooms Station. Then they fetched his belongings.

Bishop Bell overlooked: Fisher gets the job

January 4th: Geoffrey Fisher, the 58-year-old Bishop of Chester, has been installed as Archbishop of Canterbury, with all the ceremonial pageantry afforded to such occasions. He succeeds the charismatic William Temple who died suddenly in October last year.

Fisher, well-known as the former headmaster of Repton School, is a fairly controversial choice for it was widely expected that George Bell, Bishop of Chichester, and the man who started the *Friends of Canterbury Cathedral* in the twenties, would be the automatic choice.

Bell, then Dean of Canterbury and the tireless Margaret Babington raised thousands of pounds for the Cathedral fund and he continued to show great interest in the progress of the "Friends" even after his appointment at Chichester in 1929. He was succeeded at the Deanery by Dick Shepherd and then Hewlett Johnson.

So why didn't this charming, knowledgeable Bishop become Primate? Perhaps it was something to do with his support for appeasement and opposition to war. Bell's views would not have been acceptable to Churchill.

Archbishop Temple will be sorely missed. He had described Canterbury as "the cradle of the nation's spiritual enlightenment" and had constructive views on the way the city should be rebuilt after the bombing.

The boys are coming home: another troop ship arrives at Folkestone.

PLUTO supplies vital fuel for the advancing army

February: One million gallons of petrol today is now flowing beneath the English Channel in a pipeline under the ocean, better known as PLUTO.

Easily enough to quench the thirst of the Allied vehicles moving steadily towards the German border, the pipeline is made of 12,000 tons of lead and 5,600 tons of steel. The tubes, manufactured in 750-yard lengths, were welded together at Littlestone railway station. They were then wound on to massive drums and towed across the Channel by two tugs.

The first PLUTO line was laid between the Isle of Wight and Cherbourg immediately after the peninsula had been captured. As the Allied armies advanced it was replaced almost immediately with a line from Dungeness to Boulogne.

The idea of a pipeline first came from Lord Louis Mountbatten who said victory could not be achieved unless the Allies had a constant supply of petrol. Trials were held and PLUTO was born.

In order not to arouse suspicion, "holiday bungalows" were built to conceal the pumping plant and high pressure pumps were hidden in the sand dunes. A network of pipes link the pumping stations to ports and oil refineries.

Death from the stratosphere at 3,500 mph

January: Thousands of people who made their homes in Chislehurst caves and the old lime pits at Swanscombe during the blitz have returned as rocket attacks on Kent and South London continue to claim many lives. A few weeks ago V2 rockets, launched in Holland, crashed in the centre of Gravesend. The first fell in Portland Avenue and killed five people. The second missile destroyed four homes and an engineering works in Milton Place, killed eight people and injured over 50. There was no warning. Just a flash, a double explosion and then...chaos.

At last Churchill has admitted that Britain is under attack from the second of Hitler's vengeance weapons. For several weeks the Government spoke of mystery gas-main explosions, but the Prime Minister told Parliament before Christmas that casualties caused by the long-range weapons have not been heavy.

He is right. Many have crashed harmlessly in rural areas. In fact Knockholt, Eastchurch, Chislet, Lullingstone, Borough Green, Bexleyheath, Orpington, Yalding, Ditton and Penshurst have all experienced the ghastly horror of a ballistic missile appearing from the stratosphere — at a speed that has revolutionised military strategy.

It is believed that the rocket travels at 3,500 mph, carries a ton of dynamite in its nose and is launched from mobile launching machines in The Hague. Churchill has said the rocket sites in Pas de Calais and Belgium have already been captured and it will not be long before Allied forces destroy the bases in the Netherlands.

The worst rocket incident of the campaign so far occurred on Saturday (November 25th) when a missile fell to the rear of Woolworth's in New Cross Road. The store, which was full of women and children, bulged slightly outwards then collapsed inwards in a great cloud of dust and smoke which mushroomed high in the air. Those inside stood no chance. Next door the Co-op also disintegrated, passers-by were lifted high in the air and thrown great distances. A bus spun round like a top, lorries overturned and people in nearby offices were killed at their desks. It took many days and nights to extricate the bodies and the official death toll has been given as 160.

It is believed that the rockets were intended to be launched from huge concrete firing bunkers in Northern France but these were destroyed by B17 Flying Fortresses in 1943. Eventually the A4 (as the V2 is known to the German scientists) was launched from mobile firing tables in Holland.

The Orpington rocket — is it the last?

March 28th: The liberation of Paris and Brussels and the steady advance of the Allies across the Rhine and into Germany means the rocket attacks on south-east England will soon be over.

Yesterday one exploded on a small estate at Kynaston Road, Orpington, injured 23 people and killed a 34-year-old housewife, Ivy Millichamp. She could well be the last victim. Unconfirmed reports suggest the Allies have captured the last rocket battery in The Hague.

Since the campaign began in September, 1,115 rockets have been fired at Britain and 64 have landed in Kent. Eight died when one exploded near the centre of Swanscombe, 10 died at Sutton-at-Hone a few days later. There have been further fatalities at Whitstable, Strood, Stoke, Woolwich, Sevenoaks, Westerham and Beckenham.

March: From photographs and maps captured from the Germans, more information is reaching the Allies about the A4 rocket. This shows a rocket in position on a Meiller trailer next to the inspection platform. It is believed that many of the early launch attempts failed but the scientists, led by Werner von Braun — the mastermind behind the ballistic missile — made constant improvements. More than 1,000 have now been fired at Britain and many have landed in Kent.

How this picture helped to win the war

Having taken several shots of the children in the trench, John Topham invited mums and dads to pose in a similar way. Few people have seen this photograph. It did not have the same appeal.

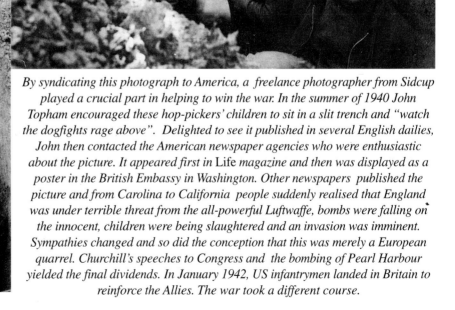

By syndicating this photograph to America, a freelance photographer from Sidcup played a crucial part in helping to win the war. In the summer of 1940 John Topham encouraged these hop-pickers' children to sit in a slit trench and "watch the dogfights rage above". Delighted to see it published in several English dailies, John then contacted the American newspaper agencies who were enthusiastic about the picture. It appeared first in Life *magazine and then was displayed as a poster in the British Embassy in Washington. Other newspapers published the picture and from Carolina to California people suddenly realised that England was under terrible threat from the all-powerful Luftwaffe, bombs were falling on the innocent, children were being slaughtered and an invasion was imminent. Sympathies changed and so did the conception that this was merely a European quarrel. Churchill's speeches to Congress and the bombing of Pearl Harbour yielded the final dividends. In January 1942, US infantrymen landed in Britain to reinforce the Allies. The war took a different course.*

The last survivor of Rorke's Drift dies at Beckenham

May 9th: Frank Bourne, one of Kent's most famous soldiers, died today just hours after learning the war had officially ended. As the last survivor of the defence of Rorke's Drift, Natal, where 130 British troops successfully fought off 4,000 Zulu warriors, Lt-Col Bourne had seen more than his fair share of tragedy in a particularly active life.

Bourne OBE DCM was a Colour Sergeant and later Lt-Col with the 24th Regiment of the South Wales Borderers in South Africa in January 1879 during the height of the Zulu War.

He knew little of the massacre at Isandhlwana where more than a thousand officers, NCOs and blacks were slaughtered by Zulus, because he and his men were holding the garrison at Rorke's Drift, some miles away.

In what has become a legendary battle the Welsh Borderers threw up defences and somehow held out for 12 hours as 4,000 Zulu warriors repeatedly attacked.

Bourne, who lived in Beckenham, will be interred in Elmers End Cemetery.

Front-line county celebrates freedom at last

May 9th: The second world war is over. The Third Reich, which Hitler said would last 1,000 years, is dead. Hitler is also dead having shot himself just 36 hours after marrying his mistress Eva Braun.

Today, Kent celebrated the first day of peace since September 2nd, 1939, in a variety of ways. At Ramsgate the deck chairs on the sands were fully occupied and people swam in the sea. At Folkestone, airmen from Hawkinge and Lympne appeared in the streets in their pyjamas. At Dover a few people climbed Shakespeare Cliff and looked across the Channel waters to Cap Griz Nez. No longer could they see the great guns of Calais or the intensive German activity. There were no fighters or bombers in the sky, no high explosives, incendiaries or parachute mines. The last doodlebug had long since left its launching ramp and the rocket men in Holland had retreated or surrendered to the Americans.

To mark the occasion all schools in Kent will be closed for two days. Public houses have been granted an extension of licensing hours. On Sunday thanksgiving services will be held in every church in the county.

The civilian casualty list shows that more than 1,608 people in Kent were killed and nearly 2,500 seriously injured. Of these many more may die of their wounds. In the north Kent metropolitan boroughs of Beckenham, Bromley and Erith and the districts of Chislehurst and Sidcup, Crayford, Orpington and Penge, a further 1,366 died with 3,670 seriously wounded.

Dover, Canterbury and Ashford have suffered the most fatalities while Dartford Rural is easily the most bombed borough, having received more than 5,000 explosives and approximately 200,000 incendiaries.

During the next few weeks there will be many speeches praising the work of the Civil Defence personnel for their vigilance, devotion, high standard of efficiency and most of all for their defiance during the dark years.

The Home Guard and Fire Watching Parties stood down in December. NFS stations have now been amalgamated and the ARP rescue teams disbanded. Today (Wednesday) Kent units of the Civil Defence will stand down.

On Sunday after the church services there will be big parades, the majority against the background of blitzed buildings and bombsites. Already there are Union Jacks everywhere and large bonfires are appearing. On top there are no Guy Fawkes. The effigy is that of Hitler.

No one deserves this moment more than the people of Dover where 199 people died and nearly 4,000 homes were severely, if not completely, wrecked. Many children under six years old do not know what it is like to sleep in their own beds.

Yesterday, Dover harbour greeted Churchill's official declaration by sounding the sirens. Ships were dressed for the occasion. For more than an hour no-one could speak for they couldn't be heard. The sirens were deafening. On Sunday, Dover Castle will be floodlit as a final symbol of the defiance of Hellfire Corner.

The war is over.

May 13th: One man who has not been able to join in the victory celebrations but did more than most to bring about peace is Admiral Sir Bernard Ramsay who was in command at Dover from 1939 until 1942. Sir Bernard was killed in an air crash near Paris in January.

Today (Sunday) a special service will be held in Dover to remember the man who masterminded *Operation Dynamo* in 1940 and eventually became Commander-in-Chief of the naval forces for *Operation Overlord*, the allied invasion of France.

Labour takes eight Kent seats in election landslide

July 26th: For the first time in history, Labour is in power with a decisive and overwhelming majority and Winston Churchill — regarded everywhere as Britain's wartime saviour — has been rejected. With a landslide majority of 180 seats, Clement Attlee is the new Prime Minister.

In Kent, Labour has eight seats in the 16 constituencies, gaining six and holding two. The greatest surprise is that the Tories have lost one of their major strongholds. Dover was captured by Labour for the first time and they also won the new constituency of Bexley.

The Labour gains were at Chatham, Chislehurst, Faversham, Gillingham and Gravesend. The Conservative Party has held onto — Ashford, Bromley, Canterbury, Hythe, Thanet, Maidstone, Sevenoaks and Tonbridge.

The new Government has been elected for its "Let Us Face The Future" manifesto which has a detailed programme of social reform and public ownership. With the death of Roosevelt there will be two new faces at the Postdam conference tomorrow — Attlee and Harry Truman.

Full results are as follows:

ASHFORD: E.P.Smith (Con) 18,800, H.W.Lee (Lab) 12,575, H.V.Strong (Lib) 4,804. **Cons majority 6,225.** No change.

CANTERBURY: J.White (Con) 24,280, J.D.Bell (Lab) 14,115, Mrs Williamson (CW) 1017. **Cons majority 10,165.** No change.

DOVER: J.R.Thomas (Lab) 17,373, J.Arbuthnot (Con) 15,691. **Majority 1,682:** Labour gain.

MAIDSTONE: A.C.Bossom (Con) 21,320, O.Shaw (Lab) 18,295, G.Murray (Dem) 416. **Cons majority 3,025.** No change.

ROCHESTER/CHATHAM: A.G.Bottomley (Lab) 19,250, L.F.Plugge (Con) 15,534. **Majority 3,716.** Labour gain.

SEVENOAKS: C.E.Ponsonby (Con) 18,893, J.Pudney (Lab) 14,947, Miss Muspratt (Lib) 6,906, K.Thompson (Com) 676. **Cons majority 3,946.** No change.

BEXLEY: Mrs Adamson (Lab) 24,686, J.C.Lockwood (Con) 12,923, W.Smith (Lib) 5,750. **Lab majority 11,763.**

CHISLEHURST: G.Wallace (Lab) 25,522, N.Fisher (Con) 19,243, C.Hawkins (Lib) 6,824. **Majority 6,279.** Labour gain.

DARTFORD: N.Dodds (Lab) 36,666, R.E.Grubb (Con) 16,951. **Lab majority 19,715.** No change.

FAVERSHAM: P.L.Wells (Lab) 23,502, Sir A. Maitland (Con) 21,037. **Majority 2,465.** Labour gain.

HYTHE: H.R.Mackeson (Con) 8,048, D.Widdicombe (Lab) 6,091, Capt A.James (Lib) 3,152. **Cons majority 1,957.** No change.

ORPINGTON: Sir W.Smithers (Con) 20,388, Col A.R.Mais (Lab) 15,846, F.R.Goodfellow (Lib) 5,140, D.G.Milner (Ind) 528. **Cons majority 4,542.** No change.

GILLINGHAM: J.Binns (Lab) 15,110, J.B.Dodge (Con) 13,254. **Majority 1,856.** Labour gain.

TONBRIDGE: Lt-Cmdr William (Con) 23,081, Miss V.Dart (Lab) 16,590, J.Metcalf (Lib) 5,351. **Cons majority 6,491.** No change.

GRAVESEND: G.Allighan (Lab) 21,609, Sir I.Albery (Con) 14,553, R.Goodfellow (Lib) 5,033. **Majority 7,056.** Labour gain.

ISLE OF THANET: Hon F.Carson (Con) 15,023, T.C.Boyd (Lab) 12,075, P.J.Willmett (Lib) 3,732. **Con majority 2,918.** No change.

Albert Tester of Broadstairs may have been Gestapo chief

May: Ramsgate's pre-war dentist, Brigadier J. Morley Stebbings, has confirmed that the "mysterious" German intelligence agent killed by the Russians in Castle Mintia, Rumania, is Dr Albert Tester.

Dr Tester lived at Naldera, a clifftop mansion immediately below the North Foreland lighthouse, but disappeared a few days before war broke out in the summer of 1939. Locals say he escaped by rowing out to a waiting submarine having heard that Kent police were becoming increasingly suspicious about his motives.

People in Broadstairs thought that was the end of the story but last year a German officer, believed to be Dr Tester, was shot and killed by advancing Russians when his car swerved and plunged into a ditch after crashing through a road barrier. No positive identification was made. A few weeks ago, at the request of Britain, the Russian authorities exhumed his body. Confirmation came from Brigadier Morley Stebbings who examined his teeth.

No definite details have been issued but it is believed that Dr Tester was a Gestapo chief in Kent preparing the ground for the control of the county in the event of a successful invasion. He lived at Naldera for a number of years with his wife and five children.

VJ tea parties have been held all over Kent. Here are the happy children and residents of Lower Road in the Foster Clark Estate, Maidstone.

Atom bomb vaporises Japanese cities

August 14th: The Japanese War is over. Tokyo surrendered unconditionally today following the explosion of the most devastating bomb mankind has known. On August 6th, the USAAF B29 bomber *Enola Gay* dropped the atom bomb on Hiroshima killing an estimated 80,000 people from blast and burns. Others may die from the effects of radiation. Three days later the target was the shipbuilding port of Nagasaki.

A British physicist, working for the Government's top secret armament research and development establishment at Fort Halstead, near Sevenoaks, was one of the prominent scientists behind the "wonder weapon". Dr William Penney who lives at Belgrave Road, Sheerness, carried out the basic research for the bomb before the US came into the war. It was his plan to implode segments of plutonium to form a critical mass in which neutrons would split the atomic nuclei.

When the full scale of the enterprise became clear all work was transferred to the United States where it was designed and built and renamed the "Manhattan Project".

Four days ago Dr Penney was the British observer along with Wing Commander Leonard Cheshire in the American bomber which flew over Nagasaki. He saw the bomb in its descent and then the smoke and dust and debris rise five miles in the air in a giant mushroom-shaped cloud. Tokyo claimed that a further 70,000 people had perished and demanded peace talks immediately.

The world's first atomic bomb has 2,000 times the blast power of Britain's "grand slam" bomb which was dropped on German cities. It exploded with a force equivalent to 20,000 tons of TNT. It fused sand into glass and released

(continued next page)

Now comes the task of rebuilding

so much energy in a chain reaction that scientists themselves were terrified by the power. It is already being described as one of the most controversial acts in history — "an atrocity," says Tokyo — a device which could end the world.

The US troops in East Kent were the first to show their delight at the news of the surrender. People asleep in Folkestone were woken by an announcement from a jeep. In the Thames Estuary, at Gravesend, the ships' sirens signalled the good news. County Hall made the official announcement at 3pm today. There will be victory celebrations again, perhaps a little more muted because many feel the Japanese surrender is a distant affair and the dropping of the atom bomb a revenge for the bombing of Pearl Harbour.

Tonight, at 9pm, the King will broadcast to the nation. He will call for the people to restore the shattered fabric of civilisation. Nowhere is the fabric more shattered than here in the front-line county of Kent. It is going to be a long task, but surely a rewarding one.

Civilian casualties, damage and bombs

(excluding the Kent boroughs in London Civil Defence Regions)

Local Authority	Killed	Seriously injured	Slightly injured	Property wrecked	Severely damaged	HE Bombs	Incendiary bombs (approx)	Flying bombs
Ashford area	103	162	245	184	393	974	12,645	184
Bridge-Blean	29	35	84	81	151	1,364	18,300	13
Broadstairs	7	6	48	18	163	278	300	3
Canterbury	115	140	240	808	1,047	445	10,000	1
Chatham	47	47	225	297	454	267	1,535	nil
Dartford MB	92	72	205	174	357	553	11,982	14
Dartford RD	50	80	280	120	894	5,359	200,000	76
Deal	64	55	198	172	718	173	118	nil
Dover MB	199	307	420	910	2,998	464	1,500	3
Dover RD	5	10	8	36	141	389	2,380	21
Eastry RD	20	32	57	27	65	667	1,700	8
Elham RD	15	15	57	27	203	930	6,500	64
Faversham	17	26	60	12	29	442	1,283	15
Folkestone	85	181	484	290	1,486	378	1,113	29
Gillingham	57	68	184	168	359	275	3,885	3
Gravesend	38	81	202	45	211	292	300,000	3
Herne Bay	9	21	39	12	45	104	1,090	1
Hollingbourne	10	20	38	11	170	946	1,720	81
Hythe	24	36	106	96	385	79	nil	11
Maidstone MB	60	105	182	127	210	264	1,000	6
Maidstone RD	9	16	59	22	198	689	7,000	63
Malling RD	46	62	164	36	287	1,979	11,332	97
Margate	35	40	201	268	592	584	2,489	nil
New Romney	12	32	52	61	218	718	3,823	149
Northfleet	40	47	39	35	104	362	11,000	4
Queenborough	Nil	nil	5	nil	1	52	1,000	nil
Ramsgate	84	89	139	393	418	860	283	nil
Rochester	75	86	360	276	1,221	238	14	5
Sandwich	Nil	2	8	7	107	52	1,000	nil
Sevenoaks UD	22	59	111	42	133	98	4,000	5
Sevenoaks RD	62	70	188	86	169	3,259	53,500	137
Sheppey RD	8	13	8	12	39	633	680	5
Sheerness	2	nil	18	8	4	23	150	nil
Sittingbourne	31	47	109	64	153	828	17,000	19
Southborough	Nil	1	18	nil	45	23	15	5
Strood RD	8	32	74	29	162	1,983	22,987	35
Swanscombe	62	105	141	93	367	211	5,000	10
Tenterden area	21	64	151	34	235	704	3,500	238
Tonbridge UD	9	27	101	17	232	142	1,200	11
Tonbridge RD	11	45	30	14	157	673	3,400	95
Tunbridge Wells	15	31	36	13	113	186	660	6
Whitstable	10	35	118	84	735	232	700	2
Total	1,608	2,402	5,492	5,209	16,170	29,272	727,784	1,422

Sixth baron is among Kent's 12 VCs

A PEER of the realm is among the 12 Men of Kent or Kentish Men who have won the Victoria Cross for conspicuous acts of bravery on the battlefield — and they represent all three services.

Major William Philip Sidney, aged 37, of Penshurst Place, who became the 6th Baron de L'Isle and Dudley on the death of his father last year, won his award for a conspicuous act of bravery in Italy. Lord de L'Isle is a descendant of Sir Philip Sidney, the poet-soldier, who died for his country in 1582.

Major Sidney and his 5th Battalion Grenadier Guards were among the Allies of the Fifth Army who landed in the Anzio district on the Italian coast south of Rome, in January last year. They found themselves surrounded by the enemy who had brought up fresh troops, supported by tanks and big artillery concentrations.

During the night of February 7th-8th Major Sidney led successful attacks against the enemy, engaging them with his Tommy gun at point-blank range. His action inspired his men to regain lost ground with a brilliant succession of counter attacks.

Later in the year, also in Italy, **John Henry Cound Brunt** of Paddock Wood also confronted the enemy single-handed and showed similar aggressive and inspiring leadership.

Brunt, a captain with the Sherwood Foresters, attached to the Lincolnshire Regiment, was at Faenza with his platoon when their post was destroyed by mortar fire.

Brunt, who is 22, held the enemy on his own while his men moved to an alternative position. Firing a Bren gun he killed 14 and then fired a Piat and a 2m mortar left by the casualties. He was able eventually to get his wounded away. The enemy withdrew.

Wing Commander Roderick Learoyd of New Romney won his VC in August 1940 when he was a Flight Lieutenant with 49 Squadron and briefed to bomb the Dortmund-Ems canal.

He took his plane into the target at only 150 feet, in the full glare of searchlights and flak barrage all round him. Although his aircraft was badly damaged, the bombs were dropped and he managed to get back to England without further damage or injury to his crew.

There are two posthumous Victoria Crosses for Kent's Arnhem heroes. **Captain Lionel Ernest Queripel** of Warwick Place, Tunbridge Wells, was trapped with his unit of the Royal Sussex Regiment during the bid to seize the bridges over the Rhine.

For nine hours his men were involved in a bitter battle and Captain Queripel was wounded on three occasions.

Major Philip Sidney receives the Victoria Cross from General Alexander. Among those present at this ceremony was Viscount John Gort, Major Sidney's father-in-law.

Eventually he decided to cover his men's withdrawal and was last seen facing the enemy alone with a pistol in one hand and a hand grenade in the other.

Lance Corporal Henry Eric Harden of Colyer Road, Northfleet also died. He was with the Royal Medical Corps and on two occasions risked enemy fire to bring in wounded colleagues, ordering a Bren gun to give cover. He was wounded and his smock ripped to pieces but he carried on. On the third occasion he attempted to bring in a wounded officer who was fully exposed to enemy fire. He reached the man but fell with a sniper's bullet through his head.

Squadron Leader Robert Palmer of Gillingham was leading a formation of Lancasters with 109 Squadron in December 1944 with a mission to attack marshalling yards in daylight. He came under heavy anti-aircraft fire but managed to keep the badly damaged aircraft on a straight course and release his bombs. His Lancaster was last seen spiralling to earth in flames.

Two Kent men who were fighting at St Nazaire, France, on March 27th, 1942, have also won the Victoria Cross. **Sergeant Frank Durrant** of the Royal Corps Engineers, whose family live at Green Street Green, near Orpington, was in charge of a Lewis gun on a motor launch which came under heavy fire.

Sergeant Durrant had no protection and was wounded in several places but he refused to surrender and continued

Captain John Brunt

Squadron Leader Robert Palmer

Captain Lionel Queripel

Lance Corporal Eric Harden

Wing Commander Roderick Learoyd

Lance Corporal John Harman
see page 148

firing until the launch was boarded and those who were alive taken away. He died the next day.

Lt Colonel Augustus Newman of Sandwich was the first man ashore with his commando unit in the St Nazaire raid, directing operations quite regardless of his own safety. He and his men were eventually overwhelmed and taken prisoner.

A Bexleyheath man, **Lieutenant (later Captain) Richard Stannard,** received his VC for action in Norway where his ship *HMS Arab* survived 31 bombing attacks in five days. He also saved a pier from being destroyed by fire and shot down a bomber.

Lt-Commander Eugene Esmonde (second left) with officers and ratings, decorated for the part they played in the sinking of the Bismarck. Esmonde was posthumously awarded the VC in February 1942. See page 130.

Green Belt will protect rural Kent from the giant sprawl

November: The drift of England's population from the industrial north to the south east has been threatening the integrity of the "green belt" for some years but thanks to Professor Patrick Abercrombie there will be no development in the countryside that surrounds London and a limit will be placed on the size of towns which encircle the capital.

The Abercrombie Report, just published, is of enormous importance to a town such as Sevenoaks which stands out as an island surrounded by deep emerald. There, the population will be limited to 17,000 — and, unlike Bromley, Beckenham and Sidcup, it will never be allowed to be swallowed by the metropolis. The chalk Downs to the north will remain a physical barrier.

The report also recommends the creation of a ring of small new towns around London and the setting up of a regional planning board.

Although the ladies of the WVS did their best to "protect" the American GI's from what they called "good time girls" by setting up welcome clubs and encouraging private hospitality, hundreds of young women from Kent have, not only danced with and been wooed by but also, married their gum-chewing, jitterbug-dancing friends from the other side of the water. About 80,000 "GI brides" are leaving England — many with children— to join their husbands in the United States and dozens come from Kent. Here they are at Waterloo Station on their way to Southampton and the Queen Mary. One girl from Tenterden said: "It wasn't only the PX nylons and cigarettes but their charm which took us by storm. Those gorgeous boys could shoot a line and it gave an enormous lift to the female population in my locality."

'I wish peace to the world' — The last words of Joachim von Ribbentrop, Foreign Minister in the Nazi regime at the execution chamber in Nuremberg.

January 1st: British exports are half the pre-war figure and government expenditure abroad is four times greater than that before the war. The country is heavily in debt and vast sums are needed to reclothe, feed and house the people. The Government is planning the introduction of a Welfare State.

Test flights have begun at Heath Row where a major new airport is planned.

February 7th: A world food crisis means that all rations are to be reduced.

February 23rd: Lilian Mabel Miller, 30-year-old wife of a Canadian soldier, has been found dead in allotments near the Sturry Road, Canterbury. It is believed she was strangled and a murder hunt is under way.

February 25th: Grocer's shops in Maidstone are selling bananas for the first time since1939. For many children this is their first taste of the Caribbean fruit.

March 1st: The Bank of England has been nationalised.

March 5th: Winston Churchill has spoken of an "iron curtain" descending across the Continent. In a speech in America he said Russia might even be preparing to spread Communist tyranny across the whole free world. He said: "The dark ages may return on the gleaming wings of science".

March 9th: 33 football fans were killed today and 500 badly hurt when steel barriers collapsed at the Bolton Wanderers' ground.

March 28th: Kent schoolchildren along with those in the rest of the country are to get free school milk and dinners.

May 16th: The Prime Minister, Clement Attlee, has unveiled plans for a united and independent India.

June 14th: The television pioneer John Logie Baird died

The black chiffon blouse and the lilac pink hat have been made from old evening dresses. This is still the age of "make-do and mend".

today at Bexhill-on-Sea. He was 58.

July 15th: The Kent County Agricultural Show has resumed on 30 acres of land at Mote Park, Maidstone.

July 16th: Number 46 Transport Command has taken control of Manston aerodrome. For the past few months it has been used as an RAF and Civil aerodrome with Dakotas appearing in increasing numbers.

September 29th: The BBC has announced plans for a Third Programme on the wireless.

Clement Attlee has opened the Temple Hill housing estate at Dartford.

October 12th: Ten days after his DH 108 jet plane exploded in mid-air and crashed into the Thames Estuary, the body of Geoffrey de Havilland, 36-year-old ace test pilot, of the de Havilland Aircraft Company, has been washed ashore at Whitstable. The coroner said: "This fine young man has given his life for the future of England."

October 16th: With the notable exception of Hitler's deputy, Martin Boorman, who is believed to be dead, and Hermann Goering, who has committed suicide, ten top Nazi war criminals have been hanged at Nuremberg. First to enter the execution chamber was von Ribbontrop who was so well known in Thanet before the war.

November 6th: A carriage museum in the former stables of the Archbishop's Manor House, Maidstone, is open to the public.

November 22nd: An Hungarian journalist, Ladislao Biro, has introduced a new pen which can write 200,000 words without refilling, blotting or smudging. It is known as "The Biro".

November 28th: According to a report today a "tidal wave" of divorce is sweeping Britain.

December 18th: MPs have approved the nationalisation of railways, road haulage and ports. No decision has yet been made on the iron and steel industry.

John Aris, one of the last Wealden hoop makers has retired after 60 years in the business. Hoops have been used by coopers or barrel makers for hundreds of years and the industry once flourished in the Weald of Kent.

Obituary: Lord Hayter of Chislehurst has died at the age of 98. Better known as Sir George Chubb, founder of the lock and safe company, he lived for many years at Newlands, Chislehurst Common.

Obituary: Major the Hon Bowes-Lyon, uncle to Her Majesty Queen Elizabeth, died at his home in Crockham Street, Westerham. Bowes-Lyon was well known in Edenbridge where he had been a church warden for many years.

Obituary: Viscount John Standish Surtees Prendergast Vereker Gort VC, DSO, MC GCB, KCB, Commander-in-Chief of British Expeditionary Forces in the Second World War, ADC to George V1 1940-44, Governor of Malta 1942-44, then High Commissioner for Palestine 1944-45. John Gort is the father-in-law to Lord de L'Isle of Penshurst. He has been interred in a vault at St John the Baptist, Penshurst.

GREAT HITS OF 1946

It's a Pity to Say Goodnight
A Gal in Calico

1946

Knole and Chartwell are given to the National Trust

Churchill and Lord Sackville will have lifetime tenures

January: Two of Kent's finest historic houses, Knole at Sevenoaks (above) and Chartwell, near Westerham, have been presented to the National Trust.

Winston Churchill, now facing the harsh realities of an austerity-ridden peace, will continue to live at Chartwell — thanks to an anonymous group of friends who have purchased the house and given it to the Trust on condition that Winston has a lifetime tenure of the property.

The gift came in the nick of time for Churchill, who with last year's election defeat still weighing heavily, had contemplated selling Chartwell and moving away. Now he can continue to write and paint and prepare his war memoirs. He also plans to buy Chartwell Farm and Bardogs and take up farming.

Lord Sackville's decision to present Knole to the Trust, together with an endowment for its upkeep, is less of a surprise. With 365 rooms, numerous courtyards and a garden of four acres, it is more like a fortified mediaeval town than the home of a single family, and the tax burden is tremendous. Lord Sackville cannot afford to maintain the house and its valuable contents at his own expense.

Kent writer Richard Church says: "I cannot begin to describe its treasures, either indoors or out. There it stands, among its monumental trees and groves, with the deer drifting like the ghosts of heraldry over the bracken and under the shadows of the castle walls."

For the National Trust, the once-tiny charity founded by Octavia Hill and her friends almost 50 years ago, the acquisition of Knole and Chartwell represents a milestone in its history. Both Lord Sackville and Churchill believe it is natural and reasonable that such magnificent houses should come into public ownership so that the right to use them and enjoy them may be for ever secured for the community.

Mosaic pavements and Christian warriors discovered

January 19th: The archaeologists who are carefully uncovering a fourth century Roman mosaic pavement in Butchery Lane, Canterbury, this week have had another thrilling surprise. Not far away, in the village square of Lenham, workmen have unearthed human skeletons believed to be Saxon.

The skeletons, which are in good condition, are of two men and a woman. The men are of average height, one with a perfect set of teeth and each buried with his shield and sword. With the woman is a small bronze buckle. It is believed they may be Christians.

They were found in the corner of the Clock House, part of a late fourteenth century house, recently occupied by a watchmaker.

The mosaic pavement in Canterbury has been uncovered in the cellar opposite the City Arms. Samian pottery has also been found along with a small bronze coin, circa 350 AD. The archaeologists are now uncovering a second mosaic pavement nearby and work will begin on a third in the Easter holidays.

King and Queen tour the desolate wilderness of Canterbury

July 14th: The King and Queen and Princess Elizabeth visited Canterbury yesterday to attend a special service of thanksgiving for the preservation of the Cathedral from destruction during the war. Their tour included a drive through the devastated streets with the Lord Lieutenant, Lord Cornwallis.

They saw what was left of the main shopping area on either side of St George's Street and the rickety tower of the church, which some people feel can be saved. They saw the huge area of devastation from Watling Street in the south-west to Burgate. They saw the remains of the Corn Exchange and Longmarket, the fenced-off rubble of the Royal Fountain Hotel and the damage in the Precincts. The royal party heard that the city received 445 high explosive bombs plus an estimated 10,000 incendiaries and that 800 buildings were demolished.

The day was also a great occasion for King's School, the oldest and worst-bombed school in England, for the King presented a new Charter exclusively for the school as distinct from the Cathedral.

August 15th: For the first time in history a commoner has been installed as Lord Warden of the Cinque Ports. Resplendent in his ceremonial uniform and accompanied by his wife Clementine, Mr Winston Churchill yesterday heard the Archbishop quote his famous speech — "Never in the field of human conflict......" He then said: "In the new Lord Warden we have a man who, during the years of our greatest peril and achievement, kept watch and ward over England, over the Empire and over freedom." For the citizens of Dover and for the thousands more who had come to the town the highlight of the day was the procession from the church to St Martin's Priory. At one time the Lord Warden vied with the King himself in power and influence and Dover made the very best of the occasion.

OBITUARY

H.G.Wells — "the man who made everyone else seem like a dull dog"

August 14th: Herbert George Wells (better known as HG), novelist and pioneer of science fiction, died yesterday just a few weeks before his eightieth birthday at his home in Hanover Terrace.

The son of a Bromley shopkeeper and former Kent cricketer, Wells wrote a series of novels about lower middle-class life but was better known for his original works of science fiction.

He used the dislocation of time and space to comment on our own society in *The Time Machine* (written in a flat in Sevenoaks), *The Invisible Man, The War of the Worlds* and *The First Men in The Moon*.

Wells lived at Spade House, Sandgate, Folkestone, for a number of years after the turn of the century. He was an active member of the Fabian Society until he fell out with its most famous member, G.B. Shaw, and a firm believer in sexual freedom.

In 1912, Wells published *Marriage*, advocating free love. It was so brilliantly reviewed by Rebecca West, the writer and feminist, that Wells suggested they should meet. The result was a 10-year love affair.

In the early thirties, Wells predicted there would be another war within 10 years and, in 1936, he wrote a film script *The Shape of Things to Come* warning of the perils of an atom bomb. Just before he died he spoke about the explosion in Hiroshima and how he hoped to treat it for a film sequel to his original script.

An obituary notice today by his great friend, J.B. Priestley says: "Of all the English writers I have known, he was the most honest, the frankest, the one least afraid of telling the truth. If he has offended public opinion, that is chiefly because English public opinion feeds itself with cant and humbug.."

George Orwell in the *Manchester Evening News* writes: "No writer has so deeply influenced his contemporaries. He was so big a figure, he has played so great a part in forming our picture of the world that in agreeing or disagreeing we are apt to forget his purely literary achievements."

It is alleged that Wells has seduced and then abandoned scores of women. Rebecca West says: "He was no Don Juan who discarded women so readily; he was more often discarded himself. This tale of multiple disaster is the more extraordinary because the women who left him all felt enduring affection for him and were his friends in old age. His hold over them derived from his charm....with no personal advantage but a bright eye he made everyone else in the room seem like a dull dog."

Biggin Hill's memorial chapel destroyed by fire

The little memorial chapel, established at RAF Biggin Hill in memory of the 453 aircrew who lost their lives during the war, has been destroyed by fire. Padre Cecil King made the gruesome discovery yesterday and found that little could be salvaged apart from the charred visitors' book in which one name is still legible — Winston S. Churchill.

The chapel, housed in a disused army hut, was dedicated in 1943 by the then station commander,

'Sailor' Malan. During the service he unveiled a reredos which bore the names of Dunkirk, Dieppe and the Battle of Britain and contained the names of every pilot who took off over under the colours of the Biggin Hill Wing never to return.

Knowing that Biggin Hill has never lost a battle, Padre King is devoting his energies into building a new Chapel. An appeal will be launched soon.

October 19th: Kippington Court, an impressive mansion in Sevenoaks, has been formally handed to the British Legion to be used as a convalescent home for ex-servicemen and women. The house, re-named Churchill Court, was acquired recently by Mr C.A. Hopkins who presented it to Mr and Mrs Churchill. Mr Churchill, in turn, presented it to the Legion.

'Meopham New Town' offers hope for the homeless

September: The picturesque village of Meopham, famous for its windmill and large village green, is one of the localities earmarked to become a new satellite town of London where the homelessness problem becomes more acute every day.

Villagers are incensed but new homes will have to be provided somewhere for the "blitzed" Londoners. Every day more and more men are being demobilised, bitterness is growing and squatters are moving into empty military camps and gun sites.

Of the 60,000 new houses planned by the Government, two-thirds will be prefabricated buildings and, in the Dartford area, the first 40 have already been opened at East Hill, South Darenth. A further 100 are being erected on sites at Swanley and Stone.

The first "prefab" to be officially opened at South Darenth is occupied by Mr and Mrs James Adair and their daughter Maureen. The family have been trying for three years to get a house of their own.

Many homes are woefully inadequate with outside toilets, no bathrooms, no running hot water and oil lamps for lighting. A lucky few are getting council flats or houses.

The really lucky people are those who will soon move into permanent brick houses. 140 are under construction in Canterbury and the first two will be opened soon by the mayor. At Erith, 120 houses are available and the council is planning a lottery among the 1,300 who have applied.

There is also considerable building work scheduled in the Kennington and Kingsnorth areas of Ashford.

Distressed Duchess may have to sell her treasures

September: It has been revealed that the beautiful and elegant Duchess of Kent, one of the busiest and most popular members of the Royal family, has no public income whatsoever and will soon be forced to sell art treasures collected by her husband.

Sources close to the family are shocked to learn that the former Princess Marina of Greece, who married the Duke of Kent in 1934, does not receive an income from the Civil List. That ceased when the Duke was killed in 1942. Apparently he was not a rich man and the little money he left was placed in trust for his children.

It has also been revealed that the Duchess does not receive an RAF pension as the widow of an Air Commodore. She had refused to accept it because she wanted to make a contribution at the time to the war effort. Today she is in desperate financial straits with three children to look after (Prince Edward, Prince Michael and Princess Alexandra), a large establishment to run and a high standard to maintain.

Fortunately she is able to sell her late husband's collection of antique furniture, pictures and silver amassed, wisely as it turns out, from his legacy left by King George V. The auction will be conducted by Christie's early next year.

Ever since her marriage to Prince George, the Duchess has enjoyed an adoring following but she feels a little humiliated by having to sell his treasures, particularly pieces made by Hepplewhite and Chippendale.

There is even talk of the Duchess being offered a contract to star in a Hollywood film. That has been denied.

Triumphant miners say goodbye to their 'capitalist' owners

January 1st: This is the moment the Kent coalminers have been waiting for. As New Year's Day dawned, the flags, the speeches, the bunting and the excitement among the men signalled that the new era in the coal mining industry had finally arrived. From today the pits belong to the nation. It is the first part of the new Government's nationalisation programme.

On Saturday (January 4th), Tilmanstone will hold a large party and the following day the Betteshanger Colliery Band will march through the village where the oldest underground worker, 72-year-old George Walker, will hoist the National Coal Board (NCB) flag. Socialist heartbeats are quickening in the Kent collieries. This is goodbye to Pearson and Long — their former "hated capitalist owners".

Rear Admiral H.R.M.Woodhouse, chairman of the south east divisional board, said the NCB and the miners now want to work together as a family. "The board are going to introduce pit launderies and improved canteen standards," he said. In reply the chairman of the Betteshanger branch of the National Union of Mineworkers said his men would set a target of 20,000 tons of coal per week.

Kent currently has four pits with an annual turnover of £3 million. There are 1,600 colliery houses at Aylesham, Betteshanger, Elvington and Hersden and other facilities include the aerial ropeway to Dover Harbour, the central repair depot at Richborough and the briquette making plant at Tilmanstone.

There are also plans to open two new collieries and improve the ventilation shafts on the coalface. The miners and the coal board know there are still billions of tons of coal under the Kent countryside.

Mixed in with the celebrations and enthusiastic plans, however, are doubts for the immediate future. A fuel crisis is looming. Coal exports are down. There is considerable absenteeism in the collieries. The Kent miners may have to wait awhile for the New Jerusalem.

January 1st: Miners of the Snowdown Colliery, Nonington, have just completed their best weekly output — and smashed their target by 40 per cent by producing 13,863 tons in a week. Photograph shows the undermanager (right centre), J.Griffiths, congratulating his colleagues. The scoreboard is above.

'We must build a United States of Europe. In this way only will hundreds of millions of toilers be able to regain the simple joys and hopes which make life worth living' — Winston Churchill.

1947

January 8th: A strike by road haulage workers has left thousands of tons of meat and other food-stuffs to rot in warehouses. The army has been called in to help with supplies.

January 22nd: The meat ration has been cut to even less — only one shilling's worth per person per week. There has been an increase in the allowance of corned beef.

January 29th: As the weather deteriorates, power cuts cause chaos throughout Britain. Steelworks have been closed through a lack of coal.

January 31st: Following the massacre of eight Britons by Jewish terrorists, British women and children and "non-essential" civilians are being evacuated from the UN mandated territory of Palestine.

February 8th: Thomas Lamont, partner in the famous American banking firm of J.P. Morgan and Co, has given £124,000 towards the restoration of Canterbury Cathedral.

February 12th: More than four million workers have been made idle by power cuts. Thousands of homes are without heat or light.

February 20th: Lord Louis Mountbatten has been appointed Viceroy of India in order to preside over independence plans.

February 22nd: The atrocious weather has led to the cancellation of most matches in the football championship this month. Domestic fuel rationing seems likely as the cold spell continues.

March 3rd: Power has been restored at last and Britain returns to work.

March 11th: Sir Waldron Smithers, MP for Orpington, told the House of Commons today that Lord Nelson's arm has been removed from the figurehead at the Royal Naval Barracks, Chatham, and he feels there is Communist influence behind this vandalism.

March 18th: Philip Mountbatten has become a naturalised Briton.

Summer: Thanks to German prisoners of war who have helped to restore the New Romney, Hythe and Dymchurch miniature railway to its pre-war glory, the line has now re-opened and is already proving very popular among holiday-makers to the area. The opening ceremony was performed by the two funniest men in show-business, Stan Laurel and Oliver Hardy, on tour in this country, who brought their slapstick humour to Hythe. It is only a few years ago that the little train was equipped with an anti-aircraft gun to defend itself and the locality from the Luftwaffe. When it was handed back to its owner the line and rolling stock were in a sorry state.

April 2nd: A report says that the recent flooding in England has killed two million sheep and damaged 500,000 acres of wheat.

April 7th: The American motor car pioneer, Henry Ford, died today aged 83.

April 11th: James Mason and Margaret Lockwood have been voted Britain's favourite film stars.

May 1st: Christian Dior has introduced his controversial New Look which gives females an hour-glass shape and says farewell to austerity clothing.

May 23rd: Lord Mountbatten has proposed that India be divided into two states - one Moslem, the other Hindu.

June 5th: George Marshall, American Secretary of State, has said his country will help the nations outside the Russian orbit.

July 9th: The engagement has been announced between Princess Elizabeth and Lieutenant Philip Mountbatten. The Princess who is 21, will be allowed extra clothing coupons for her dress. Her fiance, 26, is the son of the late Prince Andrew of Greece.

July 18th: A party of British naval ratings have refused to allow 5,000 Jewish immigrants on board the ship *Exodus* to disembark at Haifa. They have been transferred to three waiting ships and taken to Cyprus.

The Old Soar manor house at Plaxtol, an original Queen Anne farmhouse, has been acquired by the National Trust.

July 19th: Reports say several Jews died in the fighting on board the *Exodus*. The clamour for a Jewish state in Palestine is rising. Britain has been called upon to remove immigration restrictions.

August 15th: British rule in India has ended after 163 years. Today, the new independent dominions of India and Pakistan are born.

August 27th: As a new financial crisis hits the country, the Government has announced the first instalment of austerity cuts. They include a ban on pleasure motoring and foreign holidays and more stringent food rationing.

The Elham Valley railway line, Canterbury to Folkestone has closed.

October 14th: American Test pilot, Chuck Yeager, has become the first man to travel faster than sound. His Bell XI rocket plane broke through the "sound barrier" at more than 600 mph .

November 20th: Princess Elizabeth, the heir to the throne, today married Prince Philip, the Duke of Edinburgh at Westminster Abbey. It was a glittering ceremony.

December 23rd: In the largest migration in history it is estimated that 8,500,000 refugees divided between Moslem and Hindu have crossed the India-Pakistan border to their respective countries. It is also estimated that almost 500,000 have been slaughtered or died of starvation.

GREAT HITS OF 1947

Maybe it's Because I'm a Londoner.
They Say It's Wonderful.

Airliner crashes on farmland at Stowting

January 12th: A BOAC Dakota airliner, carrying 16 passengers, crashed in the village of Stowting yesterday with the loss of eight lives and serious injuries to the other occupants.

The aircraft, which had set out in the morning from London to West Africa, was prevented by fog from refuelling in France and was returning when it crashed late in the afternoon.

Five people died immediately and three succumbed to their injuries later in hospital. The injured were taken to Willesborough and Ashford Hospitals.

The pilot, first officer, navigator and radio officer are among the dead.

It is believed the pilot was flying to Manston airport where flares had been prepared; an earlier wireless message had spoken of shortage of petrol. It seems the airliner crashed into the steep hillside at Highfield Farm and then slithered into some trees.

A number of people from Stowting and Brabourne rushed to the scene but rescue work was difficult because of the darkness on the steep and muddy hillside. Ambulances could get no nearer than 400 yards.

The final touches to the cake for the wedding of Mary Churchill and Christopher Soames — badges of the Coldstream Guards and the ATS — are applied by Mr Philip Boreham, whose family have been bakers to the Churchills at Westerham for 25 years.

Churchill: 'We must build a United States of Europe'

February 8th: Winston Churchill continues to talk about the "tragedy" of a divided Europe. Last year he travelled to the Netherlands, France, Switzerland and Belgium, addressing Parliaments, receiving honours and expounding his beliefs: "We must build a United Sates of Europe. In this way only will hundreds of millions of toilers be able to regain the simple joys and hopes which make life worth living. The process is simple. All that is needed is the resolve of hundreds of millions of men and women to do right instead of wrong and gain as their reward blessing instead of cursing."

As well as stressing the need to uphold democracy, Churchill is nearing the completion of the first volume of his war memoirs which will be published at the end of the year.

On Tuesday next week (February 11th) he has another pressing appointment at St Margaret's Church, Westminster, where his youngest daughter, Mary, will marry Christopher Soames, a captain in the Coldstream Guards.

January 28th: *Heavy snowfalls, aided by abnormally cold weather, are producing transport chaos in many parts of Kent. Village stores and inns are running short of supplies. Pictured here struggling through the snow is a baker and his assistant from Rainham who have trudged for two miles in order to reach the village of Bredhurst, cut off by snow.*

Snowbound Kent loses villages and even trains

March 18th: As warm air finally arrives to melt the snow and temperatures rise to a commendable 57F, the people of Kent are mightily relieved that the bitterly hard winter of 1947 may finally be over. In towns and villages it has been the worst eight weeks in living memory, a winter of endless grey skies, raging blizzards, sub-zero temperatures, power cuts, strikes and frozen pipes. On top of that, coal has been in short supply and rations cut even more drastically.

It was towards the end of January that an easterly wind sent temperatures plunging. By the 23rd the freeze had intensified and ice floes were forming in the Thames and Medway and it just became colder and colder.

On January 28th at West Malling, the temperature had fallen to a perishing 3F, the River Medway was frozen solid and it was now snowing heavily. Whipped up by the icy winds, drifts formed across the county. Gangs using snowploughs, with the help of German prisoners of war, battled to keep the roads clear but they were fighting a losing battle. Villages were cut off and rescue parties were sent out to find those living in isolated cottages. Kent was lost under a complete blanket of snow.

There were frightening experiences. At Gravesend a shopkeeper walking in from Buckland couldn't tell where the roads ended and hedgerows began and sank to her shoulders in a drift. Somebody heard her cries for help. The Isle of Sheppey was cut off from the mainland and the light railway to Leysdown snowed under.

In Folkestone danger signs were erected on public buildings warning of the massive icicles which hung menacingly above.

Day after day it snowed, stopping all shipping in the

continued on page 176

February 26th:
How often has this happened? A huge field of ice-floes extending for miles along the seashore at Whitstable and for more than a mile out to sea is chilly proof that this is one of the most extraordinary winters ever known. All rivers in Kent are also frozen and there is no sign of any let up in the Arctic conditions as harbour barges and fishing vessels continue to be ice-bound.

People work by candlelight as cold intensifies

(continued)

Channel on February 12th which strengthened fears of new food shortages. Fishing fleets were forced to stay in port, airports were closed, children could not get to school and the road system was paralysed. In the Weald of Kent snowploughs disappeared, a train was lost on the Isle of Grain and at Hythe Brewery a bottling plant had to be operated by hand.

February continued to be an unforgettable month. Cinemas closed, factories had to lay off workers and old people died of hypothermia. In the poorer areas of north-east Kent fireplaces were stacked with broken furniture and even shoes in order to keep the embers glowing.

The coldest night had yet to arrive. At Tunbridge Wells on February 23rd the reading was -2F and it was now three weeks since the people of Kent had seen anything but grey, cheerless skies.

Sunshine at the end of the month was all too brief. The arrival of March heralded rain which fell onto frozen ground-coating everything with a layer of ice. Trees, telephone wires and poles were encased. The Folkestone Herald commented: "Nothing has escaped the ice. Even the tiniest blade of grass had its coating."

Now telephone wires sagged to the ground and pulled down the poles. Trees collapsed under the weight.

By Tuesday March 13th the ground was clear of snow in some places of Kent and a high of 49F was attained but yet again cold northerly winds gathered forces for a new onslaught.

As blizzards and power cuts hit the country again and people lit the candles the cry went up everywhere. Is this winter ever going to end?

Cars negotiate the floods in Maidstone.

High Streets flooded as the great snow thaws

March 21st: As the great snow thawed and turned to rain last week, so the Rivers Medway, Darent, Stour and Rother burst their banks, inundating farmland and causing the worst flooding in the county for 20 years.

In Tonbridge and Maidstone the floodwater easily overtopped the bridges and rushed into the High Street. People had to be lowered from their bedroom windows into boats in Fairmeadow, Maidstone, and the Corporation's electricity works and Mason's Waterside Brewery were under several feet.

The worst area was the Medway valley at Yalding, East Peckham and Beltring. The hop farm was waterlogged and most of the roads were impassable.

It was the same story in the Weald where the River Beult burst its banks and cattle and horses were marooned. The rush of water also covered hundreds of acres of ground either side of the Stour. Bucksford Bridge, Great Chart, Hothfield and Little Chart were cut off and the most serious flooding occurred at Worten Farm, Great Chart, the home of the archaeologist Sir Leonard Woolley. There, staff had a terrifying night.

Up the 'Addicks': Charlton Athletic wins the FA Cup

April 26th: Charlton Athletic is the toast of Kent. Thousands of football supporters from all over the county, but particularly those from the north, were at Wembley yesterday to see the "Addicks" beat Burnley in the final of the FA Cup by the only goal of the game.

The hero was Chris Duffy who broke away from centre-half Alan Brown to volley the winner and send the partisan crowd ecstatic.

Charlton have come through this difficult season of snow and ice and rock-hard dangerous pitches in great style by beating Rochdale, West Bromwich, Blackburn, Preston and Newcastle. It is their second successive appearance in the Wembley final and they fully deserved to avenge last year's defeat by Derby in extra time.

Manager Jimmy Seed is the inspiration behind the club's success. In 1935 Charlton were in the Third Division South. They won promotion to Division Two that year and, the following year, came second to Manchester United to earn a place in Division One. No other club in history has equalled that climb.

In fact it was only 26 years ago that Charlton entered the Football League. Its ground, The Valley, was little more than a swamp and not very popular, so a move was made to Catford. This was even less popular so the "Addicks", as they are called, went back to the Valley and improved the ground.

In 1938, 75,031 spectator watched the match with Aston Villa. It is believed the capacity may be even more for there is plenty of space on the banked terraces.

Today, Charlton Athletic is Kent's only representative in the Football League. Sadly Gillingham failed to gain re-election in 1938 and now play in the Southern League. They have high hopes, however, of re-entering the professional game when, and if, the southern section is enlarged. In the meantime they must continue to play with the zest and ability which everyone knows they are capable of.

September: It has been a vintage summer of glorious sunshine. For several weeks in July children enjoyed lessons out of doors and even the little ones at Woolwich nursery took their rest time in the park . It was August, however, which provided the climax. There was a drought of 50 successive days at Wye and, over England as a whole, it was the warmest August on record.

For cricket fans Kent returned to their winning ways, finishing fourth. Supporters saw a galaxy of entertainment with three players, Fagg, Todd and Ames, all exceeding 2,000 runs. None could match the achievement of a Middlesex player, Denis Compton, who has ended the season with a record 3,518 runs and 18 centuries.

Appropriately it was Lord Cornwallis who presided over this memorable summer as President of the MCC.

Bell Harry, the 250-foot pinnacle of the Cathedral and the richly ornate twin towers, stand above the rubble in this depressing picture of post-war Canterbury. The rebuilding will begin soon and red brick has been chosen for the devastated central area. There are also more changes "in the wind" including a proposed relief road and car parks. Sadly, the Guildhall, said to be too dilapidated for repair, has been demolished. Large areas of so-called slums are also in the process of being cleared.

A plan for Canterbury after six bitter years

Almost six years after the central area of Canterbury was laid waste by the June 1942 Baedeker blitz, the city council has approved a central area plan incorporating a modified inner ring road.

This decision, greeted with considerable relief, follows months of bitter arguments and public conferences, of optimism and idealism, of resistance and resignations and debates so strenuous that many have wondered if an agreement could ever be reached.

Today the blitzed central area of desolation is still picturesquely covered by willowherb and buddleia. Only Marks and Spencers, Woolworths and the battered tower of St George's church rise above the open cellars, pockmarked by archaeological diggers. In the Precincts the ruined Deanery is in the process of repair but in the dark passages around the cloisters there are still signs of horrible destruction.

It was in 1943, less than a year after Hitler's bombs destroyed nearly one-third of the main shopping area, that Dr Charles Holden was appointed as consultant planner to prepare a redevelopment scheme with the city surveyor, Hugh Wilson.

The plan included a new road parallel to the High Street,

a Civic Way, linking Cathedral and Civic Centre and the purchase by the council of the land in the damaged areas.

The Holden proposals alarmed powerful interests and at a public indignation meeting a Citizens' Defence Association was formed. "Their aim," said town clerk, John Boyle, "was to fight to the death. They considered the plan would destroy the traditional character of Canterbury and that the acquisition of land was a gross injustice to the owners."

Problems followed problems. The mayor, Charles Lefevre, died having succumbed to the strain and, at the municipal elections which followed, every councillor who supported the Holden Plan was defeated.

That was three years ago. Since then there have been various alternative proposals to deal with traffic congestion and centre redevelopment. The council, the Citizens' Defence Association, the Chamber of Trade, the Ministry of Planning and Transport have failed to reach agreement, until now.

The modified scheme omits the parallel road but approves a relief road. In the blitzed area proposals have been drawn up for new shops, service areas and car parks. The development plan actually includes a designation area covering some 33 acres in the centre of the city.

'So long as there are tears and suffering, so long our work will not be over' — Pandit Nehru, first Prime Minister of India.

January 1st: The railways will be nationalised from midnight tonight.

January 30th: Mahatma Ghandi, the man who campaigned so long for India's freedom from British rule, was assassinated today in New Delhi.

January 31st: Rioting has broken out all over India as people mourn the death of their leader.

February 13th: The ATS and the WAAF have become the Women's Royal Army Corps and the Women's Royal Air Force. A House of Commons Bill has made them permanent.

February 18th: The majority of doctors have voted against a National Health Service. The ballot was carried out by the British Medical Association.

February 26th: Lord Cornwallis, Lord Lieutenant of Kent, today married Lady Esme Walker of Slinfold, Sussex, at St Mark's Church, North Audley Street, London. A reception was held at Claridge's Hotel for 200 guests.

April 1st: With headquarters remaining at The Godlands, Tovil, an old country house, control of fire-fighting in Kent has been handed over to the County Council. The new authority takes over 79 fire stations from the now-disbanded NFS, many of which will be manned by part-time personnel.

April 14th: MP's have voted to ban the death penalty over a trial period of five years.

May 14th: The new State of Israel is born today with David Ben Gurion as Prime Minister of a provisional government.

May 19th: There was great excitement at Manston today as a "borrowed" Czech airliner landed at the airfield with eight Czech exiles on board.

HRH The Duchess of Kent yesterday opened the new landing stage of the Royal Harbour in Ramsgate.

Miss Richmal Crompton Lamburn, the former classics mistress at Bromley High School, continues to write books about that scruffy, rebellious, lovable 11-year-old called William Brown, and she is keeping pace with the changing world. Her latest, William and the Brains Trust, *follows* William and the Evacuees *and* William and the ARP. *The Bromley area is the background to all her stories which are earning her a great deal of money. Her first book* Just William *appeared in the spring of 1922 and sales since then have topped an estimated five million. Miss Lamburn, now 58, still lives on Bromley Common. She says she is working on a new younger child character called Jimmy. He will be introduced next year.*

June 2nd: At a special service in Rochester Cathedral, the bell of the 8th *HMS Kent* has been entrusted to the Dean and Chapter. The ship has now been broken up.

June 20th: The British Dental Association has now told dentists not to join the NHS.

June 30th: In an operation called *The Berlin Air Lift*, 200 aircraft are landing every day in the British zone of the city with supplies to beat the Russian blockade of Berlin. At present there is just enough food to last a month.

July 5th: Despite powerful opposition from doctors and dentists, the National Health Service has come into being together with a national insurance scheme. Offering free medical treatment for the entire population, it is a triumph for the Health Minister, Aneurin Bevan. Cottage hospitals throughout Kent now cease to be voluntary supported institutions.

July 13th: An Armstrong Siddeley Lancaster car was loaded aboard a Bristol Freighter at the newly commissioned Ferryfield Airport between New Romney and Lydd yesterday. Silver City Airways will operate the route to Le Touquet.

July 16th: The Vickers Viscount, the world's first turbine-propeller aircraft today made its maiden flight.

July 26th: Londoner Freddie Mills beat Gus Lesnecich today to become the light heavyweight champion of the world.

August: The Americans, with 38 gold medals, have dominated the Olympic Games held in London. The greatest hero has been a Czech athlete, Emil Zatopek, who won the 10,000 metres by a full lap, setting a new record. The Games will be notable for being inexpensive amid the strictures of post-war austerity.

August 8th: The Buffs (Royal East Kent Regiment) have been granted the freedom of the City of Canterbury.

October 4th: Churchill has published *The Gathering Storm,* the first volume of his history of the second world war.

Author Richard Church of Curtisden Green, Goudhurst, has published a book about Kent — an unfolding pageant of two thousand years.

November 14th: Princess Elizabeth and Prince Philip have announced the birth of a son, Charles Philip Arthur George.

Shepherd Neame, the long-established brewery in Court Street, Faversham (the brewing capital of Kent), has celebrated its 250th anniversary. The company is believed to be the oldest brewery in the world.

GREAT HITS OF 1948

Slow Boat to China

Tragedy for Medway Towns as Shorts move to Belfast

April 8th: Today the last aeroplane built by Short Brothers at the Seaplane Works will leave the concrete slipway on the Rochester Esplanade. The luxurious *Solent,* built for BOAC, with accommodation for 37 passengers, signals the end of an era. Short Brothers' three factories have been relocated to Belfast and all attempts to keep the company in the Medway Towns has failed. Workers have been offered employment in Ireland but hundreds are now redundant.

The first rumours of a total shutdown were heard two years ago. By then the work force had been reduced from the peak level of 11,000 in 1942 to 5,000 and there were fears of further redundancies.

Trade unions took the initiative with a series of mass meetings and the establishment of a working party to draw up an industrial plan linking aviation with the Medway Towns. But then the bombshell came. In June 1946, the Government announced that all factories would close and work would be transferred to Belfast. Technical staff only would be offered redeployment.

Within a week the largest procession ever seen in the Medway Towns marched to Jackson's Field, Rochester, to demonstrate. There were more than 8,000 people. Traffic in the High Street was completely jammed as the long column from the seaplane works, led by a brass band, proceeded from Willis Avenue to Corporation Street and Star Hill. Scores of banners were carried and one said: "Food is going to Germany, Work is going to Belfast. We are going to hell fast."

The workers appealed to their MPs for support but Arthur Bottomley (Rochester and Chatham) and John Binns (Gillingham) declined to oppose their Government's decision. They said they would urge ministers to give every encouragement to attract new industry to the area.

In an article in the *Daily Sketch,* Oswald Short, chairman of the company before it was taken over by the Labour Government, says that the aerodrome at Rochester is not big enough for the super giant aeroplanes to take off or land.

"When I was chairman," he wrote, "I made it a duty to go up with our chief test pilots to any first trials of an aeroplane or flying boat. I know what it is like to make a forced landing on the Medway when the wind is blowing across the river. Either the seaplane works or the bridge at Rochester flash before your eyes and often I wondered if the planes would stop in time."

The "good old days". This picture was taken in 1937 when nannies and their charges, on the banks of the Medway at Rochester, had a perfect view of the Empire Class flying boat built by Short Brothers. This was hailed as one of the finest and sturdiest marine aircraft ever built. The hull had two decks — crew and mail compartment in the upper deck and accommodation for 24 passengers and additional cargo in the lower. Hundreds of local people were involved in the construction.

Kent has said goodbye to one of her greatest heroines. The former pleasure steamer *Queen of Kent* has been sold to the South of England Royal Mail Steam Packet Company and renamed *Lorna Doone*.

This remarkable ship was built in 1916 as a minesweeper, HMS *Atherstone*. In 1928 she was bought by the New Medway Steam Packet Company, renamed *Queen of Kent*, fitted with new paddle wheels and gave countless excursions to trippers and holidaymakers.

In 1939 she was requisitioned by the Admiralty and served again as a minesweeper. On D Day she was the Control Ship at Dungeness and then, once more, reconditioned for further service.

August 13th: Huge crowds gathered at Dover to see the Olympic flame on its way from Athens to Wembley. This famous symbol of peace was then passed from one runner to another every three or four miles across the county. In these first games since the flamboyant Nazi Olympiad of 1936, there are high hopes of British successes. Below: Arthur Galloway, of Westerham Harriers, takes the torch on the last leg of its journey through Kent. Accompanied by a police motorcycle and followed by a veritable cavalcade of vehicles, on a grey and misty morning at 6.30am, there are hoards of sightseers on the green at Westerham and all along the route to Moorhouse before it leaves Kent, and continues on its way from Oxted.

Dick Barton - Special Agent — born in Brenchley

May: In the quiet Kent village of Brenchley lives a man who crowds more thrills and adventures into a quarter-of-an-hour than most people experience in a lifetime. His name is Basil Dawson and he is the author of the serial script, *Dick Barton — Special Agent,* which nightly holds wireless listeners in thrall.

Surrounded by encyclopaedia and reference books, Mr Dawson sits at his desk in Pound Field and hammers out Dick's latest adventures on his portable typewriter.

Dick Barton has thrilled the nation. It is conceived and written in groups of 20 episodes of 15 minutes each and split-second timing is necessary in each episode.

"My greatest problem," Mr Dawson said, "is to contrive an ending to each episode which is full of suspense." His wife is also a writer for the wireless and her adaptation of Noel Streatfeild's *Ballet Shoes* is running as a serial on Children's Hour.

The couple lived at Edenbridge, Tonbridge and Horsmonden before moving to Brenchley. Mr Dawson is keen to join the local cricket club and regularly joins the players at the local.

July: Among the young ladies queueing for the autograph of Patricia Dainton who opened Dartford's annual conservative fête earlier this month is a young 23-year-old undergraduate, Margaret Roberts, who is reading chemistry at Oxford.

Manston air display disaster: death toll now 12

September 24th: Three more people have died at Margate General Hospital bringing the number of victims from last week's Manston air display disaster to 12. Many others are still in a serious condition.

The tragedy occurred when a Mosquito twin-engined aircraft stalled and crashed during a display of low-flying aerobatics. The plane struck a column of motorcars, which were proceeding towards the aerodrome, exploded and burst into flames on impact. Motorists were trapped in the vehicles and burnt to death while cyclists and pedestrians, caught in a river of flame, shared the same fate. Nine people, including the pilot and navigator, were killed outright.

At the inquest on Monday, evidence of the utmost poignancy was given for, in many instances, the bodies of the people who lost their lives were so badly burned that it was impossible to identify them except by tickets and clothing.

Among the witnesses was 11-year-old Malcolm John Andrews, a pupil at Simon Langton School, Canterbury, whose mother, brother and aunt were killed. He said they were cycling from Margate to Manston. Brent, his two-year-old brother, was riding in a carrier on his mother's bike.

"I went ahead and got there first," he said. "I looked back for them and saw an aeroplane diving. Then there was a flash and sheet of flame". One of the Andrews' neighbours said that Mrs Andrews was uncertain whether she should take her children to the show or to cricket at Canterbury. She tossed a coin to decide.

Mr Cecil Stuart Chieseman of Chislehurst said he was driving his car to Manston. Looking in his driving mirror he saw the aircraft approaching. It crashed onto the car behind in which his son, Stuart, aged 13, Frances Lewis, aged 13 and Miss Astell were riding. "I ran back," he said, "but could find no trace of the car or occupants".

The inquest heard that the pilot, Flight Lt Geoffrey Hanson, had been directed to dive to 200 feet, climb to 500 and then roll. It is believed the crash was an error of judgement on the pilot's part. He was too low for a roll.

After the jury returned a verdict of misadventure the Coroner said: "People might question whether there ought to be displays of this kind at all. Perhaps there is every reason that the Royal Air Force and the skill and bravery of its pilots should be made known in this country and abroad."

World speed records were Sir Malcolm's hobby

December 31st: Sir Malcolm Campbell, who held both the world land and water speed records, has died at Reigate, aged 63.

Born in Chislehurst, the only son of a jeweller and his wife, Campbell devoted his youth to buying cars and motorbikes and racing them. In 1909 he built his own aeroplane in a disused barn at Orpington and attempted to fly but managed no more than a few hundred yards. In 1914 he was commissioned in the Royal West Kent Regiment but transferred to the Royal Flying Corps

Malcolm Campbell in the cockpit of his car "Bluebird" at Brooklands

and became a ferry pilot. He turned to motor racing, won more than 400 trophies and set out to make world records a hobby. After many disappointments and numerous hair-raising escapes from death he set up a series of land speed records in cars which he built at his own expense, and called *Bluebird*.

He was the first man to travel at 150, then 200 mph and, in 1932, raised the record to 250 mph. In 1935, in a Rolls-Royce-Campbell *Bluebird,* he exceeded 300 mph and was knighted. Turning his attention to water speed records, Sir Malcolm managed 141 mph in 1939.

He had few other interests apart from fishing, although he did stand, unsuccessfully, as a Conservative candidate in the election of 1935.

Sir Malcolm, who married three times, has a daughter and a son, Donald, who shares his passion for racing.

This year's holiday trade is providing great business for the railways. Without cars or petrol people are travelling by train and crowds have reached record proportions this summer. This is the astonishing scene at Waterloo Station today. The queue started from the main entrance, into York Road, round the bomb site and ended down the York Road out of sight.

Broadstairs 'Billy' grows fatter despite the rationing

As the food shortage hits Kent with a vengeance one resident, who has lived in Broadstairs since 1926, seems to have ample supply. But this character, with his enormous girth and unscrupulous greed, is a hero — and is worth an estimated £1 million.

His name is Billy Bunter, and he is the fat, bespectacled boy, whose adventures at Greyfriars School have appeared in hundreds of novels and magazines.

The creator is Frank Richards of Percy Avenue, Kingsgate, Broadstairs, who is nearly 80 but still turning out Bunter stories at an incredible rate.

Better known as Charles Hamilton, this cheerful author says Bunter was based on an editor he knew

and his friends were flesh and blood people around in 1908 when the boys made their debut.

Since then generations of schoolboys (and grown-ups) have been entertained and Frank estimates he is worth a million pounds. "Don't imagine that is what I have got," he said, "but I was earning £2,500 a year until the war when my income dropped to nothing.

"That was a shattering experience," he said, "but Bunter is blossoming again and I'm producing seven novels this year, including a Bessie Bunter."

Frank also said that his publisher allows him only one copy of the book and he has to buy others from a bookseller to give to friends!

Food parcels help with Dover's new plight

A welcome gift of food parcels from far away Piet Retief in South Africa has arrived in Dover and, at the special request of the donors, 84 of the 196 parcels received have been distributed to the aged residents of Kent's worst-bombed town.

The Town Hall, previously the Hospital of La Maison Dieu, miraculously escaped the shelling and the bombing, and the elderly folk gathered in the Great Hall to receive their gifts from His Worship the Mayor, Cllr W.J. Fish.

Communities throughout Kent are receiving food parcels from South Africa, Canada, Australia and New Zealand. They are particularly welcome in view of the belt-tightening measures for coping with Britain's dollar shortage.

Sugar rationing is down to eight ounces a week, sweet rationing is back at four ounces a week and tobacco supplies have been cut drastically again.

It is the east Kent towns which are suffering the most. Because the rate product was so greatly reduced by war damage and evacuation, special Government grants were awarded. These grants will end in March.

Discussing the numerous dishes to be made from the South African food parcels, just received, are 85-year-old Mrs Jones of Beaufoy Terrace, Mrs Port of Balfour Road and Miss Axon of Lascelles Road, Dover.

January 22nd: Mao Tse-tung and his Communist troops have taken over Peking and the civil war which began after Mao's "Long March" has ended with peace talks.

February 5th: Broadstairs said goodbye today to one of its most endearing and talented residents when Uncle Mac died of a heart attack, aged 73. Born James Henry Summerston he arrived at Broadstairs in 1895 with a minstrel troupe. He began his own troupe early this century and erected a stage by the main steps in the bay in 1909. After the 1914-18 war he started a White Night held every Thursday evening. In the second world war he gave concerts in aid of charities.

March 11th: Maidstone and District Motor Services Ltd and the Chatham and District Traction Company said today they will "fight to the last wheel" against the nationalisation of their passenger transport undertakings.

March 15th: Clothes rationing has ended but the utility scheme, in which ready-to-wear clothes are made under a cloth quota system, will continue.

March 18th: Britain is among eight western countries to sign a new peace alliance to be known as the North Atlantic Treaty Organisation (NATO).

March 25th: *Hamlet* today became the first British film to win an Academy Award for best picture. Laurence Olivier also wins an Oscar for his performance in the title role.

April 1st: 12 areas in England and Wales have been proposed as National Parks.

April 5th: Water companies in the Medway towns, Sheppey and south Kent have warned the public that they must economise in the use of water. Unless there is heavy rain, they say, the position will be critical and restrictions will be introduced.

Archaeologists excavating a Roman Villa at Lullingstone, near

March: Sir Michael Balcon who made film history last year when he took Ealing Studios to Australia to produce The Overlanders, *plans another visit "down under" in May to make* Eureka Stockade, *a comedy of English immigrants starring Tommy Trinder and Chips Rafferty. (See page 191).*

Eynsford, are ecstatic. They believe they have unearthed the most important Roman site in Kent, with the possible exception of Richborough Castle and the Pharos at Dover Castle. The villa is believed to have been the home of a Romanised Briton whose family farmed the area for centuries.

April 24th: The Government announced that chocolate and sweet rationing has ended.

Kent and England cricketer Les Ames has turned down an offer to captain the county side in succession to Bryan Valentine. The county wanted him to take amateur status. D.G. Clark will instead lead the side.

May 1st: The gas industry has been nationalised by the Labour Government.

A new motorcar racing track has opened at Fawkham for Formula Three racing. The circuit will be known as Brands Hatch.

May 11th: The Ireland Bill passed a second reading today opposed by 12 Labour and two Ulster MPs. It recognises Eire as a republic.

June 10th: George Orwell has published a new book about a future frightening world controlled by "Big Brother". It is called *1984*.

July 14th: Sugar rationing has been reintroduced. The milk ration

is cut from three to two and a half pints per person per week.

July 15th: Winston Churchill, who owns several hundred acres and a herd of pedigree dairy cows at Westerham, has gained a First in the "cow in calf" class at the Kent County Show.

September 4th: A 130-ton airliner, the *Bristol Brabazon,* made her maiden flight today. It has eight Rolls-Royce engines and can carry 100 passengers.

September 18th: Britain has devalued the pound by 30 per cent, from four dollars three cents to two dollars 80 cents. Sir Stafford Cripps, Chancellor of the Exchequer, says that devaluation will boost British exports.

October 12th: The Soviet Union has established a German Democratic Republic. Stalin's move follows the failure of his attempt to strangle West Berlin by denying access to it.

An inscription on the side of the war-damaged Methodist Church near Dover Priory railway station reads: *Built 1910. Bombed 1916. Rebuilt 1920. Bombed 1941. Rebuilt 1949.*

October 26th: Britain, which has several million pounds worth of commercial interests in China, has given full diplomatic recognition to the new regime there.

November 4th: The BBC has purchased the Rank film studios in Lime Grove, West London, for television use.

Folkestone poet, novelist and botanist Jocelyn Brooke has published the second of his semi-autobiographical novels, *A Mind of Serpents.* Last year he wrote *The Orchard Trilogy.* Both books recall his childhood in Folkestone and the Bishopsbourne areas.

GREAT HITS OF 1949

Baby, It's Cold Outside

Buttons and Bows

May 12th: Two Kent airmen have played a big part in the Berlin Air Lift which ended today when the Russian blockade was finally lifted. One of them, 23-year-old Engineer Philip Fairweather from Sevenoaks, has completed the greatest number of sorties and the other, Flight Lieutenant Ronald Mortley from Allhallows-on-Sea, is an experienced Transport Command pilot who has been continuously engaged since the early days of the operation. Awards have been recommended for both men.

The two men flew through rain, fog and high winds into Berlin on hundreds of occasions, carrying both food and fuel to the Allied sector of the city. They were able to get enough supplies through to keep Berliners going. The operation has cost the Allies $200 million.

Engineer Fairweather and Flt Lt Mortley feel they have beaten the Russians at their own game. The Soviet Union blocked off the city last year to protest at what they called intransigence by Western Allies on the future of Germany.

March 14th: *Kent Fire Brigade estimates that it has taken 1,550 man-hours to fight the floods which have devastated Kent in the last two weeks. The brigade is less than nine months old but they responded to the emergency with great skill and speed.*

It was on March 1st that hundreds of messages were received that a high tide was causing flooding at various points between Margate and Crayford (see picture). A tidal surge had swept down the North Sea, into the Thames Estuary and up the river valleys, reaching 15 miles inland. So bad was the flooding that Chatham, Rochester, Strood, Upnor, Gravesend,

Sheerness, Sittingbourne, Faversham, Herne Bay, Whitstable, Dover and Margate were declared one incident. The following day the Kent Rivers Catchment Board said agricultural land and orchards were under water at Gillingham. Normal pumping operations were impossible so it was decided to operate a system of syphons, using armoured suction hoses, to reduce the water level. The syphon operated for four days and nights. In the meantime a 70 mph gale caused "sensational spring tides to pile up" around the Kent coast and there were breaches in the sea wall. Soldiers were called in to help workmen with the repair.

April: Hundreds of families from Kent are being lured "down under" to Australia and New Zealand where there is ample space and sunshine, no problem finding homes or employment and no such things as rationing or the other hardships which have plagued "austerity Britain" for so many years. Among those leaving Kent this month under the Assisted Passages Scheme for £10 a head is Mr Gordon Wing, his wife and seven children. Here they are pictured for the last time at their home in Balfour Road, Dover, looking forward to the long sea voyage ahead.

Three winners in one year for Sir Michael Balcon

June: The Oscars won by *Hamlet* and *The Red Shoes* this year prove for the first time that Britain is matching Hollywood in the quality of its films. One of the most popular producers is Sir Michael Balcon, whose determination to promote a characteristically British film industry is bearing fruit at the Ealing Studios which he took over in 1938 when he was living at Henden Manor, Ide Hill, near Sevenoaks.

The Ealing comedies combine British eccentricity, anarchy and old-fashioned humour. Among those to be produced this year are *Passport to Pimlico*, *Whisky Galore* and *Kind Hearts and Coronets*.

The latter is breaking box-office records already. Alec Guinness, who made his name in *Oliver Twist* as Fagin, gives a virtuoso performance with a set of character sketches as the eight members of the D'Ascoyne family who are murdered. Just like an earlier Ealing comedy *The Lavender Hill Mob* it is witty, eccentric and English.

Sir Michael, who was knighted last year, founded Gainsborough Pictures and between 1931 and 1937 he was in charge of production for Gaumont British Picture Corporation. He briefly joined Metro Goldwyn Mayer but left to take up independent production again and joined Ealing Studios.

Today Sir Michael and his wife Aileen live at Upper Parrock, Hartfield, near Tunbridge Wells.

Among the VIPs to visit Ealing studios and meet such stars as Alec Guinness, Jack Warner, Joan Greenwood and Jimmy Hanley are Princess Elizabeth and Princess Margaret — seen here with Sir Michael

July 29th: Prince Georg of Denmark lays a commemorative stone alongside the site at Pegwell Bay where the Hugin *is to be left and preserved.*

Vikings invade again — to a rousing reception

July 28th: Seething throngs of people covering every inch of the sands and six deep on the cliff top were in Broadstairs today to give Thanet the biggest, noisiest and longest day anyone can remember.

The occasion was the 1,500th anniversary of the reputed first landing of the Vikings who came to Kent in search of settlement. It was marked in spectacular manner by the arrival on Broadstairs beach of the *Hugin* — a replica of the open-decked longship commanded by Hengist and Horsa.

From the moment the silhouette on the skyline resolved itself there were great cheers from the flag-waving crowd — a vastly different reception from that given by the apprehensive, confused Britons who were standing on the shore 15 centuries ago.

Surrounded by escorting vessels, with the raven standard at the masthead, painted shields along the gunwhale and fierce-looking warriors aboard, the *Hugin* led the fleet in this modern Viking invasion.

It was the young men of Copenhagen rowing clubs who built a full-scale reconstruction of the fifth century vessels which ravaged the shores of Europe during the closing years of the Roman occupation.

Inspired by the wartime co-operation between England and Denmark, the *Hugin* and its fleet set sail from Frederikssund at the beginning of the month. The crew represented 30 different trades and professions. They all wore long beards, costumes and helmets and carried weapons which were authentic right down to the last buckle.

On shore an inadequate and harassed force of policemen and schoolteachers were having great difficulty controlling the throngs of children who showed every sign of rushing into the sea to greet the bewhiskered, spear-waving Norsemen.

Standing high on the vessel and holding onto the raven was the chief Viking, Erik Suell Kiergaard. He was the first ashore to recieve the official welcoming party from the town of Broadstairs.

It has also been a good summer for the swimming pool business and among the most popular has been The Strand at Gillingham (above) on the banks of the River Medway. Described in the brochures as a riverside lido it is estimated that 12,000 visitors a day were arriving at the height of the summer. Also popular is the Hilden Manor swimming pool, Hildenborough and The Woodsgate, Pembury, which is advertised as "the best swimming pool in the country with continuously purified heated water, diving chutes and showers".

A blazing summer — especially in Bordeaux

September 12th: Too much water a few weeks ago has suddenly been converted into far too little. This long, hot, dry summer is not only straining the resources of the fire brigade but causing further distress as water joins sweets and tobacco as a rationed commodity.

Fires are everywhere. On August 21st a large part of the scenic railway and show booths at Dreamland, Margate, were severely damaged. A man was killed and two injured at Canterbury when a tanker lorry unloading vaporising oil at the Invicta Engineering Works exploded. The noise was heard all over the city.

At Dartford a 250-ton stack of wood pulp caught fire in the spring. Four days later an extensive range of buildings covering three acres at Lloyd's Paper Mill at Sittingbourne was destroyed.

Kent Fire Brigade's worst incident, however, was not in Kent. Throughout June and July forest fires were raging throughout the Bordeaux region of France. They had claimed more than a 100 lives including 28 soldiers trapped in the centre of the fires. Kent responded to an SOS on August 20th and the Foreign Office gave permission for the local fire-fighters to travel without passports.

During this traumatic summer the Kent Brigade responded to a record 8,636 calls. Fireman C.A. Young of St Margaret's was killed and as many as 68 men injured.

Carmelites return home to Aylesford

November: **The Brothers of the Carmelite Order have returned to Aylesford Priory which was their home from 1245 until they were driven out in 1538 by Henry VIII during his dissolution of the monasteries.**

The church, the Priory and its cluster of buildings near the banks of the Medway have been in secular hands for more than 200 years. The last occupant was Major Copley-Hewett who suffered a disastrous fire in 1930. Since then The Friars has been mainly a heap of ruins.

The Brothers have paid £25,000 for the site. Many friends have advised against attempting restoration but they say they will employ Carmelite craftsmen from the Continent to rebuild the Great Court. They say it will be a labour of love.

The original Carmelites were hermits, driven out of the Holy Lands by the Saracens and brought to England by Crusaders. Given land at Aylesford they built the church, the house and the stone bridge across the Medway.

The inspiration behind the restoration project is Father Malachy Lynch who is keen to establish the Mother House of the Order of Carmelites on the banks of the Medway and, perhaps, one day encourage pilgrims to come from all over the world.

Canon Thorndyke, the father of actress Sybil, was Vicar of Aylesford for a few years.

Subscribers please, look out for Volume Three

THE third volume of this **Kent Chronicle of the Century** series will be published in October 1998 and will cover the years between 1950 and 1974. It will be identical in format to this book. The great difference is that many of the events and personalities will be remembered by most people — certainly those over 50.

Readers will recall the sad but exciting fifties — sad because young men from Kent were still involved in conflicts around the world and we lost our much-loved King George VI; exciting because this was the age of Rock and Roll, Bill Hayley and Elvis. "We've never had it so good," said our MP for Bromley. Perhaps we haven't! Certainly the Festival of Britain and the Coronation lifted the spirits of the nation — and we won the Ashes.

But it wasn't good in January 1953 when a tidal surge, whipped up by a hurricane-force wind, hit north Kent with a vengeance. Many people will remember the great floods, arguably the most dramatic weather event of the century. It wasn't good when those brave Sea Scouts from Gillingham were mown down by a bus at Chatham. And it wasn't good in December 1957 when 94 Kentish train passengers died in the fog at Lewisham. Other people will recall the CND marches and the spies, such as Burgess and Maclean, but how many know of their Kentish connections ?

No other decade had a greater effect on modern popular culture than the sixties. Those memorable "swinging" years permeated every level of society. The Beatles came to Kent often; their promotional film for their single Strawberry Fields For Ever/ Penny Lane was filmed in Knole Park, Sevenoaks. But the sixties were also about space travel and Concorde, about two kinds of mini, the Great Train Robbery, the death of Churchill and assassinations in America. Where were you when Kennedy was shot? Where were you on the night of July 30th when we won the World Cup? Where were you when Neil Armstrong landed on the moon?

There are Kentish connections in many of these events. If you would like to subscribe to the next volume please write (or telephone) to the address below for details. There will be a reduction for subscribers and the names will be printed in the book. We will, of course, require a deposit followed by the balance just prior to publication. All subscribers will receive signed copies.

Froglets Publications,
Brasted Chart, Westerham,
Kent TN16 1LY
Tel: 01959 562972
Fax: 01959 565365

BIBLIOGRAPHY

In writing this book I have referred to a variety of pamphlets, newspaper articles and miscellaneous documents kept in the Centre for Kentish Studies and various libraries throughout the county. Prominent among these is the monthly journal *Bygone Kent* published by Meresborough Books. I also referred to the following books:
The Pleasant Town of Sevenoaks, by John Dunlop. *A Look Back at Orpington,* John Edwards etc. *Abdication of King Edward VIII,* AJP Taylor. *Memory Lane,* James Cameron. *The Motor Bus Services of Kent and Sussex* (up to end of vol 2) Eric Baldock. *Tales of Old Kent,* Alan Bignell. *King's England Kent,* Arthur Mee. *A Portrait of Bromley 1929-1939,* Lewis Blake. *Front Line County* Andrew Rootes. *Action Station 9,* Chris Ashworth. *Kent Headlines,* Alan Bignell. *Kent Women,* Bowen Pearse. *History of the Kent Coalfield,* John Hilton. *Heroes and Villains of Kent,* Adrian Gray. *The History of Kent County Cricket Club,* Dudley Moore. *The King of Games,* Frank Woolley. *Tales of Old Tonbridge,* Frank Chapman. *Prelude to War,* Kent Aviation Historical Research Society. *Hellfire Corner,* Roy

Humphreys. *Churchill,* Martin Gilbert. *Margate's Winter Gardens,* John Williams. *Romney Marsh,* Anne Roper. *Kent Through The Years,* Christopher Wright. *To Fire Committed,* Harry Klopper. *Stories of Famous Ships,* Richard Garrett. *A History of Gravesend,* Robert Hiscock. *Lady Sackville,* Susan Mary Alsop.*Chislehurst Caves,* Eric Inman. *Spirit of Kent (Lord Cornwallis),* Henry Pratt Boorman. *Kent Police Centenary 1857-1957,* ed RL Thomas. *Kent at War,* Bob Ogley. *Kent Weather Book,* Bob Ogley, Mark Davison and Ian Currie. *Hythe Haven,* Duncan Forbes. *Hidden Kent,* Alan Major. *History of Maidstone,* Peter Clark and Lyn Murfin. *Memories of Kent Cinemas,* Martin Tapsell. *Chronicle of the Century,*ed Derrik Mercer. *Biggin On The Bump,* Bob Ogley. *Thanet at War,* Roy Humphreys. *Dover at War, Midst Bands and Bombs,* A.B.C. Kempe. *Who's Buried Where in Kent,* Alan Major. *National Trust,* Merlin Waterson. *Kent Unconquered,* Pratt Boorman. *Portrait of Canterbury,* John Boyle. *We'll Meet Again,* Vera Lynn. *Kent,* Richard Church. *Kent Bibliography,* T.A. Bushell.

SUBSCRIBERS

The following kindly gave their support to this book

Doreen Allibone
Mr L.F. Ambrose
Charmian Amos
Iain H. Anderson
Sally G. Anning
Jim Armstrong
Roy Arnold
Vic Ashlee
Mrs Anne Atkin
Mrs W.J. Baigent
Jonathan Balcon
Mr and Mrs O.C. Baldock
Charles F. Baldwin
Mr and Mrs T.A. Ball
R.A.Barham
Emily Barnett
Robert Beck
D. Bellringer
H.Belsey
D.E. Bengeyfield
Dick and Pamela Bennett
Eric Bennett
Melville Edwin Bishop
Shirley M.Blake
Miss M.V. Borner
Paul M. Boulton
G.R. Boxall
Violet Brand
Wendy Brazier
W.J. Brenton
Mr and Mrs M.A. Brett
The Briers Family
Doris M. Brown
Mrs Rosemary Brown
Ann Buckett
Jean Bunnett
Mr Sidney Burvill
A.K. Butcher
Colin Butcher
J.J. Butcher
Mrs M.C. Button
Carol Ann Bush
Robin Carden
Peter Challis
Mrs Janet Chambers
Mr and Mrs C.A. Chapman
Betty J. Church
Mrs Sheila Churches
Mrs Florence W. Clarke
Roy Cleveley
Arthur Clipstone
Margaret Cole
J.M. Cook
Mr Rodney Collins
Mr G.A.P. and P. Coombs
Cyril and Iris Crane
Mrs Jean Crisfield
June Cronk
L.J. and P.A. Cropper

Richard P. Cross
Stan Darnell
A. Davidson
Jim Davis
Glenys Davis
John Dawson
Alan Deares
Mick Dennett
M.J.K. Dodsworth
John F. Dorling
Mr J.E. Dorman
N.O. Durdant-Hollamby
Mr A.J. Dutton
Mark Dutton
Mr D.O. Dykes
Eric Edgehill
Mrs Janet Edwards
Leonard Egan
Daniel M. Egan
Dorothy K. Elliott
Peter Ellison
Douglas Elks
Elwin Francis End
Rachel and George Elvery
Evelyn M. Evans
Jennifer and David Eyre
Denis Fentiman
Harry Fenton
The Finney Family
Mr N. Folkard
Christiane P. Foster
Bill Foster
Mr C.H. Fox
MrsEmerald Frampton
Mr Bernard Fuller
Doug Furrents
David and
Jonathan Garrard
Mr M. Godfrey
Mrs G. Gurr
Kenneth W. Hammerton
Ben Hammock
Angela and Barrie Harber
Muriel Emma Harker
Alan Harmsworth
R.C. Harris
Miss June Haste
Ken Hayes
Mark Heselden
Rev M.E. Hewett
J. Hickling
Joyce Hickmott
George R. Higgs
Neil Hilkene
Guy Hitchings
David Thomas Hobbs
Angela M. Holness
B.A. Holyland
Mrs Edith Hopkins
Doreen Hopkins
John Howcroft
G. Hughes
Sue and Chris Huke
Alan Humphrey

Maureen Humphrey
Elizabeth Jaeker
Mr H.W.M. James
Gary and Bobbie Jarvis
Maria J. Jarvis
Mr A. Jeffreys
Mary L. Johnson
Mrs C.L. Jones
H.W.M. Jones
Paul and Julie Jones
Ray and Brenda Jones
Mr T.I. Jones
Lynn Jung
Alan M. Kay
Bernard Keeling
Derek Kemp
John Cornelius Kemp
Mrs Maureen Kessel
Eric Keys
Peter J. Kiff
Sue Kirkham
A.J. Ladd
The Langridge Family
G. Lawton
Angela Legood
Len Squires
Stella Lewis
Bexley Library
C.T.J. Lindsay
Linda, Alan and Daniel
Linton
John London
Gary Long
Mrs Brigid Longley
Gordon Luck
Lyminge Historical
Society
Brian McNaughton
Betty Marsh
Pat Marshall
Ian Martin
Peter Martin
Colin P. Matthews
C.N. Mathews
N.J. Matthews
M.S. Matthews
B.L. and J.F. Matthews
C.S. Mathews
Philip Maytum
Michael Mercer
Mrs P. Meridew
Beryl Miles
C.A. Miles
Caroline Mitchell
Elaine Moody
Agnes Todd Morgan
Peter Morgan
Tony and Maralyn Mulcuck
Alan Mount and
Anne Rickard
Bill Morton
Brian and Muriel Neal
Frederick G. Neville

Mrs Adriane Norris
D.C. Nowers
Pam Nye
Peter O'Sullivan
Len Olive
W.H. Orrell
Mr and Mrs B.B. Payne
Allan Pearce
Mrs L. Peatfield
Alun Pedler
John Sidney Penn
Pauline, Brian & Kathryn Phillips
Mrs E. Palmer
M. Piddock
Robert Piper
G. John Pluckrose
R. Parkes
Mr Chris Porteous
Monnie E. Potter
Jan and Chris Powis
Hugh R. Pryke
Barbara Pritchard
Sharon Proudlove BSc
Janet and Alec Ramage
Mrs E.I. Rand
Paul Rason
Paul C. Rayner
Linda Read
Mrs L. Rich
David C. Redman
Kevin F. Reynolds
Mrs I.C. Rhodes
Trevor Robbie
Bill and Vera Roberts
Mrs E.C. Robinson
A. Rodgers
Martin and Jill Rolls
Roy Rofe
Margaret Rogans
Peter Rogers
Joyce and Frank Rooney
Malcolm Round
Colin W. Rumley
Mrs D. Russell
The Ruston Family
Joan Evelyn Sale
Mr Amitha and Mrs
Colleen Samarasinghe
Eileen L. Sands
John and Kay Saunders
Mr Brian A. Sayer
St Michael's School
Mrs Rocky Scurr
Mike and Tessa Sheeres
Maurice G. Short
Ron Sinclair
Alan Smith
Dave Solley
Joan W. Spreyer
Len Squires
Maurice Stocker
D.G. Stevens
Keith Stevens

Ronald H.H. Stokes
Mrs I.H. Streeting
S.J. Stringer
Sue Swain
Mrs Joyce Frances Tapsell
K.E. Taylor
C.H. Taylor
S.E. Taylor
Hugh W. Taylor
George Taylor
Miss M.A. Thatcher
Valerie Thatcher
Mrs Joan Thomas
Mr Troye R. Thomas
R.G. Thomas
Edwin Thompson
Paul Thompson
Miss Angela Thorn
Graham Tippen
John R. Toms
Michael J. Tong
Eunice D. Towersey
Mrs Norma Towler
Miss J. Tresize
Mrs Eve Tucker
Gordon C. Turner
Mrs Stella D. Underwood
Mrs D. Walford
Mr B.A. Walker
Philip Wanstall
John H. Warner
Michael J. Waterhouse
Mrs Iris Watkins
A. Webber
Alan R. Wells
Mrs E. Whitehead
Gillian and Chris Whittingham
Mr D. Wickenden
Terry A. Wickens
Don Wiffen
Alan Wilkinson
F.H.A. Williams
John and Wendy Williams
John S. Wilmshurst
Sidney G. Willson
Mr P.F. and Mrs S.M. Winton
George Winton
David Witherspoon
Christopher Wood
Denzil, Susan, Jane and James Wood
Sylvia Wood
Lionel J. Wood
Mr S. Wooldridge
Mrs and Mrs R. Woodgate
Miss M. Wootton
John Edward Wratten
Patricia Wright
Chris Wyer
Ron Yates
Mrs A. Young

INDEX

FROGLETS BOOKS AND WHAT THE CRITICS SAY

In The Wake of The Hurricane
(Sevenoaks edition) by Bob Ogley

The wind that blew in from the sea in the early hours of October 16th, 1987, toppled six of the town's seven famous oak trees, devastated the ancient Knole Park and changed the face of Sevenoaks and district, prompted local newspaper editor Bob Ogley to take aerial photographs of the disaster, write a book and look for a publisher. Rejected, he published the book himself, sold 5,000 copies in a week and 45,000 within a few months. It changed his life. **Temporarily out of print.**

In The Wake of The Hurricane
(National Edition) by Bob Ogley

This book of photographs and stories of the Great Storm, covering every county in the south-east, is one of England's greatest-ever self-publishing success stories. Bob Ogley and his partner Fern Flynn sold over 100,000 copies, raised more than £26,000 for the National Trust and prompted *The Observer* to describe their company as a "publishing phenomenon". Warm tributes came from people all over the country including Margaret and Denis Thatcher, Sir Leonard Cheshire, Winston Churchill and Lord Astor. The Times described them as "sensational" and the Express said "because of demand the book is more elusive than Spycatcher". **In The Wake of The Hurricane** spent 28 successive weeks in the top ten list of bestsellers and for a while was number two in the country.
ISBN 0 913019 1 8. **Price: £8.95**

The Hurricane Series
by Mark Davison, Ian Currie, Bob Ogley and Kev Reynolds

So successful were the first two books about the "hurricane", or great storm of October 1987, that Bob Ogley decided to publish regional books about the brutal way in which England's landscape was rearranged and include hitherto untold dramatic stories of that night. **Surrey In The Hurricane,** written jointly by Mark Davison and Ian Currie, sold more than 25,000 copies and raised £8,000 for the Surrey Wildlife Trust. **London's Hurricane**, also by Mark and Ian, followed and **Eye On The Hurricane** by Bob Ogley and Kev Reynolds covered the drama in the eastern counties of England. These books took the money raised for conservation appeals to more than £50,000. The Meteorological Office didn't like the word "hurricane". It does not apply to our latitude, they said. So Bob Ogley

went to Jamaica to write a book about the effects of the Caribbean's latest big brush with the elements — **Hurricane Gilbert.** The Prime Minister wrote the foreword, the Governor General contributed his personal anecdotes and the book took the island by storm! **Price £7.95**

King Oak of Sevenoaks
by Ron Denney

A story for children between the ages of eight and eighty about King Oak, the only tree out of Sevenoaks' seven eponymous oaks to survive the night of October 16th, 1987. Accompanied by water colour paintings. ISBN 1- 872337- 00- 7 **Price £6.95**

Biggin On The Bump
by Bob Ogley

This is the story of the most famous fighter station in the world — an airfield now inhabited by the shadows of extraordinary men and women. Bob Ogley brings it to life and, from the first page, gives a fascinating insight into the men, the women, the machines and the indomitable spirit of those drawn into conflict from 1916 to 1945...and beyond. This is what the critics say: **"From the brilliantly named Froglets Publications comes the equally brilliant Biggin On The Bump — a glorious tribute to gallantry on and around the airfield"** — *Flypast.* **"A lively and human story of an exciting time"** — *The Royal Aero Club Gazette.* **"It makes fascinating reading"** — *Air Pictorial.* **"A glorious story"** — *Aviation News.*
ISBN 1- 872337- 05 - 8 **Price £9.99.**

Doodlebugs and Rockets
by Bob Ogley

It took Bob Ogley many months to research and write the story of the flying bombs — V1 and V2, or Doodlebug and Rocket — the unique, brilliantly conceived, indiscriminate, briefly-lived weapons that were launched by the Germans against London in a last-ditch orgy of violence designed to turn the tide of war. Appealing for reminiscences and photographs, Bob was overwhelmed by the response. Thousands remembered the ungainly monsters that roared across the skies sounding like badly-tuned motor bikes. Who could forget that moment when the engine cut out and the missile fell silently to earth followed by a shattering explosion? More than 200 photographs. **"One of Kent's best-selling books, Doodlebugs and Rockets went into reprint after just two months in the shops"**

— *Kent Life.* **"Survival, secrets, tragedy and triumph in wartime Britain — author Bob Ogley is set to storm the best-selling charts once again"** — *Clive Page, Kentish Times.* **"Not a military appreciation but a human story well told"** — *Light Aviation.* **"A model history that remembers a phenomenon too readily relegated to a footnote in other books. Thoroughly recommended"** — *Air Pictorial.* **"A vivid piece of historical story-telling"** — *Air Mail.*
ISBN 1- 872337- 22 - 8 **£16.99 (hardback).**
ISBN 1- 872337- 21- X **£10.99 (paperback)**

Flying Bombs Over England
by H.E.Bates

Described as one of the most exciting literary discoveries of the decade this is the story of Germany's secret weapons, written by the famous novelist H.E.Bates. Working at the time for the Air Ministry, Bates was asked to put together the official documentation of the flying bombs. He wrote 30,000 evocative, descriptive words explaining just what it was like to live in Southern England at the time — and, to his dismay, saw his manuscript suppressed under the "30-year rule". It then remained "lost" for another 20 years and was eventually discovered by Bob Ogley during the research into his book. Royalties have been donated by the author's window, Madge Bates, to the RAF Benevolent Fund. **"Bob Ogley quickly realised he had discovered buried treasure"** — *Evening Standard.*
ISBN 1- 872337- 04 - X **£16.99 hardback**

Kent at War (1939-1945)
by Bob Ogley

This illustrated history of the second world war relives the drama, heroism and horrors as they unfolded in the front-line county of Kent. This is not just a story of countless fighting men but of the ordinary people who played their part in this great conflict. Here are the ration queues and austerity clothing, Vera Lynn and Glenn Miller, twice-weekly trips round the bomb craters to the "flicks" and the camaraderie in the shelters and tunnels under the cliffs. Every Kent town had a British Restaurant, a rest centre and exchange store and every Kent town contributed towards a squadron of Spitfires. **"Kent at War is a rich feast, heavily laced with the voices of Kent telling their own stories"** — *Jane Bakowski, Sevenoaks Chronicle.* **"Bite-sized chunks of text complemented by well-chosen contemporary photographs —Kent at War has to be a winner"** — *Airway.* **"Bob Ogley's meticulous research has uncovered the**

human stories of terrible, desperate and even hilarious times"— *Frank Chapman, The Courier.* **"Bob Ogley covers a whole range of subjects but for Home Front buffs Kent at War would be a worthy addition to their bookshelves"** — *Michael Conway — The Home Front.* **"A remarkable story of fortitude through the horror and hope of six years of war"** — *News Shopper.*
  ISBN 1 -872337- 49- X **£16.99 hardback**
ISBN 1-87337 -18 -X **£10.99 paperback**

Surrey at War (1939-1945)
by Bob Ogley

The companion book to Kent at War. Stories of tragedy, endurance and courage. All the great events and more than 200 photographs that cannot fail to stir powerful emotions as they bring back memories of the most dramatic years of the century.
ISBN 1- 872337 -70-8 **£16.99 hardback**
ISBN 1-872337-65-1 **£10.99 paperback**

The Kent Weather Book
by Bob Ogley, Ian Currie and Mark Davison

Floods and freezes, tempests and tornadoes, deluges and dust devils, hailstones and heatwaves. Here is a unique pictorial record of Kent's most dramatic weather events. We are told that global warming may be the cause of recent extremes in the weather but in the hop fields and orchards, on the chalk cliffs and Downs and across the rich marshland of Kent, the climate has always been immensely variable. This book provides the proof — right up to 1997. The Kent Weather Book was the subject of a short documentary on *Meridian Television* and received rave reviews from every local newspaper in Kent.
ISBN 1-87337- 15 - X **£10.99 (paperback)**

The Weather Book series
by Bob Ogley, Mark Davison and Ian Currie

The Kent Weather Book sold so brilliantly that Bob Ogley and his co-authors — weather experts, Mark Davison and Ian Currie — decided to write the history of the weather in other English counties. Now there are individual books for Essex, Surrey, Sussex, Norfolk and Suffolk, Hampshire and the Isle of Wight and Berkshire. Yes, the train that should have arrived on platform two really was stranded in a snowdrift. Yes, grandad was telling the truth when he said he paddled down the High Street in a canoe. The pictures tell the story. **"The authors have done their homework meticulously and presented a thorough analysis of the region's weather. A fascinating book"** — *The Suffolk Sage on the Norfolk and Suffolk Weather Book.*

"Graphic details and excellent photographs bring many memories flooding back (pardon the pun)" — *Meon Valley News on the Hampshire and Isle of Wight Weather Book.* **"I could not put it down. It read like a horror story, then it made me cry."** — *Tom Moore, Evening Argus, on the Sussex Weather Book.*
Prices vary £9.95 - £10.99

Other books published by Froglets include

Underriver —
Samuel Palmer's Golden Valley

by Griselda Barton with Michael Tong

Samuel Palmer was one of England's greatest 19th Century landscape painters who came from London to live and work in the Kentish village of Shoreham below the verdant chalk hills of the North Downs. Through his artistic perception Shoreham was to have immortality betowed upon it as "The Valley of Vision". Palmer often walked at night to the distant hills where he could see the sun rise over "the flower of Kentish scenery. Below the hills was his "Golden Valley" — the hamlet of Underriver.
ISBN 1- 872337- 45- 7 **£9.95 (paperback)**
* colour reproductions

Westerham at War
by Helen Long

The war years in Winston Churchill's home town of Westerham seen at a truly personal level from those who lived through them. Helen Long has attracted much acclaim for her diligence and perseverance in harvesting such a fascinating array of individual recollections, including many about the great man himself. A reminder to those old enough to have taken part to say with pride "I was there — in Westerham". ISBN 1- 872337- 40 -6 **£8.95**

Tales of Old Tonbridge
by Frank Chapman

The author was editorial director of the Kent and Sussex Courier Group of Newspapers for many years and this book contains brilliantly written stories of the characters who lived in or visited his home town of Tonbridge. Among them are Frank Woolley, Kent's great all-round cricketer, General Booth, founder of the Salvation Army, Donald Clark, celebrated nationally as the "puritan prude", and many more.
ISBN 1-872337-55-4 **£8.95**

The Story of Robson and Jerome
by Bob Ogley

The pop industry is used to surprises but when Robson Green and Jerome Flynn soared to the top of the charts with their recording of *Unchained Melody* they were thunderstruck. Nonplussed critics wondered how two actors could upstage so many brilliant and seasoned musicians with a first-ever single and then turn the record industry upside down with the fastest two-million selling album in the history of popular music. Bob Ogley tells the story of the two boys — one from a mining community in the north-east and the other from an acting family in the south east — and how they were drawn into the theatrical world....and stardom extraordinaire.

ISBN 1-872337-81-3 **£14.95 (hardback)**
ISBN 1-872337-3-x **£9.95 (paperback)**

Does your club need a speaker?

BOB OGLEY was born in Sevenoaks, has lived in the county all his life and is proud to be a Kentish Man. As author of more than a dozen books he has travelled extensively in pursuit of information and photographs and is in great demand from organisations across the south-east to tell his unique story.

A former editor of *The Sevenoaks Chronicle,* Bob was a journalist for more than 30 years before he left his newspaper to concentrate on writing books and giving his talks. He is also a regular broadcaster on BBC Radio Kent.

The subjects covered by Bob in his talks are: *War in Kent (and Surrey), The History of RAF Biggin Hill, Doodlebugs and Rockets, The Weather Wherever* and, of course, *The Great Storm and How it Changed His Life.* He introduces humour and reality and has an amazing collection of anecdotes which he delivers with great enthusiasm.

On the right we quote what some people have said about Bob Ogley's talks:

If you would like to book Bob Ogley to talk to your club (whatever time of day), please write or ring Froglets. His fees vary depending on the size of the audience. But hurry. He's in great demand.

"I have attended some interesting evenings in my life but I count yesterday as the best" — Paula Rangecroft, Leigh Historical Society

"Bob Ogley's talk held us all enthralled. Everyone enjoyed it enormously" — Alan O'Hagan, Otham Historical Society.

"It was one of the best talks I have ever had the pleasure to hear and one which all present will talk about for years "— Peter Rogers, The Sevenoaks Society.

"We were spellbound by his many and varied stories" — Marion Wadley, Weybridge Friendship Club.

" We were totally enthralled by the lucidity and clarity of speech from someone who was never brought up to publish books and give talks" — Harry Clark, Rustington Heritage .

Donations

These are the totals so far raised by the sale of Froglets' books

National Trust Storm Appeal	**£24,000**
National Trust South Downs Appeal	**£2,000**
Sevenoaks "Trees for the Future"	**£12,500**
Surrey Wildlife Trust....	**£8,500**
Brazilian Rain Forest	**£5,000**
Orkney Field Club	**£2,000**
Bateman's appeal, East Sussex (on behalf of W.H. Smith Ltd)	**£1,000**
London Wildlife Trust	**£1,000**
Essex Wildlife Trust	**£750**
Suffolk Wildlife Trust	**£750**
Norfolk Naturalist's Trust	**£250**
Cambridge Wildlife Trust	**£250**
The Evening Standard Tree Appeal	**£500**
Care Village, Ide Hill	**£500**

From the royalties of *Biggin on The Bump*, **£15,000** has been donated to the RAF Benevolent Fund.

From the sale of *Coast to Coast,* which was written by the editorial staff of TVS, **£10,000** has been donated to the Royal National Lifeboat Institute.

In November 1995 a cheque for **£15,000** was presented to the RAF Benevolent Fund representing royalties from Flying Bombs over England. It was donated by Madge Bates, widow of the much loved author H.E. Bates.

OVERALL TOTAL £99,000